Mine

By

Jessica
Jones

Realizing Potentials Press
New Lenox, Illinois

Mine
By Jessica Jones

Published by:

Realizing Potentials Press
P.O. Box 1014
New Lenox, IL 60451 1014

Publisher's Cataloging-in-Publication
(Provided by Quality Books, Inc.)

Jones, Jessica.
    Mine / Jessica Jones. --1st ed.
    p. cm.
    LCCN: 00-130335
    ISBN: 0-9670829-2-7

    1. Psychoses--Fiction. 2. Abduction--Fiction.
3. Northwest, Pacific--Fiction. I. Title.

PS3560.04928Min 2000   813'.6
                            QBI00-901102

I dedicate this book foremost to my mother, who said, "Go to your room and write a book, and leave my damn TV alone!" I thank her for the years of encouragement and belief. I am so sorry she didn't live to see the dream become a reality.

This book is also for Suzi, the best friend and editor a person could have. She lived through my troubled times and distorted realities for over 23 years, and certainly deserves to see an end to it with the publication of this book. Thank you for your direction, comments, and multitudinous criticisms that kept me on the road to freedom.

This book is dedicated to anyone who is going through what I went through for 44 years. There is an end to the mountainous path, a way out of the collapsed tunnel. One can survive the insanity of spiritual horrors and the evils of mankind, and come out the other end unscathed and healed.

It is also for my many friends who have shown me that people can love me as I am, and helped me become the woman I was intended to be.

I would like to give special thanks to Ken who offered me endless support and the title for this book; Barb whose contagious excitement kept me going; and Clare whose insistent prodding and support made this a reality.

Part One

❧ The Spring ☙

Chapter One

"Katie, please. Stop doing that and let's talk about it," David pleaded, exasperation flowing from every word.

Kathryn quit pulling out what little was left in her dresser drawers and turned to face him, a sweater still dangling from her hand. She gazed up at him with a look of utter helplessness. Her swollen tear-stained face revealed she was losing the battle, falling into the slippery abyss of complete panic. The sweater slipped from her trembling fingers and dropped onto the heap of clothes on the floor. Frustration and fear were apparent in her aqua eyes. David's concerned face mirrored her pain, and she knew he too felt powerless even as his strength reached out to her.

"Katie, talk to me. Tell me what you're looking for," he begged.

She stared blankly at the rhythmic clenching of his jaw as the waves of anger flooded over him. They stood in the rubble of what looked like a tornado path, if it had indeed been a force of nature that hurled their belongings about the room. Clothes lay scattered and torn to shreds. The glass protecting each precious memory lay shattered in jagged shards. The contents of Kathryn's favorite perfumes and oils soiled the carpet and bed. Books lay sliced and carved into confetti-sized bits of words littering the tops of dressers.

Kathryn tried but could not reach out to him past her own turmoil. She stifled a new outburst as her eyes fell on a decapitated picture of her baby girl. Her bottom lip quivered as she struggled to compose herself. "What do you want me to say, David? I feel as if I've been...raped."

David wrapped his arms around her as Kathryn sobbed with abandonment, the tears dissolving any restraint. He held her tightly, trying to shield her from the stark reality of the break-in. He let her cry in silence until she emptied herself.

"I know, Katie. But whoever it was is gone now, and John doesn't think he'll be back," David whispered in a feeble attempt to soothe her anxiety.

"David, he pawed through our belongings. That animal handled my most intimate things. He broke into our house and did whatever the hell he wanted. I feel violated! No one even knew he was here! How can John say this creature will never come back?" she snapped, her voice like a double-edged saber.

David looked into her eyes and gently squeezed her arms in reassurance, but with a frown of helplessness on his brow. Kathryn tried to smile, but she lacked the strength to turn up the corners of her lips.

"He wasn't a good thief. He left everything of value. He's got to be a crackpot! And he apparently doesn't do this type of thing for a living. It's probably just a couple of kids out for a rush. That's all there is to it. It's over. They broke in, did what they wanted, and left," David said with an air of masculine confidence.

Kathryn noticed the tiny twitch at the corner of his left eye as he spoke. It was a dead giveaway that even David wasn't totally convinced with his argument. She knew he was simply trying to make her feel better, but at the moment there was little he could do or say to calm her fears.

"David, some creep has just stolen our wedding picture, two photo albums, a box of old letters, our address book, and who knows what else? And then this animal tore through the house like a demolition crew!" Kathryn tried to quell her rising hysterics. "And some of my panties...my underwear, David! That creep stole my damned underwear! What possible use could he have for them? Out of the laundry, for heaven's sake!" She was feeling worse than when she had first walked in on the nightmarish scene. She wondered how she was supposed to feel right now, and suspected she should be feeling exactly as she was—as if she had been savagely violated.

Kathryn pushed herself away from David and headed into the kitchen to make a pot of coffee. She needed something hot to drink, and since it was unlikely she would be getting any sleep tonight, coffee seemed like the best thing. She wanted to be awake when their uninvited guest returned.

I know he'll be back no matter what David and John think, she thought as she measured the coffee grounds.

The sensation of needing to beat on someone was new to her. It was a dark side to her character that she hadn't realized existed. She had always thought herself a pacifist, but realized she had never before been in a situation that might stir up her killer instinct. She now believed she was capable of defending herself and her family if necessary with the strength and conviction this vicious, deeply hidden anger stirring inside. She promised herself that no one would ever again sneak up and invade the sanctity of life she and David had created for themselves.

The coffeepot stopped its last few noisy gurgles. She filled two mugs, fortified them with a generous splash of dark Jamaican rum, and carried them into the living room. As she walked through the archway, David tried to hide his uneasiness by sauntering casually to the sofa. He had attempted to straighten the room hurriedly before she returned. It was evident that he didn't know what to say or do to help her through this crisis, and it hurt her to see his helplessness. Kathryn loved David with all her heart. He had been her entire life until their daughter expanded the circle by her birth two years ago. With the painful exception of her mother's death, they had a carefree, happy life. They were young and successful with the whole world in front of them.

Both she and David had thriving business careers. David owned an advertising firm that contracted work through most of Northwest Washington, while she had joined her father's naturopathic clinic. Kathryn had been destined to enter the medical field, having been raised in a health-orientated family. She obtained degrees in medicine as well as naturopathy and now worked to join the two sciences, using the benefits of both.

She attended a university in California with idyllic hopes of changing the world. She had been young and filled with passion back then. Gone was her mother's decade of "Make love, not war." Instead, the concerns of Kathryn's days at school were "Save the whales" and "Recycle!" She embraced demonstrations from pro-life to logging roads, each one an important current issue that carried more weight than the faded *Flower Power* of earlier decades.

It was during this time that she met Wendy, her college roommate. Wendy was a budding artist/militant activist who marched against AIDS, chanting, "You shouldn't have to die from love!" and rebelling against the limits on total freedom of expression. When she wasn't marching in gay rights rallies, she was fashioning some monstrous masterpiece out of scrap metal looted from the local wrecking yard.

Both girls had a voracious appetite for life and regularly solved the world's problems over Grande vanilla lattés and cheesecake. The two developed an immediate rapport and consequently, Wendy had introduced Kathryn to her dearest and oldest confidante, David. Ironically, the three had grown up in Nantok Falls, yet Kathryn had never met them. David and Wendy were two years Kathryn's senior, so they had not crossed Kathryn's path in their hometown.

The three became inseparable throughout David and Wendy's last two college years. They shared their experiences, hopes and fears, weaving a delicate but binding thread of intimacy that led to the natural culmination of David and Kathryn marrying right after he graduated. Wendy and David, leaving Kathryn to finish her schooling, returned to Nantok Falls. Wendy settled into a controversial sculpting career and David set up his advertising agency.

The year after they were married, David managed to purchase five acres of waterfront property up island from his parents. There he began building the home of Kathryn's dreams.

David's parents had arranged to sell their successful lumber and hardware business and retire to New Mexico after his father developed a heart problem. David's mother, who was from New Mexico, longed to leave the cold, rainy coastal temperatures and return to the dry warmth of the Midwest.

Kathryn traveled home when her classes weren't demanding all her time and attention. David worked on the house every spare moment, first camping at his parent's house before they left, and then moving into the completed basement before finishing the upper floors. Each time Kathryn returned home, she found a bit more resemblance to the house they envisioned nestled deep in the forest of cedar trees towering over the cliff. When Kathryn moved in after finally completing her internship at Seattle General, David carried her over the threshold of their finished house.

Less than a year later, Wendy married a young man from the mainland who had gone into business with David. Bill brought a certain artistic flair to the multimedia-advertising department and thus increased David's business significantly. Bill's easy, natural, creative ability inspired Wendy, who by now enjoyed a measure of renown in the area. She had two showings in Seattle that were relatively successful in terms of commercial return and exposure.

Life had been so easy; perhaps too easy, Kathryn thought in retrospect. *Perhaps that's why they chose our home to break into.* The thought flitted through her distressed mind as she sipped her coffee. *What goes around comes around. But what did we ever do to deserve this?*

"David, you don't really think it was a couple of kids, do you?" Kathryn asked as her mind wandered back over the evening. She flicked her dark auburn hair from her eyes as she watched David try to hide his own anxiety.

"I think some kids were aimlessly out for the night, saw an empty house, couldn't resist the temptation, and stole a few useless items for trophies," he said assuredly. "Don't build this thing into something more than it is."

She could see the worry crease his brow and dull his usually brilliant blue eyes. Katie knew David felt as vulnerable as she did. The thief left a dirty feeling on everything he touched, making her skin crawl with an eerie disgust.

David had called the sheriff's office as soon as they arrived home from their weekend away, then phoned Wendy to see if she would keep Meaghan another couple of days. It was Kathryn's thirty-fifth birthday, and, as a surprise, David had taken her on a sailing trip through the San Juan Islands. It had been a glorious four days filled with adventure and love, but the pleasure ended sharply when they walked into the disheveled house.

The intruder had gone through every room, stealing only those things that held sentimental value, not monetary worth. He stole little pieces of their lives that could never be replaced by mere insurance. With each newly discovered missing item, both again asked, "Why?"

When the sheriff arrived, Kathryn was glad to see it was John. She had gone to school with John Tyler, and throughout their last three high school years, they had been a hot item. They parted friends as their career choices took them down different paths. After prom night, John left for the police academy on the mainland, and no matter how heartbroken she was, Kathryn knew they did not belong together. He was a good friend and always would be.

He proved that tonight as he drove up and took over the situation with masterful ease that gave both she and David a measure of reassurance. John made them feel as if he could catch the burglar as soon as he got back to town, as if it was already a done deal.

She had thought *she* would never ever need John's services, but when he answered their distress call, she was visibly relieved. John was a good cop. He knew his job and did it well. He had quickly moved up through the ranks on the mainland, and when the sheriff's chair became available in their hometown, he immediately applied for the position. The beat was quieter than he was used to in Seattle, and Kathryn knew he preferred being a small town peacekeeper to a big city crimefighter. His work was far more personal and rewarding here on the island. In Seattle he defended the rights of *Vics*, but here he protected friends.

Until tonight, Kathryn had always felt completely safe. She had considered their seaside community to be almost family and now wondered if she had misplaced her trust. Kathryn tried to envision which local kid was capable of committing such an offense, but was unable to attach a face to such an insensitive prowler. She didn't know anyone who was cruel and callous enough to destroy someone else's life like this. The more she thought about it, the more she felt she didn't want to know anyone like that.

While Kathryn and David waited in the house, John searched the grounds for any evidence relevant to the identity of the perpetrator, but found nothing. There were no visible signs of forced entry. He suspected whoever it was gained access through an open bathroom window on the second floor, and after dusting the frame and window, he was certain of it. Whoever it was had wiped the entire area clean of any prints, even Kathryn's and David's.

Kathryn was aware of John's hesitation as he reported what he found. His obvious avoidance of certain words to minimize the trauma enforced her belief that it was not simply a couple of amateur kids seeking excitement on an impulsive thrill. The total disregard with which the person had devastated their property was frightening. Whoever it was had been professional enough to leave no sign of his visit except the shambled remains in each room.

She shuddered as the memory of the scene flooded over her afresh. Unable to resist the need any longer, she put her coffee cup down, stood up, bristled her back with determination, and marched into the bedroom to finish the work she had begun earlier. She threw all her clothes, both dirty and clean, into the laundry room. It was a task that would last the better part of two days but it didn't matter.

Kathryn had to wash the memory of his touch out of her life.

Chapter Two

Kathryn woke up to the sun peeking through the skylight above the bed. She stretched lazily, feeling refreshed for the first time in days. It was the third morning after the break-in and she was relieved to discover the incident was becoming just a very nasty memory. At first she thought the horror would never leave, but each normal day that passed pushed the trauma a little further away.

The day promised to be a hectic one. There were added appointments crammed in here and there to accommodate those patients she had rescheduled from Monday and Tuesday. Kathryn had taken those two days off to scrub the contamination out of her house after the burglary. The peace and purity it had brought to her were worth the longer days required to catch up. She was happy to be getting back to work and put the incident behind her.

After a quick shower, Kathryn headed to the kitchen. She wanted to make pancakes this morning, knowing it would be a pleasant surprise for David and Meaghan. This was usually a Saturday morning treat, but she felt it would be good today. It was a sign that their life was back on track. As she cooked, Kathryn found herself humming a little tune her mother had often sung to her when she was a young girl. While she hummed, a sense of peace washed over her, as it used to when she curled up in her mother's lap. For a moment, all seemed right with the world.

Meaghan strolled into the kitchen, sounding a wide, waking yawn. One little fist rubbed lazily at her eye as she walked up to Kathryn and wrapped herself around her mother's leg like a velcroed teddy bear. Kate swooped down, lifted her daughter up into her arms and twirled her around until Meaghan squealed with delight. Giving Meaghan a hug, Kathryn carried her to the table and set her down on the specially made chair decorated with all the latest cartoon characters.

David had taken over a year to finish carving the chair. He had also carved a swinging bassinet before Meaghan was born, adorning it with brightly painted bear characters. It was a natural talent David developed when he was a boy. A family friend—a Native American man who earned his living carving masks for customers as far away as Britain and Japan—had taken the boy under his wing and taught him to become a fine artist. David enjoyed giving his creations to family and friends as special gifts.

He strolled through the doorway, his thick red hair still wet from a shower. He reached out and affectionately squeezed Kathryn's shoulder, relieved to see her back to her old self again. Moving over to the table, he gave Meaghan a gentle kiss on the forehead. He tousled Meaghan's short, carrot-colored hair as he sat down and pretended to notice another three freckles among the hundreds on her little pixie nose.

Kathryn finished turning the last of the pancakes and heaped the remaining golden discs onto the already overflowing plate. She carried the stack of pancakes to the table when the phone rang in the living room. Handing the platter of steaming cakes to David, she dashed down the steps to grab the phone before the machine picked it up.

"Good morning, Wendy," she laughed, a melodious lilt in her voice. It was quarter of eight and it could only be Wendy this early in the morning, checking to see if Kathryn would be going to work this morning or playing hooky for another day, really to see if Meaghan needed babysitting or not.

After Meaghan was born and Kathryn was ready to go back to work, Wendy took over the responsibility of being nanny since it didn't interfere with her artistic creations. It was an arrangement that made everyone happy. Kathryn knew Meaghan was safe and well cared for, and Wendy, who loved kids, filled her home with laughter.

"Good morning, Katie," cooed the sandpaper voice on the other end.

A chill spiked up Kathryn's back, causing her to shiver. Her hand squeezed the neck of the phone until her knuckles turned white. She didn't recognize the voice. The grating, mechanical sound was disturbing. Gooseflesh popped out along her arms as the haunting familiarity of his voice flowed through the receiver and shook her with a terror she didn't quite understand.

"Who is this?" she whispered nervously. As the words tumbled from her lips, she already knew it was a stupid question. *It was him, the creep who had ransacked their home.*

"Does it matter? You don't know me yet, so it shouldn't matter to you what my name is. It wouldn't mean anything to you," he explained smugly, as if schooling a naughty, nosy child. "No, what *is* important is that I know you. In fact, I know everything about you and your puky little family. I know everything worth knowing about your pathetic friends. Is Panchez in the other room? Is he sitting at the kitchen table eating breakfast or is he out chasing windmills? Is he being a good little husband?"

The voice dripped with a chilling malice that chipped away at her heart with the piercing force of an ice pick. She hadn't heard the name *Sancho Panchez* for over five years. It was a name Wendy had given David in college after he and Kathryn were the only two who showed up for an animal cruelty rally at a mink farm. Wendy had always said that Kathryn was like Don Quixote, knight errant, and David was her trusty squire, Sancho.

Kathryn's eyes looked wildly about, trying to see where this lunatic was watching her from. She was sure he was hiding behind a tree, spying on them. He had to be close by to know what they were doing.

But how does he know David's nickname? she asked herself, her mind already forming the answer. *The letters and albums. Of course.*

"You're the animal who broke in here the other day, aren't you? You're the creep who gutted my house, aren't you? Aren't you!" she screeched, anger sharpening her rising voice with a shrillness she had never heard before in herself. His voice sounded cruel—deep, with a rasping, inhuman wheeze to it. She tried to put a face to the sound and settled on the giant with metal teeth from a super-spy movie.

There was no one outside in the yard that she could see through the window, thinking he might be talking on a cellular phone. There was a distant, hollow sound to the background noise of the call.

"You're very good. I told George you would be good. I prefer them smart. It's more interesting. It makes the game better that way. You enjoy games, don't you, Katie? I love games, but they have to be challenging. I'm very good at them when they're interesting. I need a good opponent. I knew you would be good when I saw you with your friend and daughter in the café the other day. I assume that was Wendy. You looked very sexy in that green outfit. Tight fitting and short. I appreciated that. And little Meaghan is the spitting image of you. She's gonna be a real heartbreaker someday, when...if...she grows up," he cawed. His voice oozed a sickening threat that slid across her mind, filling the spaces of thought with horrible visions that wouldn't go away.

"No, I don't enjoy games and I wouldn't ever play one with you. Who the hell are you? What do you want?" she demanded sharply, losing the battle to keep her voice from rising two octaves above hysteria.

"Now, now. Don't disappoint me, Katie..." the voice snarled. In her mind, she could see his lips curl over luminous, metal teeth.

"Do not call me that!" she shouted, trying to make sure he got the point.

The sun brightened the family room, warming the area before the window. Particles of dust danced on the rays creating streams of sunlight. Seagulls called above the cliffs as they dropped fresh clam shells onto the rocks below. Upstairs, David and Meaghan were enjoying the breakfast that was to prove that their life was again reaching normalcy. But it was all a lie. The voice of the man who taunted Kathryn was the ugly reality that would not go away.

"You're not helping your chances in the game with this attitude." She could feel the sleaziness of his condoning smile as he spoke.

"Who are you?" she screamed, more frightened than she had ever been. Kathryn collapsed in the chair beside the end table, too weak to stand any longer. The mocking tone of his voice robbed her of any peace she had regained over the last two days.

"I told you. Who I *am* doesn't matter. What I *want* might interest you, though. You see, I want Meaghan. Let's just call her...*the prize*. Now pay attention. I'm only going to say this once. This is how the game works: I try to get your little girl, and you try to stop me. Winner gets the brat. Do you think you can prevent me from getting to her, Katie? Oh, but wait. You don't want to play with me. I guess that means I win by default, so I guess I'll just drop by and pick her up," he laughed a dark, evil laugh. He then hung up the phone abruptly, as if he had just ordered pizza.

Kathryn's face blanched in horrified shock. The deafening thud of her heart pounded in her ears. In the corner of her eye an unexpected shadow suddenly loomed too close by. Startled, she let out a short squeal and dropped the receiver from her hand. The noise of the phone clattering on the cherry wood table drew her eyes away from David who had come down to the family room to see what was upsetting her.

She stared through tortured eyes at the receiver with a sense of unbelief. The thought of this maniac coming after her baby was more than she could bear to contemplate. She looked back up at David and fell on him with hysterical sobs, her burning, red-rimmed eyes filled with fear. The words of the voice on the phone still echoed in her ears.

The call cast dark clouds on what had promised to be a beautiful morning. Breakfast lay cooling and forgotten on the table as they huddled together in the wash of panic, again waiting for John to arrive. Together, David and Kathryn formulated their own plan to protect Meaghan.

The decision was already settled before John arrived. They set their plan into motion despite what John might say or do in his official capacity. David would take Meaghan to Farmington, New Mexico this very afternoon, to stay with his parents. There was a flight leaving Seattle before lunch and two seats were booked on it before Kathryn finished packing for Meaghan. Wendy would take

Kathryn to work late and pick her up afterward so she wouldn't be alone. Bill would handle the three appointments David had to deal with this afternoon. David could catch a connecting flight back to Seattle six hours later, arriving home about midnight.

John was free to do whatever he wanted as Sheriff, but they would take care of Meaghan's safety themselves. They were not willing to wait for this maniac to make a move. Meaghan would be tucked away in New Mexico until they felt secure enough to bring her back.

The sound of car wheels crunching on the driveway gravel alerted Kathryn as she moved Meaghan's suitcase down the hallway and set it by the front door. She would have to pack a few of Meaghan's stuffed toys and Blankie into a carry-on bag. John rang the doorbell and David let him in as Kathryn finished getting their daughter ready. There was half an hour before they had to leave to catch the ferry for the mainland in time for their flight, and David wanted to make sure John would keep an eye on Kathryn while he was gone.

She could hear the voices fade into the living room as she carried Meaghan to the bathroom. Kathryn was still shaking from the lingering effects of the call. She clutched Meaghan with a desperation that made her loathe letting her baby out of her sight for even a second.

"Katie, come and tell John what the man said to you," David hollered from the sofa, beckoning her to join them.

Kathryn stalked into the living room, still clinging onto Meaghan. She collapsed into the overstuffed chair opposite John and David, sighing heavily. Remembering the words the man spoke was too great a burden. She wrapped her arms a little tighter around Meaghan as she began to whisper the earlier conversation with the oppressive, gravel-voiced man, hoping her low tones would reduce her fears and protect Meaghan from understanding what was happening.

David and Meaghan drove away half an hour later, leaving Sheriff John Tyler and Kathryn to discuss the matter fully. John approved the measures taken for their daughter's safety and promised to initiate a watch on the house and a tap on the phone line. He also offered to call the Farmington Sheriff's Department and have them keep an eye on the Breslin ranch.

It was doubtful that anyone would follow the child so far away. Instead, the man would probably lose interest in the new complication and find someone else to terrorize. Now that Meaghan was out of the way, they could all breathe easier and do whatever was necessary to catch this maniac who was toying with them. Until the man discovered Meaghan was no longer in town, the police were free to set a trap for him.

As Kathryn listened to her friend list his resources, she watched his jaw clench with angry determination—things like this simply didn't happen in Nantok Falls, especially not to his friends. It gave her a sense of security against the rising tide of threats. As John said his good-byes, she could see the concern etched into his eyes. They carried the same concern for her that they had that prom night when he told her he was leaving. But now they had a mission—they said that he would use every available means in his power to protect her and her family. Kathryn felt better than she had an hour ago and let the relief give her some measure of comfort.

With the phone call distanced from her, Kathryn found herself putting a more realistic face to the voice. As she watched John vanish down the driveway, she let her imagination put that very face of her unknown enemy behind a row of dull, gray bars. She could envision John throwing away the key to the dark, musty, urine stained cell. The devilish looking man crouched in the filthy squalor, his cold black eyes glaring up at her with the uncaring indifference of a shark's stare. The man's once strong, forbidding body began to fade into a shriveled, crippled relic with graying hair and quivering voice. The gleaming evil vehemence of his crushing jaw vanished into a toothless, gaping hole that was powerless to mouth the words of his earlier terrifying intimidation. He was no longer the strong enemy that threatened her, but a demented coward who lurked in shadows. The vision of her threatening nemesis faded into nothingness, crowded out by the sunny warmth of the present reality.

"Well, I'm no longer unsuspecting. I'm prepared for you, you bastard. I won't be facing you alone. Together we'll kick your ass all the way to jail. You want to play a game? Well, I've just stacked the deck in my favor. I've taken away your *prize*. Come and try whatever you want, creep. We're waiting for you," she declared, bracing herself against the unknown. She hoped it was all just a bad dream she would wake up from any minute now, but somehow, she knew there was more to come.

Kathryn closed the door and rolled the deadbolt lever slowly between trembling fingers, the sound of the click echoing through the eerie silence of the empty house. She did not relish being alone, even for a moment. The deputy John dispatched to watch the house was already on his way from town. She steeled herself in case of another phone call and prayed Wendy would be earlier than promised. It wasn't enough to have a strange man standing guard outside her home. She needed a trusted, familiar friend close by for reassurance.

Kathryn dressed uneasily, unable to shake the thought of being watched by someone. This stranger had been in their home when they were in the San Juan Islands. She didn't know if he could come in again whenever he chose, but realized that he assumed he could. His voice was so cocky. He sounded as if he knew he could do whatever whenever he liked, and no one could stop him. It had not been sufficiently established how the madman broke into the house in the first place—at least not enough to satisfy her. He could have used a key for all she knew.

The idea of his being there, with her, evoked an uncontrollable shudder and she decided not to take a shower, shades of every horror movie she had ever seen dominating her thoughts. They now exposed her vulnerability, and that alone frightened her. After hastily dressing, Kathryn dashed into the kitchen to pack a quick lunch. She rounded the corner and screamed as she ran smack into a body she didn't know was there.

"You scared the hell out of me," she gasped, holding her hand over a pounding heart.

"Sorry, Katie. I let myself in," Wendy apologized. "Why on earth are you so jumpy? Did something happen this morning? Where's Meaghan?"

Kathryn reluctantly retold the story. Remembering the un-nerving familiarity with which the stranger had talked to her raked her spine. The entire incident was too bizarre to be real. She tried to make light of it but failed in the attempt. When she heard Wendy gasp under the weight of both the story and fear for her friend, Kathryn could no longer hold back the tears as her own anxiety and terror collided. The questionable bravery she had felt not so very long ago dissipated in the chilling reality of the situation.

Settling down through forced determination, Kathryn put together a small lunch, not sure she would even be able to eat it, and headed to the car with Wendy. She didn't relish working today but knew she needed a distraction to take her mind off this ordeal until David got back.

Work passed far too slowly although she was run off her feet. Kathryn went through the day's activities as if she were moving in slow motion. Every time she opened the door to her next patient, she expected to see the owner of the voice that still taunted her. Her ears strained to recognize a single syllable sounding identical to the ones she heard on the phone. She found herself looking deep into the eyes of every man who came into her office, no longer feeling as if she knew any of them. Some of them were old friends, but she couldn't shake the feeling that they were now suspects.

As the clock in the front hallway chimed six-thirty, she was staring absently at the paperwork lying on the desk before her. Wendy would be arriving any minute. Kathryn updated the three remaining charts and took her mail to the front desk for the girls to post in the morning. Checking the windows and turning out the lights, Kathryn waited in the front foyer for her ride.

Fifteen minutes later the two women were parked in front of the Lamplighter Restaurant down by the old marina in the bay. Kathryn decided she wanted to eat out instead of going home where she would feel vulnerable with David and Meaghan gone, just waiting for another phone call to plague her. She was exhausted from the extra workload and stress of the day, and didn't feel like making a meal.

"God, you look awful," Wendy offered as she finally saw Kathryn in the light of the restaurant.

"Thank you so much for sharing that," Kathryn said, sarcasm mixing with weary fear.

"No, really, I mean it. You look as if you've been up all night," Wendy insisted, making sure Katie got the point.

"That's okay. I feel like it. This guy's really getting to me. I tried hard to forget him. I thought with Meaghan gone that would be taken care of and I could relax a little, but it's only made things harder to bear. I don't know if that lunatic is still in town, or whether he's followed David and is at Mom and Dad Breslin's house right now. With Meaghan out of my sight, I'm worrying more about her than before because I can't see for myself if she is all right. God, my mind won't stop thinking about this. And at work...I couldn't help feeling...Oh, I don't know. It's so silly. I felt as if I didn't know anyone anymore. You know, like every person I saw could be this guy," Kathryn said, still shaken by the day's events. "My God, I even wondered about Fred Thomas, that dear old man who lives down by the river. And he's completely harmless!"

"That's not so silly, Katie. It's a perfectly natural response to what you've been through. My God, girl, some lunatic phoned you and threatened your daughter. How else are you supposed to react?" Wendy nibbled a bread stick while waiting for the waiter.

"Are you still staying the night?" Kathryn asked, knowing she was. Somehow, though, she needed more reassurance because she hadn't heard from David yet. She doubted that he would phone until he got back to Seattle since he would be spending most of his time flying and driving to and from the ranch.

"Of course I am. I'd never leave you alone tonight. Bill wanted to come too, but I told him it wasn't necessary. We'd call him if we need him. Besides, I picked up a cheesecake this afternoon and I thought we might settle the economic problems of the world tonight, without the hungry interference of the men," Wendy laughed, raising Kathryn's spirits to a higher level. It was her job to distract Kathryn tonight, and she planned to do everything in her power to do exactly that. "When did David say he'd be home?"

"A little after midnight if he doesn't miss the last ferry. If he does, he'll have to drive 'round to the bridge. But John's man should have been at the house shortly after we left this morning." Kathryn looked absently around the dining room for a waiter. The room was full of faces she knew, people who were considered both acquaintances and friends.

In a small town, everyone knew each other. There was a certain protection in that familiarity. Strangers stood out in a crowd or on the street. A person could walk alone down the streets of town at night or take a stroll in the park on a warm summer's night, knowing they were not in any danger. It was good to live in a place where people felt safe. Kathryn was angry that it was being snatched away from her.

"Oh, good. Here comes the waiter. I'm starving," Kathryn added, wanting to change the subject from the distressing reality. She'd read of these kinds of things happening, but like everyone else, she thought it only happened in L.A. or New York. She never dreamed something evil would come into her little corner of the world and throw her entire life upside down.

During their dinner, the two women chatted superficially, discussing all the latest gossip. Wendy often spent a good deal of her day on the phone, learning all the hottest local scoop about who was doing what with whom and where. Nantok Falls had a population of about twenty thousand and that made everyone neighbors, either by direct or indirect contact. If she didn't know someone personally, Kathryn knew them as a friend of a friend, or someone's cousin or even a patient. She used to appreciate it that way.

Kathryn was glad for the lightness of the banter and could almost forget what awaited her at home. As she studied the faces in the restaurant, she was relieved to see that the other patrons were involved in their own conversations and were not watching her as she expected at least one of them might be doing. The evening had turned into a girls' night out and it felt good. They laughed at the outrageous stories Wendy shared while sipping away at a liter of wine and nibbling a slice of lemon cheesecake. They decided to have it now rather than at home later.

The drive home was pleasant, lulling Kathryn into a feeling that this morning hadn't really happened. They turned into the long, hidden road that was, in fact, their driveway and the future street of a planned housing development. Their property was on the waterside of a large piece of land once owned by David's father and had been in the family almost since wagon trains first brought settlers west. Now, the property was subdivided into future contracting sites.

The sedan wove through the dark tunnel of trees until they broke into the clearing around the house. Wendy slowed her vehicle and flicked on her high beams. A white car loomed in the two circles of light, sitting just to the left of the large holly tree in front of the garage. Wendy moved slowly round the circular drive, keeping a close eye on the vehicle. As she got closer, the silver and navy emblem of the Sheriff's office began to glow on the driver's door.

Kathryn let out an audible sigh of relief. She had expected to see the police here, but for some inexplicable reason, the patrol car was a surprise. "It must be the deputy John assigned."

Wendy parked her car behind the empty deputy's vehicle.

"Maybe he's out doing rounds or something," Kathryn offered.

"I guess that's part of the job description. *Barney's* gotta keep an eye on all those old bears out there in the bush. He'll come in when he realizes we're home," Wendy snickered, pleased with her own joke.

The two women giggled at the thought of the immaculately uniformed *Barney* checking under every bush and up every tree for the intruder. They tripped up the stairs still snickering at the deputy's expense and headed to the guest room to make sure everything was ready for Wendy. Kathryn pulled several of crocheted Afghans over to the dresser and set them on top with a loud, exaggerated grunt. Her mother had been a prolific crotchetier and had worked on them nonstop before she died. She had always said it kept her hands nimble and held back the growing arthritis that finally devoured her body.

A knock on the front door pulled the two women from their joking and both sprinted down the hallway. Kathryn peered cautiously through the curtained window. The deputy nodded at her and she opened the door to let him in. He was a handsome young man in his uniform, but Kathryn couldn't remember ever having seen him before.

"Sorry to bother ya'll, ma'am. Ah thought Ah shud introduce mahself seein' as Ah pulled the night shift and will be just ahtside 'til the mah'nin'. Ah'm Deputy Mike Shaw. Sheriff Tyler is sendin' Deputy Graham to relieve mah shift before ya'll go tah work, so ya'll see a new face in the mah'nin'. Just thought ya'ld like tah know."

Kathryn stared at the pleasant young face shrouded with the blackness of the country night, far away from city lights. It seemed darker than she had ever remembered, and it stripped the deputy of his innocence. The neatly pressed uniform on his gawky frame offered no overwhelming sense of protection, and that worried Kathryn. His deep southern drawl and new face made her nervous, despite the familiar badge and hat he wore proudly.

"Well, thank you Deputy...uh...Shaw. You're new around here, aren't you?" she asked, not feeling grateful for the chance to be guarded by a stranger, especially one so youthful and inexperienced.

"Yes ma'am. Ah come from Jonesboro, Georgia. It's ah small place just south o' Atlanta. Ah moved here 'bout a month ago. Ya'll can call Sheriff Tyler to verify mah shift. I don't blame ya'll for bein' ah bit nervous. The Sheriff filled m' in on what's bin goin' on here, and ya'll can rest assured that Ah'll keep ah watchful eye out all night. So don't ya'll worrah none, ma'am." The young man grinned.

Kathryn took him up on his offer and left to phone John. He was no longer at the station, but she finally reached him at home. Apologizing for disturbing him, she was glad he verified the young deputy's story.

She returned to the door moments later with a smile of relief. He was real enough, right down to his deep Georgian accent and shock of blond hair jutting from the brim of his hat. John had forgotten she didn't know the new man but assured her Mike, Chris Johnson's brother, would be there in the morning by the time she woke up.

The Deputy offered his assistance if she needed him for "Anything t'all, ma'am. Ya'll just holler."

Kathryn appreciated his attentiveness to duty and let him know that David would be returning home in a couple of hours. Before he left to resume his vigil, she showed the officer a picture of David so Deputy Shaw wouldn't hassle David, or even shoot him, because of a mistaken identity.

The two women tripped back down the hallway, unable to repress the new peel of giggles erupting over their young sentry. Their knight in shining armor, with his innocent baby face, sounded more like a good-ol'-southern-boy cartoon sheriff than the genuine right arm of the law. It was the lightness Kathryn needed to counteract the growing fear inside. She thought she could at least sleep now, and as if to prove the point, she fell into a deep, wine-induced sleep as soon as her head hit the pillow.

A sudden cold chill in the back of her bent knees aroused her from sleep enough to make her jump away. It was a shock she was very familiar with. David's feet were always cold as ice. It was a curiosity that never ceased to amaze her. It could be ninety degrees in the shade and David's feet would still feel as if they had just been pulled from a freezer.

"David," she moaned, regretting that she was now only half asleep.

"Oh, are you awake, Katie?" he asked impishly.

"I am now. What time is it?" she yawned, wanting to curl up into a ball and drift back to sleep again. She stretched lazily, turning on her back so she could talk to David. He sounded jubilant despite the pressures of the day, and she suspected that all went well with the trip.

"Quarter past twelve," he whispered.

"How'd everything go? Meaghan okay?"

"Uh huh. Meaghan thinks she's on some sort of holiday at Grammy's house. She was thrilled with the plane ride. We went into the cockpit to watch the pilot for a few minutes. And, of course, she played shy when she saw Dad, but warmed up real quick when Mom gave her a hug." He snuggled closer to Kathryn's warm, soft body.

"Did you meet our bright-eyed deputy?" she asked through a sleepy smile unseen by David.

"I saw the car but there was no one in it," he mumbled, gently kissing the back of her neck.

"He does rounds or something. He's a nice young man. From the south. Georgia, I think he said," she mumbled, trying to remember, but it wasn't important enough to think about at the moment. She was relieved about Meaghan.

"Wendy here?" David asked as he held her tight in his arms.

"Yep. Snoring away in the guest room. Bill wanted to come to help baby-sit me, but she left him at home," she replied, trying to keep away from his feet. It was a struggle because David liked to sleep kitty-corner on the bed.

"Everything's been quiet then?" he asked, reluctantly giving up the foot wrestling, more than ready to surrender to sweet slumber.

"Not a peep," she yawned, drowsiness again tugging at her relaxed mind.

"Well, let's get some Z's. I'm bushed," he said.

"I was," she grunted, resigning herself to losing the battle yet again, and letting David plant his chilly feet on her legs. David cuddled around her and together they drifted off into a sound sleep.

A loud thudding noise broke through their dreams in what seemed to be barely thirty seconds later.

"Who the hell can that be?" David asked, jumping up, suddenly awakened in a dazed sort of way.

"Probably the Deputy. Conscientious young man. Has to introduce himself. Can't just stay outside the house without you knowing who he is," she mumbled through a loud yawn. "But I guess that's commendable."

"Who?" David asked as he found his slippers and housecoat in the darkness, and tugged them on.

"Our young southern protectorate. Just go say 'hi' and let's get back to sleep," she muttered, burying her head deeper into her pillow. *Why can't they just let me sleep?*

David pushed himself out of bed. She could hear the rustle of his housecoat as he tied it closed. His slippered footfalls muffled down the stairway and stopped at the door. She knew he was probably looking through the curtain, as she had done, making sure it was the deputy and not another surprise caller wanting to take their daughter. Kathryn heard the click of the deadbolt and the creak of the door as it slowly swung open. Voices drifted toward the bedroom from the whispered tones of the two men.

"Sorry to wake ya'll, Mr. Breslin, suh. But there's somethin' Ah thought ya'll might wanna see out here," said the deep southern accent. His voice was heavy against the quiet of the night.

"Can't this wait 'til morning?" David asked, agitated by the intrusion, his voice still sluggish with sleep.

"Well, suh. I don't rightly think so. I think ya'll should come and see it right now," the young Deputy said, a desperate urgency in his voice. His voice was deeper with the weight of his discovery, and Kathryn wondered for a brief moment if he was frightened by something. He was young enough to admit fear, unlike those, more seasoned, who knew how to hide their feelings.

She could hear the hesitating silence and then the slow creak of the door as David closed it, following the deputy outdoors.

Probably wants to ask some silly question about shadows in the bushes, she sighed.

Kathryn stayed semi-awake, waiting for David's return. He'd only wake her up anyway. It was the delight of his life to give her that first cold shock when he jumped into bed. There was no end to the things that amused David, and again she found herself hoping Meaghan did not share his peculiar passion.

She heard Wendy get up and stumble to the bathroom. A short time later, the toilet flushed and tap water splashed as Wendy presumably washed her hands. Then all returned to silence once again.

A few minutes later she heard heavy footfalls heading toward their bedroom and stop beside the bed. "What did the deputy want?" she yawned, only slightly curious.

"He wanted company," growled the deep, scratchy voice.

A cold shock of fear shot through Kathryn. She hoped it was just David playing a cruel joke. He was always one for practical jokes, although she couldn't recall any in such bad taste. David loved humor, but he wasn't nasty. Kathryn flipped onto her back, propping herself up on her elbows, and tried to detect the image of the man who stood in the shadows, her eyes well adjusted to the dark.

"David, that's not funny," she snapped still unable to see who it was in the blackness. He wasn't acting like David.

A small voice from deep inside her screamed: *Get up! Get up, now. Run! Don't just lie there. Run like hell! GET UP, DAMMIT! It's him! It's HIM!*

Before she could obey her mind and move, he was on the bed. Through the darkness of the night she could see the blackened hint of a fist moving toward her face in slow motion. It planted itself on the side of her head with all the force of a truck. Before she could gather herself from the blow, a second and third landed near the first one. She could feel a small trickle of wetness flow down the side of her face. There was a taste of metallic saltiness slipping into her mouth from a stinging lip. Dazed, she moaned from the pain that exploded in her left eye.

The man grabbed her arms and flipped her onto her stomach as if she were simply a rag doll. Slamming his knee into her back, he pinned her wrists into unyielding metal cuffs. She could hear the clicking of the locks as he pressed the circular metal bars tight into her skin. Her good eye winced as the metal pinched the soft flesh of her hands, causing a shock of pain to shoot up her arms.

Kathryn opened her mouth to scream but he shoved her face into the pillows, cutting off her breath. She struggled as best she could, flopping impotently on the bed. Fear ploughed into her stomach. She gasped for air but found nothing except a smothering pillowcase filled with her imminent death as he ground her head into its depths. Her lungs ached with a bursting pain as they screamed hysterically for oxygen. Her energy deserted her as darkness swirled about her head, pulling her into a whirlpool of black unconsciousness.

An eternity of thought passed by and she finally ceased her struggles, succumbing to the greater force demanding her life.

Chapter Three

Kathryn coughed and was immediately rewarded with a sharp pain spiking through the side of her head. She was surprised to discover she was alive, although the reason she should be amazed eluded her. Her thoughts were obscured in a panic fueled by the grinding drone surrounding her. The air that only partially filled her lungs was stifling, stale and hot. Everything was black—blacker than she had ever seen. A tightness gripped her throat. She tried in vain to move her limbs but they were incapable of obeying her simplest commands. The merest effort to move created a chain reaction of muscle spasms that surged through every limb—a torment that pit its throbbing cycle against the headache that was increasing its intense attack as she became more awake.

She tried to regroup her thoughts to remember where she was and how she got there. Her mind was foggy. It was hard to keep one idea long enough to make sense of it before it transformed into something completely different. Her tongue was thick. A bad chemical taste lived in her mouth. Her lips felt dry and rough. She felt extremely hung-over.

Drugs, she rationalized. *But why would I take drugs? Where would I get them?*

Dark images of last night drifted back to her. *The Deputy...Deputy Shaw. Standing guard outside the house. David came home. Meaghan okay. A knock at the door. David came in...no...not David. The man on the phone. Had to be. He hit me...smothered me. Shoved my face into the bed...pillow...passed out...*

It all tumbled back on her. The memories were terrifying. Someone had tried to kill her. But how could she be sure he hadn't succeeded? How could she be sure she wasn't dead?

Death shouldn't hurt so much. And I hurt a lot...everywhere. No, I'm very much alive. And I'm not in a hospital. I'm moving. I can hear the rolling of wheels on asphalt. But why is it so dark? Am I blind? Am I buried alive? How can I be buried if I'm moving? Get a grip, Katie. You're losing it.

She struggled against her restraints in a renewed fit of fear only to realize that there were ropes binding her legs and arms together. She could move her head, but the cloth around her face was secured to her neck...*My God, my head is in a bag!* A fresh rush of panic flooded over her. .

She tried to scream. A low moan escaped through...*what the hell is in my mouth?* She worked her tongue around a silky, wet mass. She tried to gulp but only ended up coughing again as part of the mass slipped a little further down her restricted throat. Fearful that she would suffocate on the wad of...*are those cotton balls?*...she concentrated on not swallowing.

Relax, she ordered her straining body. The command became a chant that kept perfect rhythm with the pulsating noise filling her ears. *Relax!* she screamed, trying to combat the growing dread clawing at her.

Highway...I'm in a car. We're driving down the highway.

She was seized with a nervous trembling. She tried to force the cotton from her mouth with her tongue, carefully working the wad back from her throat, but her effort was foiled by what she presumed to be some sort of tape across her lips.

Concentrate. Get a hold of yourself. Take an assessment of your situation. You're a doctor. Act like one, she commanded herself.

She had been in emergency situations before, but it had never been personal. She couldn't remember how many times she had tried to tell a patient everything would be just fine and there was nothing to worry about. Or how many times she had seen patient panic, making an already serious situation almost impossible. And now, she was trying to give herself the same futile advice she expected her patients to follow immediately. She couldn't help but laugh—a short, smothered type of laugh, like one given by someone who spit in the face of death just before the last gurgle erupted from their lifeless body.

All right. Start at the feet and work your way up. One thing at a time.

Kathryn suffered through the misery of moving every muscle in her body, starting with her toes. It was a slow, meticulous process. Although she was working blind, she did have the added advantage of being able to feel each symptom personally, since this time she was the patient.

She had no idea how long the examination took. Time didn't seem to be an important issue at the moment.

Considering the present situation, she was relieved to have less injury than she expected to find from the amount of pain pummeling her. The fingers on both her hands were numb from lack of circulation, as were her feet. But nothing was broken. One eye was swollen shut. What she assumed were handcuffs cut deeply into her wrists. Rough nylon cord dug into her ankles giving her a degree of rope burn. Her body was covered with contusions and lacerations of varying degrees.

Kathryn was lying on her stomach on the back floor of a car—the hump pushed into her diaphragm. Her feet were bound both to her hands and the car since she couldn't move them more than a fraction of an inch. She could feel the texture of a soft car blanket covering her, which led her to believe she was not wearing any clothes. The hood surrounding her head was porous enough to allow her to breathe with only moderate difficulty...and her bladder wanted to explode.

Think about something else. Fear makes the need worse. She had too much dignity to wet herself, not allowing him to drag her that low.

Kathryn knew it wouldn't help to focus on her predicament. There was absolutely nothing she could accomplish by worrying about it. On the contrary, fretting about something over which she had no control would drain what little energy she had left and make things a lot more uncomfortable than they already were. She forced her mind onto more pleasant thoughts—the weekend that had begun this whole nightmare. With a great deal of effort, she focused through the painful discomfort and placed herself back at the restaurant.

David had booked the dinner party to include Wendy, Bill, Kathryn's father, David's sister and his brother-in-law. It was a birthday celebration with Kathryn's closest family and friends. Wine flowed throughout dinner. The meal was delicious. The desserts were scrumptious. Conversation was stimulating. Kathryn had felt very lucky that night to have such a close-knit group of people who could be called family and friends at the same time. It had been a wonderful party.

Maybe my last. Stop it! Control yourself.

At the end of the evening, David had driven along the waterfront and, instead of turning north toward home, turned south onto the highway toward the ferry. Without Kathryn knowing about it, David had arranged with her receptionist that there were to be no appointments Friday or Monday at the clinic.

He had planned a marvelous four days in and on the water on a private charter yacht called the *Nor'Westerner*. The vessel was glorious. They had sailed through the bay and out to the islands, skirting independent splotches of land jutting out of the clear waters.

The San Juan Islands were a splendid sailing paradise. Many sailors touted them as the best sailing waters in the world, in terms of both pleasure and challenge. Each of the one hundred seventy-two islands had its own distinct personality, many with ideally secure harbors. The entire area was created by the tips of a sunken mountain range protruding from the ocean floor, so every island was a different size, shape and height.

David could not have chosen anything more special for a birthday getaway. Thinking about the memory of his touch and the romance they shared gave her a warm feeling even now, in the back of a lunatic's car. A wail lodged in her throat, pinned by the spur of fear that assaulted her.

That first night they stayed in the same bed and breakfast they had visited on their first sailing trip. David was such a romantic...

God, David. Where are you? Where am I?

He loved the water as much as she did, and when they couldn't be on it, they tried to be either in it or near it. There was something magically compelling about the ocean. It called to them. It beckoned them to come and play. The ocean was so full of life, so demanding and uncompromising, while being generous and loving at the same time. Those who showed their fear or arrogance quickly saw how cruel the sea could be. But when you showed the water its due respect, it was the best friend in the whole world.

Diving into its cold, quiet depths made Kathryn feel as if she were cradled in its bosom. She could almost forget the artificial means of life support she was forced to wear in order to enter the mystical, watery world. She had played with starfish, swam with whales, frolicked with sea lions and bodysurfed on the waves. Together, she and David had explored a few of the many sunken galleons and smuggling boats that littered the underwater coasts around the San Juan Islands' archipelago.

Although they had never actually found their own Spanish Pieces of Eight gold coins, they had purchased two from one of the local diving shops the first year they had gone diving. For years, both wore a coin strung on a gold chain under their scuba suit for good luck, and for fun, they had worn them that last weekend as well. David had given Kathryn her gold chain in the car on the way to the ferry as a hint of what he had planned for them.

That was the weekend her line feed tube had broken, which prevented her from being able to inflate her suit enough to withstand the greater water pressures of the lower depths. She was forced to stay close to surface and watch with envy as David explored the cliffs for sea life and hidden treasures.

She had laughed, as much as anyone could with a breathing bit clamped between her teeth, when David was whisked along by the current. He sped along the cliff walls like a doll caught in the current of a river, moving so swiftly she doubted he had time to see anything. *Payback,* she had thought smugly. But, a true adventurer, he still flashed his camera to take as many pictures as possible as he was whisked along the cliff wall. She watched in amazement, her eyes following the flashes of light that floated off into the darkness of distant waters as David persisted in his shutterbug defiance.

We haven't picked up those pictures yet. I haven't even seen what you saw, David. Oh God, David, where are you?

It had been an eventful four days. The second night a small twenty-foot yacht had drifted into the bow of their vessel, the noise of the benign collision waking everyone up. The smaller craft's anchor had slipped and it could not prevent itself from drifting aimlessly on the tide. Their motor would not turn over, leaving them powerless against the current. The next morning the *Nor' Westerner's* captain, Davy, towed the smaller craft into Friday Harbor at the owner's request so that it could undergo necessary engine repairs.

Kathryn had applauded David's choice of vessels. The *Nor' Westerner* was a sixty-three-foot craft of opulent luxury, complete with a ruggedly handsome captain and two crewmembers. Their aft Master Stateroom was paneled in deeply oiled teak with hunter green accents, giving it a warm earthy feel that smelled of a life on the ocean. The water view and indirect lighting gave the room a soft, airy atmosphere. Kathryn could not imagine a more romantic place.

She had been delighted to see a full walk-around queen size bed and private head complete with separate shower stall and vanity. As David opened the door, displaying the walk-in clothes locker, Kathryn had checked out the drawers on both port and starboard sides of the stateroom, thrilled with how spacious their living quarters were. She hadn't expected to walk into such lavish conditions. The largest boat she had been on besides a ferry was a twenty-eight-foot sailboat they had considered purchasing.

But that was a whole lifetime ago, she moaned through the knot of soggy cotton threatening to choke her.

After stowing their gear, Kathryn and David had walked through the galley to the upper deck. They settled into two casual chairs, put their feet up and gazed out the windows, ready to watch the vessel maneuver through the sail boats, fishing scows, and ferries. Muddy Waters softly drifted from a built-in cabinet that served as the entertainment center.

Between the two chairs, the captain had placed a small teak table that held two blood-red champagne glasses, a chilled bottle of dry white wine, and two plates of crepes topped with fresh whipped cream and strawberries. David filled the two glasses and they toasted the beginning of the wonderful thirty-sixth year of her life. He wished her long life and happiness as he kissed her slowly and passionately; a lingering kiss that lasted until the crew had cast off and they were slowly leaving the pier behind. Kathryn felt more like twenty-five as she dug hungrily into her crepes and sipped the sparkling wine as the cruiser maneuvered northward through the waters, leaving the town of Everett behind.

Right now I feel like I'm eighty. Well, happy birthday, Katie! Now, you've left everything behind! She grimaced, fighting against the cuffs one more time, as if suddenly they would let go and release her from their painful hold. Resigning herself again to the metal's unyielding force, she let her mind wander back to the weekend.

It was the first time either of them had felt so completely relaxed in three months. Both their businesses kept them active and too often pushed into long hours. That weekend was more than a nice surprise...

It might have been the last weekend we ever have together, she cried, hopelessness finally swamping her. Kathryn began to sob uncontrollably—deep, gut-wrenching sobs that racked her body with spasms of stiff agony. She tried to calm herself, but failed.

Oh God, David. How did I ever get here? Where was the deputy? Where are you? And Wendy? Oh God, let me live through this. Let me escape, be rescued, something, anything...just don't let me die like this. Not horribly. I don't want to die. Meaghan needs a mother. David needs a wife. Oh God, I want to live...

Kathryn wept, choked on the cotton, and then wept some more. She had no idea where she was or where she was headed; who it was who had taken her...or why. She just knew she was a prisoner.

A prisoner. What the hell does that mean?

It was a foreign concept to her. She had read stories in magazines and books as recently as last year about different prisoners held around the world. But the notion was so strange she couldn't quite grasp the reality of it. No one had ever confined her in any way before, and now, she did not know what to do. It was odd not being able to freely move...or breathe...or swallow...or think. She could not comprehend needing someone else's permission to live. Or die...

The rhythm of the car slowed, yanking her away from her thoughts. He was pulling off the road.

Was it a truck stop? Oh God, was it wilderness? Is this where he's going to kill me? Rape me?

She held her breath, the fear driving her almost mad. Her whole body tensed against the bonds, increasing the agony that already throbbed through every muscle and sinew. The car pulled to a complete stop. Her mind raced frantically through a thousand unfinished scenarios of what she could—should—do to escape. He could untie her...to rape her...then she could kick herself free. She was a doctor. She knew what things most hurt a man. She could use her knowledge against him.

The hum of the engine stopped when he turned the motor off. The car wobbled slightly as he climbed out of the driver's seat. The door closed with a loud shudder as he slammed it behind him. She waited.

The quiet was deafening. The silence gnawed at her. What little strength she had regained vanished. Her wrists felt as if they would break with the alarm coursing through her. The pain in her head clubbed what little remained of her rational ability to conceive thought. She felt as if she swallowed a cotton ball and began to choke madly. She couldn't breathe...

This is it, she realized, glad that she would die before he killed her. Although short lived, it was somehow a small victory for her to be able to steal that moment of glory away from him.

There was a strange acceptance of death while it hung in the very air she tried to breathe. She had lived a good life and had a wonderful family. She had experienced more than many people ever know. Death could come now and she would still be the winner.

Blackness swirled around her mind, sucking her deeper into the fissure of unconsciousness. She was vaguely aware of a warm wetness spreading over her legs. Without any further struggle, she rode the wave, willing to not only accept her fate, but to embrace it. This way would at least be less violent than what he had planned.

She choked again, gasping for air and gagging as the silky cotton mass slid up from her throat and out her mouth. Air rushed into her lungs between spells of retching. Acidic bile erupted from her stomach until the only thing, left were agonizing dry heaves.

Her eyes were covered, but the hood had been removed. The air was cool and sweet, fresh, with the heavy, musky smell of mountains. She breathed in the aromatic odor of cedars that seemed to surround her in the darkness.

To her surprise, an unexpected hand suddenly caressed her cheek. Kathryn jerked back as far as she physically could—which wasn't more than an inch or two. She gasped. Her stomach settled into a dull throb. Her breathing slowed to a near-normal rhythm. An ominous stillness oppressed her.

"Please," a pitifully weak and quiet voice rasped. She was shocked to discover the strange sound belonged to her. "Please. I can't feel my hands."

Kathryn hated herself for begging, but it was so automatic, so natural, she was helpless to stop the attitude of words. It was the only thing left for her to do—breathe and beg for mercy.

She heard the jingle of metal coins close to her head. A hot metal disc slapped her on the cheek.

"Here's a quarter. Call someone who cares," the darkness growled.

"Please, don't hurt me. Don't kill me," she begged again, feeling her cheeks flush with shame.

A sharp pain pierced the flesh on her arm. A cool liquid pushed its way into her vein. A black cloud swirled around her, dragging her back down to the pit of unconsciousness.

Drugs, her mind screamed. Panic crowded in on her in that brief moment between consciousness and unconsciousness. She tried one last futile attempt to reach out to whatever humanity this creature may have hidden deep inside.

"P...l...e...a . . .." and then she slipped into the land of not knowing, or caring, what happened to her, or why.

Chapter Four

Hard, cool metal dug into her back, pinching her skin when she moved the slightest bit. Straps bound her tightly to what Kathryn assumed was the metal spring frame of a small cot. There was no mattress. Nothing protected her skin from the cold chill.

Kathryn tried to shift her arms and legs. She was taller than the bed, thinking it was most likely a child's cot. Her legs were bent at the knees. A rope bound each ankle to the base of the bed. Her arms were stretched above her head and hung from the wall or pipe behind her head. A cord dug into her throat, pinning her neck to the metal springs. A final strap bound her hips to the cot, preventing her from easing her position even slightly.

A hood wrapped her head in the inky blackness of confusion. An itchy tightness was caused by a pulling sensation across the inside her left forearm. She assumed the prickling was from tape as she was allergic to the common adhesive. It was the area of the most accessible vein in the body...the one she always used...*most likely from a needle...or an IV. They probably had to use that vein because of the straps across my hands.*

Kathryn could not imagine why she would be positioned in such unconventional traction. She had never seen any spinal damage that would require such an absurd posture. She had witnessed certain victims strapped between two metal frames that formed a tight body-width cage, but that was not her case. There was nothing on top of her, not even a blanket.

Kathryn wished she could see where she was. Straining to listen for any recognizable noises proved futile. The rustling of her hair against the material of the hood muffled the small outside sounds whenever she moved her head from one side to the other. The tightness at her throat prevented Kathryn from moving more than a few degrees, compelling her to remain as still as possible. The labored wheeze of her breathing was magnified to deafening levels by the hood. The smothering confines of the hood forced her to breathe in stale, recycled air.

Her lips were parched and hot. An itchiness plagued both upper and lower lips, increasing its annoying irritation until she thought she'd go mad. Kathryn tried to lick them, to scratch them with her tongue and teeth, but tape prevented her from opening her mouth.

Where's the oxygen hose? Why don't I have an endotracheal tube? Is this real? Or is it just a bad dream? she asked, more confused than ever.

Kathryn stretched her fingers and toes through the tingling numbness. Considering the way her circulation was cut off by the metal bars, it was a sensation she would have expected.

Everything feels real. Katie, if you're asleep, wake up and get the hell out of this nightmare, she ordered herself, hoping it would stimulate her enough to wake up.

Nothing changed. She was not asleep. Beyond any doubt, Kathryn found herself trapped in the most uncomfortable position she could imagine.

Her head was thick. She could hear Meaghan call from the other room, but couldn't get up to go to her. Perhaps Meaghan would search for Kathryn and find her strapped to the bed. Kathryn wondered why Meaghan was with her. If she were in a hospital, Meaghan should be at home with David or Wendy. *Was Meaghan strapped to a bed as well?*

Kathryn heard a distant choir singing a soft mourning chant outside her window and wondered why they weren't all singing the same tune. It was a song she knew well as it was one of her favorites. On their first anniversary, David had flown her to Broadway to see her first live production play. The vibrating acoustics of the music that flowed through the audience captured her imagination. When they had returned home, Kathryn purchased the Broadway soundtrack and played it on the way to the clinic almost every day for three months.

It was nice of David to have the music piped into her hospital room. He was always doing something special for her. It was his way. He was the most thoughtful, caring man she had ever met. When they discovered she was pregnant with Meaghan, David seemed to instinctively know it was a baby girl. To celebrate the occasion and let everyone know how he felt, he had filled Kathryn's clinic with a dozen bouquets of roses and wildflowers.

Wait a minute. What window? she asked herself, unable to find any area warmed by the sun in the cool, crisp air. Kathryn tried to call out to David...or a nurse...to tell them to close the window...to tell them that she felt cold and damp...but she couldn't speak or budge, so gave up the attempt.

Perhaps someone will come in and notice I'm shivering. I must have been in an accident. Maybe I've been in a coma since the accident. *That's why there's restraints. I might have damaged the automatic nervous system, causing me to thrash around. Perhaps I'm tied down for my own protection. And I must have serious facial injuries. It's not a hood at all...my head is wrapped in bandages. My eyes...did I get shattered windshield glass in my eyes? Am I blind? I must be in ICU. That's why I have no clothes on.*

She thought she remembered being in a car. *Maybe it was an ambulance. But...wasn't I on the floor? It must have been David's car. We were probably on our way home. I could have been thrown in the back seat during the accident. But why wasn't I wearing a seat belt? I always wear a seat belt.*

She tried to think it through clearly, but her sluggish mind inhibited her ability. She lay back, trying to release the pent-up tension that had seized her body, holding it captive. The creaking sound of the metal frame echoed distantly in the room as she tried to shift her position. Kathryn succeeded only in shifting her shoulders a millimeter in any direction.

I'm lying on springs, she realized as the cold metal cut into her back. She forced herself to lay as still as possible against the growing cramps seizing her muscles.

Did I break my back? Is that why I'm on this torturous rack? Is that why it tingles with pain? Patients have said they feel like this after they've broken their spine. They say they can't feel an outside source touching them, but there is pain in their lower body and limbs. That has to be what's happening. It's the only possible explanation. I can't imagine any sane doctor putting me on a bed of springs. It only feels like that.

Kathryn strained her ears, trying to listen through what she assumed to be gauze and tape wound about her head. *I can hear it,* she told herself. *There! There it is again. I must be in Intensive Care. That's why it's so quiet. Is that the blip of a heart monitor? Maybe it's mine. It must have been a very bad accident. I must have almost died.*

She tried to remember the car...how she got in it.

God, why doesn't someone come and talk to me? I want to know what's going on! she screamed as loud as she could inside her head. *If I'm here, where is David? Is he alive?*

Kathryn could not remember ever feeling so helpless, not even in the wake of the break-in. Unlike now, she was at least able to move and see. The useless limbs and inability to call out ate at her with a hungry frustration. Anger was mingling with terror as the unknown element of her situation nagged at her.

Wait a minute, wasn't I in bed sleeping? she asked herself, a dim memory of David's cold feet jarring her awake.

The thick daze clouding her thoughts lifted like a slow dissipating morning mist on a cold mountain lake. She remembered mentally doing a physical examination when she woke up on the car's floor after the crash. Kathryn hadn't thought anything was broken, but clearly, she must have been wrong. *After all, I can't remember the accident.*

The foggy recollection of thinking she was someone's prisoner drifted into her thoughts, making her smile at the silliness.

Hysteria, shock, hallucination, she rationalized. *Probably a combination of all three. That would explain everything.*

Kathryn could remember being away for the weekend with David. Meaghan had gone to Wendy's. It was a wonderful weekend. After coming home, though, everything fell apart.

Perhaps we had an accident on the way home. That would explain everything. There had been no break-in or phone call. We were driving home, got into a very bad car accident, and I've been in a coma, hallucinating an entire ugly nightmare since the moment of unconsciousness.

Kathryn was unsure she was able to think clearly even now. *Natural response,* she assured herself.

There was a certain amount of peace earned by fitting all the pieces of a puzzle together. Now that she had done that very thing, Kathryn decided to relax and accept her current predicament. Someone was certain to come by eventually and verify her conclusions. Then it would simply be a matter of learning to cope with the hand dealt her, and overcoming any lingering disabilities.

The sound of a vehicle crunched on the ground outside. Kathryn was absolutely certain that's what it was. She could hear a car door slam shut.

I must have a concussion. I'm still hallucinating. What would a car being doing in ICU? she asked herself, sneering at the absurdity of the tricks the mind plays on itself. *This entire situation will help me in my practice when I get back on my feet. If I can just keep focused on the good that can be gained, the bad will is easier to cope with. I will definitely have more understanding, empathy, and appreciation for the struggles of my patients.*

Kathryn had enjoyed a life of good health until this incident. She had never had so much as the measles or a sprained ankle. It did make her try harder to bring people up to the level of health she enjoyed, but there was a definite gap in understanding just what her patients were feeling. It was difficult to empathize with a painful knee that prevented someone from walking, or how the constant ache of arthritis became unbearable just before a rainy afternoon.

The door to her room creaked like old wood on rusty hinges, pulling her from her reflections. She did not remember there being a door separating the cubicles on an ICU ward. Beds were usually arranged in a circle around the nurses' station. The nurses had to maintain constant vigilance of each patient. *However, different hospitals had different arrangements. Maybe it's just a squeaky med cart or wheelchair.*

Heavy footfalls slapped across the rickety floorboards. Hard-soled shoes stopped beside her bed and she desperately wanted to ask the nurse about her condition. Hoping the woman would notice she was awake, Kathryn tried to signal by forcing her head to turn from side to side, struggling against the strangling cord holding her neck. The wet splash of water droplets landed on Kathryn's arm as the nurse emptied the syringe of air bubbles. Kathryn felt the instant pinch of a needle prick...cold liquid pushed its way against the current of her bloodstream...then the swirl sucked her back into the whirlpool.

Chapter Five

Kathryn first felt a rigid ache in her bones. This was replaced by a gradual sluggish awareness of a blinding light that pierced her eyelids like a white-hot dagger. She groaned from the stiffness, wondering how she could have slept in so late in the day—especially on such a hard, uncompromising floor. She tried to remember how she had come to be sleeping on the kitchen's cold linoleum and vaguely questioned why David or Wendy hadn't woken her before now, or at least moved her somewhere a bit more forgiving.

They wouldn't have just left me here like this, without a pillow or even a blanket. She moaned, wishing she was in her own bed, under Oma's comforter.

Kathryn's grandmother spent years making feather Eiderdowns, one for each of her eight grandchildren. Oma lovingly hand-stitched each comforter in the manner she had learned from her mother. Each was set aside to be presented as a gift on their wedding day. Kathryn, the youngest and last grandchild, received her comforter five years after her grandmother had died. The day Kathryn opened the box, tears had flowed down her cheeks. It was an unexpected surprise. Kathryn had not realized her grandmother made the old country Eiderdown well ahead of time, and now, it was a precious memory.

And David was hogging it all to himself in our warm, comfortable bed, she thought, easing herself off the growing bruise on her hip.

"What a night!" she groaned, remembering the awful nightmares that had assaulted her. Kathryn struggled to shake off the thickness that imprisoned her mind, but rational thoughts were not readily forthcoming. "I'll never drink again!" she promised herself.

"David! It's time to get up!" she hollered as loud as she could manage, ready to chide him about his obvious lack of concern over her horrendously uncomfortable sleeping arrangement.

Kathryn supposed they had drunk more wine than she should have done. They always drank a little too much on the rare occasion she and Wendy had a girls' night out, although she couldn't remember ever having so much to drink that she had passed out on the floor.

Assuming she was already late for work, Kathryn tried to summon some energy, becoming aware that she couldn't quite command enough strength to rise from her position and get Meaghan up for breakfast.

Wait a minute. Meaghan's not here. David took her to Farmington yesterday, she reminded herself. The nightmares had been bad, but saying good-bye to Meaghan for an indefinite time was the worst thing Kathryn had ever done.

Time will be tight, she thought, clearing her mind of the image of Meaghan waving from the rear window of the sedan. She rolled over, letting the other hip take the brunt of the floor's unyielding hardness.

Was today a holiday? she asked herself, trying to focus. *What is today? David left for New Mexico Wednesday. That would make today Thursday.*

It was hard to remain where she was, but somehow she lacked the necessary motivation to move. There was a residue of dizziness that plagued her every time she stirred. The floor remained inflexible and impersonal. A thirst increased its nagging annoyance as she became more alert. It overpowered the growling pangs of hunger that rolled and thundered in her stomach. A full bladder cramped with spastic, lightening stabs of pain that charged throughout her guts with enough force to double her over in crippling agony.

Kathryn could no longer ignore the urgent call of nature and, reluctant to move, she pushed herself up despite the growing stiffness where the floor had bruised her. She stumbled to the bathroom by sleepy memory and staggered straight into a cold metal table that hadn't been there when she came home last night.

Kathryn opened her eyes and hugged a throbbing knee. The realization that she was not at home unmercifully blindsided her at the same time.

"What the...?" she mumbled, stunned. The brilliance of the white room assaulted her now widened eyes, bathing them in uncomprehending fear and shock.

Is this a hospital? Am I in a psych ward? she asked herself, not really expecting an answer. There was nothing about this room that looked even vaguely familiar.

Kathryn pirouetted in a small, slow circle, allowing her mind to absorb the full scope of the room with its meager and threateningly sterile furnishings. Her mouth fell open with stunned silence. Fear, which had been lurking in her subconscious for the last two and a half days, raised its serpentine head like a poisonous viper.

The brilliance of the room brutally slapped her, forcing the encroaching dread to rapidly swell to brazen panic. Confusion crushed Kathryn's reason as she observed the room in all its horrid luminescence.

The room was compact—almost claustrophobic. The walls, ceiling and floor were smothered with antiseptic high gloss white paint. Over the paint were fastened sheets of plastic or glass...she wasn't quite sure. One complete wall was covered with several sheets of mirror from floor to ceiling and wall-to-wall. Facing the mirror, she could see the outline of a door cut into the right hand side of the reflective glass. Instead of a knob or handle, there was only a small metal box with a slit in its side... she assumed it was a card-keyed security mechanism.

The ceiling was easily ten feet high and had metal cages that protected the four rows of radiant lighting recessed into panels. The floor was coated in the same sheets of glass or plastic...*must be Plexiglas. Glass would be too fragile*, she decided.

There were only three pieces of furniture in the room: one six-foot-long stainless steel table in the middle of the floor; one stainless steel sink; and one white porcelain toilet by the far wall, behind the table and opposite the mirrored door. The room was devoid of any warmth or personality.

No natural light entered the windowless cell. The offensive artificial brilliance of the light panels reflected off the paint and Plexiglas, desperately seeking a way of escape; but, like Kathryn, it too was held captive. The reflective glow off the walls and floor hurt her eyes, leaving Kathryn with no protection at all from the merciless assault.

Eight stainless steel airshafts were evenly spaced around the ceiling perimeter. Strong streams of cold air blew down on her and offset any possible heat from the banks of lights. Each of the vents was covered with plastic squares, into which were drilled twelve small holes the diameter of her pinkie finger with protective screening inside the holes. Kathryn suspected the precaution was to prevent insects from falling down the vents...*or me from crawling out.* Yet she was given no way of reaching the vents to attempt escape.

The complete silence of the room was frightening and oppressive, broken only by the sound of her own terrified breathing as a panic attack seized. She struggled with the reality of her situation.

"But where *am I*?" she asked the silence.

Kathryn tried to pick out some reference point but couldn't find any in the strange Plexiglas room. *I haven't ever seen a hospital room like this. What in hell is going on?*

Kathryn attempted to remember the last thing she did before going to bed.

Wendy...we had supper. Kathryn leaned against the table. *I was at home.*

"But where the hell am I now?" Kathryn buried her head in her hands. "Oh God, where am I? How did I get here? I don't even know what day it is." She decided that her previous assumption that it was

Thursday was wrong, realizing for all she knew it could be a year from Wednesday.

A violent tremor seized Kathryn's body as the panic rose to unbearable heights. She fell against the table, overwhelmed by a sudden light-headedness, probably caused by drug-induced grogginess and an unreasonable thirst and hunger. She held her head in quaking hands, feeling vulnerable, desperate, and very alone. Kathryn prayed to wake up from this nightmare, but was all too much aware that she was, unfortunately, already very much awake.

The lights bore through her lids mercilessly. Kathryn decided to make the search of the walls for a dimmer switch her priority. Through squinted lids, she fought against the glare to examine the barren, bleak, white walls buried beneath the reflective Plexiglas. There was nothing remarkable, nor were there any controls of any kind available to her.

She sighed, the quivering hiss of her escaping breath exposing her paramount fear.

Kathryn's mind wandered without conscious direction. Images, partial thoughts, and random memories flitted through her panicked mind. The last thing she could recall...*No, wait. After I went to bed. A noise. Someone in the bedroom. He surprised me while I waited for David. Attacked me.* Kathryn slumped to the floor in a pool of hopelessness as tears gushed from her eyes.

"What happened? What the hell happened? Where are you, David? Where am I?" she asked the cold, uncaring stillness of her cell, repeating the words in a pathetic, halfhearted chant as what little energy she had disappeared.

No one answered. Silence swallowed her up in a terrifying eeriness.

"Think, Katie. Think, damn it!" she commanded, trying to take control of her rising panic, and wake herself up from the stupor induced by lack of food and overabundance of drugs.

Does David know I'm locked in this strange place? Has he called the Sheriff? Where was the deputy? Did someone kidnap me? I don't remember anyone taking me.

"Oh God, why can't I remember?" she cried, despair blanketing her words as her questions only fathered more questions.

Kathryn remembered hearing the strange, deep voice. *He was on me before I could move. Hitting me. And then...*

Nothing...nothing but blackness.

Kathryn couldn't remember any more. Pounding her head with shaky fists to encourage her memory to function better didn't help.

"Oh, my God," she whispered with sinking hopelessness. She could make no sense of why she was locked in this offensively brilliant room instead of being at home, in her bed, with her husband.

"Why is that wall mirrored?" she asked the room, which crushed in on her as if it had a life of its own.

Kathryn cautiously approached the silver glass, her steps awkward and unsteady, and placed her hands on the smooth coldness of its shiny face. She stared into the soul of her prison, looking beyond the reflection of her own half-naked body and tortured fear.

"Hello?" she cried out suddenly as panic forced her to bang on the mirror in an attempt to attract someone's attention on the other side. "Anybody there? Can you hear me?"

Her breathing marked time as she waited an eternity in the pitiless silence for a simple answer to her useless pleading. But no one responded. There was not even an echo from her own futile hammering as the suffocating stillness absorbed her very life, smothering her under an unseen pillow of impending death. She continued her vigilance, begging someone...anyone...to come, at the same time afraid they would, hoping and praying they wouldn't.

After another twenty minutes, Kathryn was obliged to give up her feeble attempts and head to the barren porcelain toilet across the room, unable to refuse her painful bladder one second longer. She hesitated, aware that the mirror was most probably a one-way window with the very real possibility that someone was on the other side watching her every move.

"Who are you?" she screamed, ranting at the frantic reflection of herself. "What do you want from me? Why have you brought me here? Answer me, dammit. Answer me!"

There was no acknowledgment, no indication that anyone was paying the least bit of attention to her. She resisted no longer and gave into the pressing need to relieve herself. Kathryn gave up in dismal resignation, accepting that there wasn't a damned thing she could do about whoever was on the other side anyway, and tried to ignore the thought of being studied while attempting to urinate as quietly as possible into the porcelain echo chamber.

Sitting on the toilet, hoping to take her mind off being watched, Kathryn studied the only real piece of furniture in the room. With growing distress, she wondered just what a stainless steel table might be used for. Shuddering uncontrollably at the indistinct images and possibilities that swept through her mind, she recognized it as an operating table before it had the added feature of a metal cuff soldered to each of the four corners. The very sight of such a table in this aseptic environment unnerved her.

Why is everything covered with Plexiglas sheets? The over-whelming chill from the lack of human atmosphere gnawed away at her. She felt as if she were in the sterile environment aboard a UFO

As she wiped herself, Kathryn was shocked to discover that her legs were covered with urine and dried fecal material from previous days. Disgusted with her condition, she tried unsuccessfully to remember how she got that way.

"Who are you?" she screamed at the top of her lungs, no longer able to contain the terror that swelled within her pounding breast. "What do you want from me? Damn you, answer me!"

Kathryn began to tremble as tears streamed down her cheeks, terror seizing her soul.

She leaned over the sink and turned on the cold water, splashing her face with its welcome coolness. There was no soap, face cloths, or towels. There was only cold water. Bracing herself, she removed her T-shirt and washed as completely as she could, shivering as much from the vulnerable exposure as the wetness. Cleansing her body helped to somewhat clear her mind after she lapped some frigid water from a cupped hand. Momentarily refreshed, Kathryn tried to collect her thoughts and gain some degree of control, but failed. She let her body drip dry before donning the T-shirt again, trying to retrieve what little modesty it afforded her.

She turned to face the mirrored wall, noticing her reflection in all its unflattering honesty for the first time. The hellish reality of the room had eclipsed her thoughts, not allowing her the clarity to wonder why she was so scantily dressed.

Kathryn barely recognized herself. Her hair stood out at all angles as if she had been through a windstorm. The plain white T-shirt was three sizes too big for her, hanging down to her mid-thighs, but she was grateful for that little concession. She looked pale and disoriented. Fear was carved into every feature, giving her a haunted, tortured appearance. Kathryn's left eye was swollen into a deep purple color. Two lacerations adorned the swollen bluish flesh of her left cheek and upper lip. Circling her reddened neck, digging into the tender skin, was a raw reminder of a rope burn. Deep gashes dug into the flesh of her wrists and ankles, giving them a bloodied, torn appearance amid the general bruises and cuts.

Her legs and arms were varying shades of blue, purple, and yellow, making her look more like a patchwork rag doll than a successful and confident doctor.

Kathryn stared at herself coldly. If she were a patient, Kathryn would have assumed she was in a padded cell on the fifth floor of the hospital. *Perhaps a woman who has suffered from long-term spousal abuse and couldn't remember killing her husband yesterday morning between the first and second cup of coffee.*

Without warning, she sprinted toward the table, skirted round it, and lunged at the door, pounding it with all the unsatisfied fury that overflowed from her in a monsoon of despair. Each useless blow only accomplished draining that much more of her energy and hope.

"What do you want from me?" she cried, the repetition of her words falling in synchronous desperation to the beating of her heart until she finally slumped to the floor in huddled frustration.

Am I having a nervous breakdown? How long have I been here? And where the hell is here? Kathryn asked, her growing fears strangling her.

"What do you want? Who are you? Please, answer me," she begged. The words that now trickled from her lips became unintelligible as they were buried further under inevitable sorrow. She drifted into a deep sleep, exhaustion smothering her with a cruel despondency. The grumbling of her stomach roared its displeasure to an uncaring master.

Kathryn slept fitfully for what must have been a long time, although she was unsure how long it had actually been. It felt as if only a few minutes had passed, but her bladder told a different story. Kathryn woke with an urgent stab of fear. Again the displacement of where she should be was starkly exposed by the reality of where she found herself.

How long have I been here? There was no way of telling.

When did I leave home? There was no way of remembering.

Who brought me here? There was no way of knowing.

The accursed room ravaged all concept of time and refused to allow her the luxury of clear thought. She had no familiar point of reference to anchor herself to, and that made her feel as if she was floating in some kind of alternate reality.

Emotional exhaustion refused to allow her to climb to her feet. Kathryn could only manage to thump on the mirrored door from where she lay, accepting the fact that this act was probably a futile gesture at best. But there was nothing else for her to do.

After exhausting that scanty supply of impotent strength, Kathryn crawled to the sink and drank more water to stave off the hunger that stalked her with cruel abandon.

"I'm hungry. Do you hear me? I need some food," she demanded, pointing her frustration at the mirror. "You can't just let me starve in here." However, the slow revelation dawned upon her wearied mind that they could quite easily do that very thing.

Perhaps that was the plan. But that made even less sense than being taken in the first place. *And if I'm in a hospital, that would never happen.* But Kathryn instinctively knew she wasn't in any legitimate medical facility, not even an outdated psychiatric facility.

Kathryn had heard of people who had been kidnapped and buried in a box with only enough water to last them a few days. Maybe she too had been buried in a more elaborate box, one she could walk around in, but nonetheless a coffin.

The emptiness in my stomach must mean I've already been in here more than a day, most likely three or four. But if that's so, why hasn't

whoever is hiding behind that mirror come in here to confront me?
Maybe they don't plan to, she thought suddenly, afraid of the
implications brought on by that line of thinking.

She stared at the glass wall trying to envision the face behind it.

Or maybe you have come in, while I was sleeping. Maybe you've
come in often and I just didn't know it! the very idea giving her the
terrifying feeling of a stranger's hands touching her body everywhere.

Kathryn flopped down on the toilet and leaned back on the cool
porcelain to calm her increasing panic. A reality began to surface in
the pool of pungent alarm that threatened to choke her.

Maybe you've drugged the water? she wondered. *It would*
certainly explain the drugged hangover shrouding my mind, and the
confused loss of time.

It doesn't matter, she realized. It was necessary to drink whatever
liquid was available just to stay alive.

"Who are you?" she screamed. "What do you want?"

There was no reply. She hadn't expected one.

It simply doesn't make sense for someone to go to all that trouble
to kidnap me only to let me starve to death. Kathryn glared at the
smooth, reflective shininess of the mirror, its glistening face an
unwelcome contrast to the blinding light surrounding her.

"No, you won't let me starve to death. You've put far too much
effort into this room. You'll come in. I know you will. Maybe not today,
but you'll come in before I die," she stated with the unquestioning
confidence that she was right.

It might be a good thing he hadn't come in, at least while she was
awake. Kathryn had enough to deal with without that added terror.

What would a maniac want from a woman...to steal a total
stranger from her home in the middle of the night? She had no idea and
was even more afraid to find out.

There can be only one logical explanation, she reasoned. "Ransom.
That's why you aren't concerned whether or not I have food, isn't it?
You just want the money without the hassle."

Kathryn mentally tallied up the money she thought her family
could probably raise in such a short time. *Between David, Dad, Mom*
and Dad Breslin...maybe somewhere over a million dollars.

"But if that's so, then why am I still here? Surely its been paid."

Kathryn rose listlessly and began to pace the small barren room
before finally leaning her forehead on the mirrored door, hoping its
steadiness would help her think.

There is no reason. I know they'd raise the money even if they had
to borrow against everything they owned. It should only take a
day...maybe two at most.

Again, she didn't relish the implications. She slumped to the floor
in front of the door.

Maybe you didn't send a ransom note. Maybe it's not for the money at all.

Kathryn shook her head to clear it, but it didn't help much. She couldn't imagine why anyone would have gone to such elaborate preparations just for her.

Who are you? Have you done this before? This room looks like you must have done it often. You've gone to an awful lot of trouble to make an escape-proof cell. The thought was almost more than she could bear.

Is that why you've covered the room with plastic? So you can easily clean up the mess you make after you torture and kill us? How many women have you had in this room? The image of some maniac shackling women to the table, one by one, and slicing them to slivered bits of fleshy debris dug into her thoughts. It would be worse than any autopsy she had witnessed.

She rose to her feet, turned to the mirror, and screamed as her frustration threatened to implode in upon her. Silence howled back at her and she thought she would go mad with its oppressive secrets. Kathryn fell face down on the floor as new tears overflowed already red, swollen eyelids.

"You do kill us, don't you? That's why I'm here...in this room. You starve us till we're too weak to fight, and then you kill us on that stainless steel table. You cut us into little pieces for easier disposal of the body," she accused the mirror. She felt as if she were Alice, who had just slipped to the insane world beyond the looking glass.

Only my world doesn't have a rabbit...just a mad hatter. And I can't find the way out.

Kathryn was working herself up into utter hysteria, no longer able to get a grip on the thoughts that were flitting through her mind.

You shackle us to that table and then you cut out our hearts...or something worse. The new reality mentally slapped her. She shuddered as the thought ripped through her mind. Kathryn was beyond hysteria now. Her voice rose in peaking shrillness.

"What other reason could there be? Why else would anyone build a room like this? The only thing missing is a drain in the floor."

She glared at the three pieces of furniture, scrutinizing their existence, but unable to find one scrap of evidence, even a small clue that might offer her the slightest bit of consoling balm for her burning questions. The white impersonality of the room mocked her.

"There are no answers, are there? At least nothing that makes any sense."

Kathryn sobbed as she sank again to the cold floor. The tears did little to relieve her. There was no way of telling how many women had been in this room before her. Or how many were in other rooms just like this one. Pictures of a deserted hospital refurbished for evil intent flashed through her frantic mind. She had seen the odd horror movie, and this situation fit right in with their worst setting.

David, are you still at home? Is Meaghan still safe? The agony of not knowing anything struck her trembling flesh. Kathryn felt as if the vile creature that had made her a prisoner had already ripped out her beating heart.

"Who are you? ANSWER ME!" she shrieked. There was no answer. She would just have to wait until this lunatic—whoever he was—came in and presented himself.

She wondered how long it would take for him to make an appearance.

Through reeling thoughts, she tried to remember how long it would take to starve to death. There were different ways to die of starvation, but she was healthy and had all the water she could drink...unless her captor turned that off.

Seventy-two days. Just two and a half months. She gasped, horrified by the unpleasant revelation. *That's all the time I have left to live if things don't change.*

Death seemed inevitable. Her life was no longer her own. The tenuous control she may have had was now ripped from her hands. Her life and death were in the tight grip of someone she had never seen.

Kathryn realized she would have to rely on what little ingenuity she had left if she was to have even the remotest chance of survival.

"What are you willing to do to live, Katie?" she asked herself in whispered tones, not wanting *him* to hear.

It depends on what he wants, she answered, reasoning that there could only be a set number of things he could want.

It doesn't matter what he wants. Money, sex, whatever! It doesn't matter what he asks for, Kathryn told herself, taking authority over her weaker, subconscious fears.

What if he doesn't ask for anything? That thought terrified her more than anything else.

"He will...eventually. And whatever he asks for, it doesn't matter. You will do whatever it takes to survive, Katie," she whispered with a stern hiss.

No matter the cost? Was she ready to sacrifice her pride so completely? Kathryn wasn't so certain she could do that.

Whatever the cost, she concluded, not leaving any opening for an alternate course of action. She would submit to whatever he demanded.

Perhaps she was only a last minute thought in his routine. Maybe she had been taken on the spur of the moment by being in the wrong place at the right time. Kathryn didn't know anyone who would want to do her any harm. She couldn't think of anything different in her life, *except the phone call...the threat against Meaghan...the game.*

"Were you looking for Meaghan that night? Did you take me instead, after finding she was no longer available?" Kathryn asked, grateful if that were the case. It would mean, then, that he had given up on her baby girl and she would be safe.

By the look of her prison, it couldn't have been an impulsive act. He had to have put a lot of planning and preparation into it. It had cost him an incredible amount of money.

Even underneath the brilliant white paint, the grain in the wood behind the glass shows quality, she decided, examining the wall beneath the Plexiglas overlays. David had taught Kathryn to recognize the different qualities of wood, both in his carpentry work for the house and his carvings. David had an appreciation of fine wood, and knew how to bring out the best in every individual grain.

She looked at the glass and could only assume it was some form of unbreakable, reinforced Plexiglas to prevent her escape. Plexiglas, she knew, was not cheap.

Yes, you planned this, didn't you? This was not by chance. Do you do this all the time? No, I was not an accident. But why me? You weren't after Meaghan at all. She was a ruse...a distraction so you could get to me.

But why me? Why would you decide to kidnap someone you don't even know? And if you do know me, how do you know me? Are you one of my patients?

The thought of actually knowing the sick creature that did this to her made Kathryn more upset than if he was a total stranger. She looked around the desolate room.

Have you designed and built this room just for me? Oh my God. There is no ransom. You plan to keep me!

Fresh panic washed over her and she involuntarily brought her hand up to her mouth in horrified shock. Kathryn again threw herself at the mirrored door as pure desperation controlled her moves. She pounded on the unbreakable glass until her hands were raw and red from the beating.

Are you going to sell me into slavery? Am I going to be sent overseas? Is this wall see-through so prospective buyers can examine the goods? Is this how you make your living?

"Let me out of here! Show yourself, you bastard! Who are you? Are you there? Are you watching me? I want to see you!" Kathryn screeched at the silent image jumping about wildly in the mirror before her.

Are there other women in other rooms like this one? she asked, edging up to the glass, placing her nose on the flat surface. Kathryn cupped her hand around her eyes to shade them from the glare in hopes of seeing through the mercury to the other side.

Suddenly, she saw it. On the other side of the mirrored glass was the faint, yellow glow of the burning tip of a cigarette floating in a sweeping movement from his mouth downwards.

So you are there...watching me...my discomfort...my fear...my shame. You're watching me to satisfy your sick, perverse pleasure.

She knew he was enjoying the show by the leisurely way the cigarette moved.

She closed her eyes against the brightness...against seeing him behind the glass...against the floating yellow tip...against her predicament...against the growing hunger that stalked her.

"I can see you there! Smoking your goddamned cigarette! I see you, you bastard!"

She hoped he would come in and face her now that she had exposed him. Maybe he would come in and give her something to eat if she was lucky enough.

Maybe. But she suspected her luck had run out.

Chapter Six

The whispery click of the release mechanism in the little metal box exploded into the room's ruthless silence. Kathryn held her breath as she fixed her eyes on the mirrored door that reflected her shattered appearance. The terror chiseled into her face overshadowed the image of her battered body. Her fingers quivered and her legs quaked under the pressure of expectation. Fear threatened to stop her heart; the pounding thud of her panicked heartbeat drowned out her fragmented thoughts.

Kathryn recoiled as she anticipated the action of the door popping ajar. An eternity passed.

The door slid inward, invading the confined space of her room. A dark wooden wall lay flush with the door's right edge. The restful darkness beyond the doorway called to her. Despite the chill of the room, perspiration covered her forehead. Her body reeked with the rancid smell of fear. She cowered in the twenty-inch space between the sink and the wall, deciding too late that it was a foolish move. She was boxed into a corner. But it didn't matter. Fright would not allow her to move one inch from her ludicrous hiding place.

A deep terror darkened her eyes as gooseflesh rose on her skin. A tense gulp lodged in her throat. Her eyes darted back and forth. She watched the calm demeanor of the stranger who lurked just beyond the doorway, staring at her from the shadows.

He left the door open as he stepped to the center of the room, keeping the table between himself and Kathryn. The dark, sullen man exuded an air of absolute authority.

Random thoughts bolted through her mind. *Run past him. Push him down. Escape! Do something! Don't just sit here and wait for him to make the first move.*

Her body refused to obey the barrage of commands her mind issued. Instead, it forced her to shrivel into a corner, quaking in terror. The noise of the tray clattering onto the metal table yanked her thoughts away, focusing her mind on her captor. Searching his eyes,

Kathryn could see the cold cruelty of a heartless animal. *This one only lives to cause others pain.*

She had seen the same lifeless stare before in the hollow eyes of street bullies when she interned in Seattle. She had witnessed the senseless fulfillment of their bloodlust for power in the victims that crossed her tables in ER The wanton destruction of so many lives had sickened her. It was something she doubted she would ever understand, not even in many lifetimes. Kathryn tried to swallow, but her throat was paralyzed with fear.

The thin angular features of his face were rigid and pale, giving him the appearance of a corpse in the morgue. She doubted he had ever experienced a genuine, heart-felt smile in his entire life—it would have made him human. The calculating scrutiny of his stare plunged through her heart. The icy blue inspection from his unblinking eyes herded her to new levels of terror, searing her mind into crippling arrest.

To her surprise, Kathryn discovered she was holding her breath. Her lungs began to scream for oxygen. She drew in air as quietly as she could, trying to make herself invisible before him.

He turned and headed back to the shadows of the open door, leaving her alone with the tray of food. The tantalizing smell of breakfast—coffee, fried bacon, and toast—reached out to her. Cursing, she tried to move to the table, but not one muscle followed her pleading. Instead, she trembled violently in the cramped space between the sink and wall.

From beyond the door she could hear the soft squeak of an unoiled wheel. He returned, pushing a padded black office chair into the room. The noise of the wheels creaking across the Plexiglas floor echoed off the Plexiglas walls. She watched as he moved the chair to the table, turned, and strolled back to the door. The scowling man closed the mirrored door with transparently calculated movements intended to emphasize his position as captor...and hers as prisoner.

Returning to the table, his face cracked into a menacing smile. He was unable to hide his excitement as he collapsed into the black chair. His eyes clung to her face. The man's fingers trembled as he fluffed the napkin across his legs with great fanfare. He began to shovel food into his mouth as if it were him that hadn't eaten for days.

Kathryn's stomach growled in angry response to his sadistic cruelty. She wanted to cradle her belly and comfort it, but the enticing odor of bacon and coffee refused to allow her any consolation. Kathryn hunched down by the sink, too afraid to move as she watched him devour the food before him.

He gobbled his meal in silence, too busy spilling food out of his mouth to speak. She watched him enviously as bits of egg and toast tumbled over his lips back onto the plate, only to be scooped up again in the next shovelful. He slurped coffee and orange juice with all the grace of a child not familiar with drinking from a cup.

Kathryn studied his face .and mannerisms. He was a boorish man...*probably not much need to be civilized.*

Deep creases emphasized the sides of his sallow cheeks, giving him the appearance of an emaciated derelict. His green tartan shirt was at least two sizes too big for him, and his cuffs were rolled back so the sleeves did not hang below his wrists. He had shaved his hair into a fuzzy brown brush cut.

Heavy dark circles outlined his eyes. His movements were awkward and erratic. An energy of irritation hovered about him, erupting momentarily over spilt orange juice and dropped toast. He acted very much like a man who suffered from serious sleep depravation, and she wondered just how much sleep he had gotten since kidnapping her.

She was hungry but rested. He was frail and exhausted. Kathryn thought she could probably take him. He certainly looked weaker than she had imagined. If he hadn't hit her so unexpectedly and fast the night he took her, she doubted he could have taken her at all. He appeared to have half her stamina and strength. The visual revelation of her captor's condition caused the possibilities and plans of escape to storm through her fevered mind.

A voice barked at her from across the middle of the room. Kathryn shrank from the sudden shock. Looking up at him, disgust masked her fear. The haunted man sprayed words at her through mouthfuls of food, while stabbing his spoon into the air between loads.

"Come on. Get some breakfast. You must be hungry," he said as little bits of chewed toast and scrambled egg flying through the air in her direction.

Kathryn shivered. *Move, dammit! Run, you moron! Do something! Don't just sit here!*

"Suit yourself. I'll only have to force-feed you later," he smirked. The prospect was an enjoyable anticipation to him.

Kathryn's eyes squinted her refusal to surrender. Her previous resolve—at any cost—dissipated in the presence of the enemy. She would not do anything he asked or take one thing he offered. She would not give him that power over her.

"I'm quite a good cook when I put my mind to it. Really, you should try some," he said through a smile that didn't quite reach past his lips. "I made a cheese and veggie omelet and hash browns. It's my specialty. Sorry, no forks. I wouldn't want you hurting yourself...or me."

Kathryn pursed her lips and pulled her eyes away from him as what little color she had drained away. From the corner of her eye she could see his face grow with the deep scarlet of unchecked wrath.

"I really want you to eat something. In fact, I want you to eat now," he ordered, his voice cracking with suppressed anger.

"Why have you brought me here?" she asked, unable to choke back the tears. She tried not to look at him, not wanting to give him the pleasure of her terror.

Kathryn cringed as he deliberated each of his movements, devouring his meal with obvious malice. The man placed his spoon on the plate, leaned back in his chair, and eyed her coolly. He struggled to keep self-control as impatience churned deep inside. Thin lips curled into a ghastly sneer as his brows knit into a straight ledge of bubbling fury.

In a split second, the maniac picked up the paper plate of leftover food and heaved it at her face. The plate whisked past her head and slapped into the wall, falling to the floor after depositing its contents onto the Plexiglas. From the corner of her eye, she watched as the food slid down the smooth surface in slow motion and plopped onto the clear floor, six inches from her feet, while keeping her concentration on the madman before her.

Kathryn flinched, surprised by the sudden physical outburst. Tears burst unchecked as what little self-control she possessed was pushed beyond its limit. Without warning, she sprang from the floor and found herself racing toward the man who was now standing between her and door. Her arms shot forward and knocked him down as she escaped past him toward the mirrored wall. Kathryn's mind screamed with panic, yelling instructions and directions at her so fast her body had trouble understanding them. She clumsily ran to the door where her fingers clawed at the metal box like a wild woman.

"Help! Let me out! Please, somebody help me!" she pleaded through hysterical screams. Kathryn pounded her fists against the door with ebbing strength.

She could see his reflection rise from the floor. With pent up breath, she watched as he set the chair upright. Unable to break through the door, she turned to face him, flinging her back against the mirror.

He moved toward her with methodical, deliberate determination.

Her voice ranted futile pleading. Her eyes darted back and forth in an attempt to find a new avenue of escape. There was none. There was no way around him and no way out of the room without him. Kathryn shrieked involuntarily as he came to within a hair's breadth of her face.

He was taller than she had thought. The man towered above her. His flesh was not as bony as she had imagined. She could see the veins of anger bulge from his lean, muscular neck. His body remained close to hers. Her eyes found his.

An unseen fist flattened against her face. Kathryn heard her jawbone crack as she fell against the wall before crashing onto the hard floor. He was also very much stronger than she had first thought. Certainly stronger than she was.

"If you won't eat like a human, then you'll eat like a damned animal," he grunted, towering over her cringing body.

Kathryn jammed her quivering hands between her already battered face and his exploding rage. She watched through the latticework of interlaced fingers as he reached a menacing hand toward her. He wove his fist into her unkempt hair and pulled her up from the floor. Pushing her before him, he propelled her across the room.

The corner of the unmoving table jabbed into her side and she groaned from the sudden stab of pain. She could feel him yank her head back and she thought he would snap her neck as she tumbled backward into his iron fist. Instead, he launched her body toward the floor where the food lay splattered.

"I told you to eat," he bellowed.

When she again refused to move, the man lunged at her and crashed a fist into the wall beside her head. Kathryn recoiled, flailing her arms against the air in an attempt to ward off another ruthless attack.

"And I asked you why you brought me here. Who are you? What is it you want from me? I have the right to know!" she screamed, wrapping her fingers into tight fists before her face.

His contorted face snarled and snapped at her as he towered over her recoiling body. Without warning, he pounced on her to haul her up from the floor, but landed empty handed, sprawling into the vacant space of the wall.

Kathryn had decided not to wait for another attack. She was up and off the floor, sprinting passed him as he was grabbing for her shadow. She darted round the opposite end of the table, keeping it and the chair between them.

He flipped over, jumped to his feet, charged at her with arms swinging, and tripped over the chair she shoved at him just before she sped toward the closed door. He climbed to his feet and was on her before she reached the mirrored wall. His hand lashed out and seized her by the hair. With a grunt, he yanked Kathryn off her feet and backward on top of him.

He wrapped his legs around her waist, struggling to pin her hands above her head. They rolled over each other until, finally straddling her, he crushed her face into the unyielding floor, causing her nose to bleed. Stretching her arms overhead, he clenched her wrists with a vise-grip hold, and then twisted her arms behind her back.

Kathryn cried out in pain.

Shoving her face closer to the floor with his foot, he cuffed her wrists behind her back with all the brutality and urgency of a cop subduing a drugged-up child-killer.

He flipped her onto her back. The blood pumped through his heart with the exhilaration of a hunter gloating over the triumph of a very challenging kill. He shoved his face close to hers. The veins at his temples pulsed rapidly. His breath smelled of coffee and bacon. His skin reeked of aftershave.

Kathryn reeled with a growing dizziness.

His hand reached out and caressed the tear-soaked skin of her face. He wiped a thumb beneath her eye, wiping the tears away in an unexpected display of tenderness, as if this futile attempt could actually win her confidence. He wiped at the blood on the corner of her mouth where he had smacked her.

She could feel the strong pulse in his thumb as it lingered on her cheek.

This is it! her mind screamed.

He rubbed her blood onto her T-shirt.

Don't resist! she ordered herself.

The man's fingers traveled from her left ear down to her chin. Her skin was oily from sweat and fear, and as adrenaline poured into her system with each terrifying moment, her skin became more clammy.

Don't be a moron! her mind shouted back.

He licked his lips and brought his other hand up to her face.

Fight back! she howled deep within. As she thought of herself on the floor in handcuffs, bloodied and bruised, she knew that the advice was too late in coming.

The man swallowed hard in a feeble attempt to constrain his mounting anxiety, compelling himself to take slow, regular, deep breaths in an attempt to control himself. The battle raged within him as he straddled her. The sickening-sweet odor of sweat mingled with aftershave filled her lungs as he peered down at her. His look was faraway as he chewed his bottom lip.

Fighting the urge to vomit, she tried not to move one muscle.

His eyes stared through her as if he were watching a television screen on the floor behind her head.

It's like he's forgotten I'm here.

Abruptly, he hopped to his feet and dragged Kathryn along the floor. He hauled her kicking, screaming body over to the table, picked her up, and threw her onto the cold stainless steel table, knocking the tray to the floor with a loud crash.

Kathryn broke into a peel of shrieking sobs that caused him to wince with obvious distaste and impatience.

Standing beside her as the moments ticked by, she could see him try to think things through and calm himself down. Perhaps he hadn't expected her to be a fighter. Maybe he thought she would just lie down and let him do whatever he wanted. She had determined herself to do that very thing, but, when the crunch came, it wasn't in her. She had to fight him every step of the way and he was just learning how stubborn she could be.

Didn't find that out in those bloody letters, did you, you bastard?

"You obviously don't know the ground rules. In here, you're not the same person you were out there. Out there, you were a nothing. In here, you're what I tell you to be," he stated with great effort. His hand clamped over her shoulder. His tongue licked at his bottom lip as his eyes combed every inch of her skin.

"What do you want from me?" she asked, her voice shaking as much as her body. "Is it money?"

He laughed a guttural, deep laugh that raked her spine. "Nope. There's not enough money in the whole world to buy you back from me. And I certainly don't need the pitiful amount your people can come up with." The fingers of his hand released their hold on her shoulder, massaging the feel of her flesh into his hand as he grinned with perverted pleasure.

"If it's not the money, then why am I here?" she asked, gasping against the disgusting intrusion of his touch. Her flesh bristled with goose bumps, causing her skin to tingle in a most unpleasant way.

"Let's just say you're my...uh...prisoner." He smiled, the sickening grin on his face further unsettling her.

"You can't just take someone prisoner. What century do you live in?" The bands of metal around her wrists dug into her spine, making it difficult to lie still. His grip on her shoulder pinned her down with the assurance of unmerciful strength. Sweat dotted her forehead as the gripping fear her exploded and overwhelmed her.

"Oh, but I did!" The conspicuous effort he exerted to hold himself back hewed great fissures into his already worn face. A frown entrenched itself deeper into his brow. He munched his bottom lip between strong, white teeth as his fingers dug deeper into the soft tissue of her shoulder.

Kathryn winced with pain, moaning under his grip. "You can't do that. I haven't done anything to you. Hell, you don't even know me!" She fought against the hard metal cuffs bruising her back. She kicked her feet in a feeble attempt to reposition her body, but he pushed her shoulders into the hard metal, forcing her to stay right where he wanted her.

He didn't answer. Stepping round to her head, he scrutinized her. His cold eyes feasted on his prize. The man reached out a hand and ran his fingers through her matted hair. The intense stare of his dark blue eyes caressed her skin with possessive pride.

"Who are you? What's your name? What do you want with me?" she whispered, finally working her hands to the side of her spine. It didn't feel any better. The metal threatened to cut through the T-shirt and into her flesh even though she knew there were no sharp edges on the handcuffs.

"No one is innocent, Katie. Everyone gets exactly what he or she deserves. Fate does that. Fate's never handed out anything that wasn't earned," he said, as if repeating a formula learned long ago. Thin lips curled back over his teeth as he snarled with vicious hate.

A shock of static electricity leapt from his palm into her skin. She flinched.

He huffed a loud whistling hiss of air, expelling the force of his erupting anger through clenched teeth. His blue eyes turned black. The features of his gnarled face contorted as he felt at her pulling away from his touch.

"What will it take to buy my freedom?" she asked, cringing a millimeter deeper into the table. She forced herself to remain calm. Kathryn gaped at the cruel stare highlighted by large purplish circles. The deadness she found in his eyes terrified her more than the ghastly cell which imprisoned her. Those eyes told her that she had never before imagined what she was about to find out at his hands. They told her she would be there until death rescued her from this lunatic's grasp.

Kathryn summoned all her available strength to pull her gaze from his.

"Nothing. There is nothing you can do for me or give me that will ever convince me to let you go," he whispered, his icy eyes devouring her features.

Kathryn pulled away from his hand. "You can't just keep me here. You'll have to let me go sometime. They'll find me. I'll escape."

"Oh, I don't think so. I'm much too clever for that. No one is going to find you...or this room. This room is hidden so expertly no one will ever find it, not even by accident. And there is no way of escape," he whispered, kissing her ear before pulling his face away from the side of her head.

Kathryn glared up at him, daring to show full detestation of her captor.

"You'll see I'm right...in time. I suggest you do whatever I tell you if you want to avoid certain...how shall I say...unpleasantries. Remember the rules. Memorize them. Do not break one of them if you want to live. All right, Rule Number One: there will be no questions, no arguments, no hesitations, no doing things your way. You'll do everything exactly the way I tell you without delay. Understand?" He was muttering in her ear, his lips brushing against her trembling skin.

Kathryn said nothing. She pulled away from him, repulsed at the thought of living in this room for however long it amused him.

"We're going to have a very long time to get to know each other," he crooned almost lovingly as his lips again brushed her ear.

"David will find me. He'll call every cop in the country and they'll all be out looking for me. Kidnapping—that's federal. The FBI will be looking for me," she cried, fresh tears streaming down her cheeks.

"There is no David. You have no family. There's not one person in the entire world who cares enough about you to look for you. Not the police. Not your husband. Not even your father. You no longer exist to them. I'm all you've got, and all you'll have until the day you die. And I'm not looking for you because I know exactly...where...you...are. So don't piss me off or you won't even have me, and you'll die in here all alone." Giving way to his obvious anger, he slammed his fist on the table beside her head.

The noise echoed off the Plexiglas walls. She jumped from the suddenness of the noise, swallowing hard at the lump of terror in her throat.

"I know they're looking for me. They'll find me. You just can't keep me here," she cried helplessly. She was beginning to know he could do exactly that. He seemed to be able to do whatever he wanted. The knowledge gave her an odd, displaced sensation. She felt as if his world was all she had ever known, as if the life she had with David was only a remote dream or a memory from a previous life.

He slammed his fist again into the table, the slap of its force capturing her attention, forcing her to focus on him.

"There's no one looking for you. Now or ever," he whispered through clenched teeth, his mouth less than two inches from her ear. "And I intend to keep you here as long as you interest me." His implications were transparent, and he grinned as his words dug into her mind.

"You're wrong. Someone will find me," she insisted defiantly, hoping she appeared more confident than she actually felt. His breath was hot against her face. The smell of his breath knotted her stomach into heaving convulsions.

"I've left no clues. I have no association with you or anyone who knows you. I haven't sent a ransom note. I haven't left fingerprints. I haven't even left a damned stray hair. I have been very careful. No matter how hard they look, they'll never find anything that will lead them to me. And if they don't find me, they sure as hell...won't...find...you," he laughed with gruff malice.

The sound was cruel, forcing her to fight back as if she were a petulant child. "You're not perfect. You've made a mistake. You..."

"Stop it! Shut up. Just SHUT the hell UP!" he roared. "No one will find you. Not in this room. Not now. Not ten days from now. Not ten years from now. They can look all they want. They'll never find this room. I've spent too damn much money and put too much hard work into making absolutely sure of it." His face puffed with anger as his eyes changed into shards of ice.

She could see he was losing what little control he might have had. "You'll never get away with this," she cried. His fingers pressed into her shoulder. The offensive stench of his breath as he wheezed into her ear suffocated her. Her body froze from the touch of his tongue as it flicked out of his mouth and licked her lobe.

"You better hope I do. You better pray they never find me, because, if they do they'll take me away and you'll die. Hidden behind the walls of a soundproof, bulletproof room with absolutely no possible way of escape," he promised.

Kathryn bit her lip to stave off another impending deluge of tears.

"You better hope I live a long and healthy life because your life depends on it," he snarled, again the cruel laughter cutting across his face. Hatred seemed to be the only emotion able to touch him.

"Why have you brought me here?" she asked, pleading through the horror and confusion that seethed in her mind. His fingers were like little rods of iron pushing into the soft flesh of her shoulder, and she winced against the increasing pain and tenderness.

"You were given to me," he answered with a controlled tone, revealing that he was regaining his earlier cool composure.

"Who gave me to you?" she asked, disbelieving the insanity she was hearing. She struggled against his hold, trying again to move her fists out of her spine. He refused to allow her any comfort and pinned her down harder onto the table.

"George said I could have you. George said I could teach you things, and that you're mine until he comes for you.". He looked at himself in the mirror. His eyes were vacant and dark, and he stared at himself as if he were seeing a stranger for the first time.

The flat, expressionless voice was beginning to alarm her. She had heard it in patients whom no longer had any grasp on reality. It was the voice of someone devoid of logic and stability; someone who should not be allowed loose on the streets without a team of keepers.

"Who is George?" She now understood he was more than a mere kidnapper. He was completely insane. She also understood that she would find no reasonable motive or logic to her predicament.

"You'll find out soon enough. Right now, however, I want you to eat the breakfast I made," he ordered, bringing his focus back to her.

"I'm not hungry," she lied.

He yanked her head up by the hair, pulling her face close to his. The foul heaviness of his breath nauseated her.

"Don't you EVER dare argue with me again, Katie. Now, I told you to eat," he growled, the sound of his teeth grinding in her ear.

"How can I eat with my hands cuffed behind my back?" she asked, stalling.

He hauled her off the table, dropping her to the floor. "That's your problem. Figure it out."

Kathryn stared up into his deadpan eyes and froze, unable to comply. She shivered under his gaze. "I said I'm not hungry," she repeated, again hoping to appear stronger than she felt.

He grabbed her by the arm and backhanded her across the face, catching her as she reeled backward from the force of the blow.

She struggled through stunned shock to stand on unsteady feet. He was not beyond being physically brutal to her and she wondered what else was not beyond his scope of possibilities.

He struck her again. The force of the blow pushed her into the corner of the steel table, causing her to squeal from the sudden stab in the small of her back. Kathryn stumbled to the wall as she tried to stabilize herself from his beating. She worked her jaw to ease the growing soreness. Dismayed, she looked at the food on the floor. Her stomach lurched with repulsion at the idea of eating off the floor, the thought made worse because some of the food was leftovers from his plate. She gulped back the nausea and tried to force her head to stop reeling with dizziness. She was hungry, but she wasn't at all sure she was hungry enough to give into *him*.

Anything to survive. Whatever it takes, she reminded herself. *Whatever he asks.*

Kathryn struggled to kneel on the floor without revealing more of her body than the T-shirt already showed. The cuffs and bruises greatly hindered her efforts. She bent down and worked her way through the egg, the bacon and then the toast, eating with relieved greed as the hunger took dominion over her pride.

He watched her eat. Towering over her, his blood boiling with excitement as he witnessed her debasement.

She could smell his excitement as he overshadowed her with his strength of presence. The doctor in her told Kathryn it was simply the adrenaline flowing through his body, but the knowledge didn't help.

"Goddamn it, what is it about you that affects me like this?" he asked, his voice coming from a distant place within. "The rush...it feels so good . . . .."

Kathryn slumped to the floor when she finished lapping up the food. She was revolted at the thought of giving into him, of being treated like an animal...but she had food in her stomach, and now she could deal with whatever might come next.

He pulled her up from the floor. Tugging the key out of his pocket, he unlocked the handcuffs. "I don't want to hurt you, but you have to stop fighting me. You must do what I tell you. If you don't learn that I am the boss it can be very bad, and you don't ever want to feel that kind of pain."

"If you don't want to hurt me, then let me go." Kathryn tried to massage the tenderness from her wrists.

"There's no place for you to go. You no longer have a life other than the one I offer you. You'll never see the outside world again. You'll be here, in this room, forever. And what happens between now and then is entirely dependent on how willing you are to obey," he said. His eyes, for a brief moment, took on a tenderness that could not be found in his tone.

"This doesn't make any sense. If it's not for money, why are you keeping me here? Just tell me what you want so I can get out of here," she pleaded, daring to look into those eyes that changed immediately again into the cold, blue glare of hate.

His drawn complexion grew darker. "I already have everything I want and everything I need. I have you." He smiled a ghoulish, skull-like grin.

"Why have you brought me here?" She tugged her hand out of his. He took it back, holding it tighter between his two hands.

"I waited for you my whole life. When I saw you, I knew you were the one. There's something special about you. Different. Something I want. Something I need." His eyes again looked across a horizon she could not see.

"What are you talking about? This is crazy. How can I be having this conversation?" She cried, her voice filled with exasperation. She ripped her hand from his grasp, twirled in a circle, and flung her arms up in frustrated resignation. When she again faced her captor, he was sitting on the edge of the table watching her.

"You have a quality about you that I've never seen before. I've never met anyone like you. You have an understanding and depth most people can't imagine. Can't you see that?" he asked, shocked that she had difficulty seeing his viewpoint. He shook his head at her hopelessness.

"All I understand is that you need professional help," she argued. "I could help you get that. I'll tell the police you showed me mercy. They'll understand," she said, trying to make the tone of her voice as pleasant as possible.

He slammed his fist into the table, visibly fighting the urge to push it right into her face. "I am NOT crazy. I'm quite possibly the only sane person in this whole bloody world. As a disciple of George, I see things more clearly than you."

"No sane person would ever build a room like this. Or kidnap a woman for a pet," Kathryn snapped, no longer pretending to be nice. She glared in his angry eyes, her own outrage momentarily overcoming her fear.

The man eyed her with violent rage. He wanted to beat her into submission. His hands clenched into spastic fists. He rolled on the balls of his feet. His body trembled with pent-up violence. He struggled with the animal inside.

She took his hesitation as a revelation that she might have a chance to get out of this thing alive.

"You will do as I say either the easy way...or the hard way," he hissed. His face bulged into a deep scarlet.

"Why are you doing this? Who are you?" she asked, desperate to know why she was in this situation.

"You, my pet, are going to help me become a god. You'll learn to be obedient in all things. Like I am. You'll accept your role in this life...and in the next. Like I did," he intoned, his voice even, cool and hard. "You'll learn that pain is a fact of life. You can either enjoy it and find some way to accept it so you can live with it, or you can fight it and your life will be a complete hell even after you're dead."

He jumped down from the table and faced his reflection in the mirror. Smoothing his hair, he smiled with a fiendish grin. He had learned to enjoy the pain, letting it excite him. He had learned it was the only way to survive.

His frigid eyes told her that she would learn it too. Eventually. One way or another. She wondered what pain she would have to learn to like.

"If you let me go, I won't tell anyone. I'll never let them know it was you who kidnapped me. I'll tell them that I went away on a...ah...a sabbatical to get my head straight. I'll tell them it was a sudden decision and I just had to get away. They won't look for you. I promise I'll make them believe me," she pleaded, hating him for forcing her to beg.

"They won't believe you because you won't tell them anything. The minute I let you go you'd run to the nearest sheriff's office. They'd have an APB out on me in a second. Surely I don't look that stupid," he mocked, arching one eyebrow until he looked almost comical.

The stranger's laugh grated her spine like sandpaper, making her feel more hopeless than before. She looked around the stark room, trying to fathom the finality of her predicament and the insanity of his. It was with resigned despair she appreciated this was no accident.

"You've planned this a long time, haven't you?" she asked his back through a fresh flood of tears.

"All my life. It's been the one driving force that carried me through all the hell I've felt, all the pain I've caused. George promised you to me when I was seven. It's taken three decades to fulfill. but I found you. Finally, I have you. You're mine and nobody can take you away from me. You are my soulmate forever," he answered. His voice was as flat and lifeless as his expression had become. She shuddered at the reflection staring back at her.

"You couldn't have had me in mind when you built this," she said, not wanting it to be true.

"I've known you all my life. I've been pulled toward you through a set of circumstances that has guided me right to your doorstep. When I saw you, I recognized you. Yes, all this is just for you," he said, turning to face her.

Fear danced across her face as the implications of his words dug into her heart. There were no other rooms. There were no other women waiting as she waited. It was one thing to be kidnapped for money or to be one of many for kidnapped sexual abuse, but this...

"You'll be everything I want," he continued in a bland voice.

She trembled under the increasing weight of hysteria.

"You're going to become just like me," he answered, this time staring right into her eyes. His hot breath was only inches from her.

"This is all so insane. You're deranged. I'm crazy for sitting here listening to this," she screamed and turned to get away from him, facing the wall beside the toilet, leaving him standing by the table.

"You don't have a choice," he said.

"I won't cooperate in any way," she yelled, slamming her fists into the air.

"It doesn't matter. You'll capitulate. Inevitably. You'll have to," he said as he cleaned up the tray of paper cups and dishes. His gaze glanced over the messy residue still clinging to the floor. "Clean up this mess. Rule Number Two: Keep everything spotless." He headed toward the door and pulled the card-key through the slit, releasing the lock.

As he pulled the door open, ready to walk through it, she screamed in sheer desperation. "Who are you?"

He stopped just on the other side of the doorway, turned and faced her. His right hand held the door firm while the other held the tray almost level.

Kathryn stood absolutely still, afraid to move or breathe.

"Dylan," he said. "My name is Dylan Johnson."

"Well, Dylan, I will not cooperate with you," she reaffirmed, hoping her stubbornness would convince him to release her.

"You will give in..." he whispered. As he closed the door, abandoning her again to the silence, she could hear Dylan's quiet, calm, lifeless voice whisper, "I did."

Chapter Seven

Kathryn was dumbfounded. Unsure of exactly what she had expected from their first meeting, she knew it wasn't what had happened. This Dylan character was a certifiable psychiatric case and she wondered how he had managed to stay out of captivity himself.

Where did he get all this money? she questioned, estimating the cost of such renovations as he put into this room. *Drug money? Drug lords think they can do whatever they want. Who else has money like that to throw away on a room like this?*

Kathryn's throbbing jaw demanded attention. Her tongue licked the acrid taste of stale blood at the side of her mouth. She shuffled to the sink and washed her face, hoping the cold water might help keep the swelling down, suspecting it was already too late. Holding handfuls of cold water on her swollen lip felt almost pleasant, but she wished she had access to a little more treatment.

Nothing had changed. She still had no idea where she was or why. *At least this lunatic now has a name. Not that it does me much good*, she lamented. He still had not told her his plans.

Kathryn's eyes drifted over the splattered remains of breakfast. *Hot coffee would have been so very good*, she thought, covetous of the drying brown spill on the floor. The eggs and coffee seemed to swirl together into different patterns. *Just like clouds*, she mused, realizing how pathetic and ridiculous it sounded.

Shrugging her shoulders, Kathryn walked to the opposite side of the table. *I'll clean up later. Maybe. After all, who made the mess in the first place? It certainly wasn't me.*

She rolled her neck to loosen up her shoulders. *A sauna would be wonderful*, she thought as her muscles ached from more than the beating. *Anything would be better than this fridge he's locked me in.*

Standing near the padded, black chair, she fingered the cushioned upholstery. It was not cheap. The seat was formed to protect the lower lumbar region, helping it endure those long days at the office. The cushions and arms were quilted and reinforced for comfort and long life. The lever under the seat allowed the chair to be raised and lowered by air pressure. The back could be adjusted for optimum posture protection. It was a well-constructed chair.

It was perhaps the most beautiful chair she could ever remember seeing.

Fifteen hundred dollars, she figured. *Maybe more.*

It didn't matter how much it cost. The chair was soft...inviting...black. He left it for her. Dylan left it so she could try to get comfortable.

He may be crazy, but he's not all bad, she reasoned. Kathryn hated herself for being grateful for such a small token. She was amazed that she would ever scrutinize a piece of furniture with such intent appreciation.

Kathryn let her eyes probe the black texture of the material, allowing them to weave deeply into the holes in search of any safe port against the glaring lights of the room. She gently eased herself onto the cushion. *Marvelous.*

Swinging her feet onto the table, she crossed her ankles and leaned back in the comfort of the fluffy, luxurious, black chair from a world she could only remember.

Absolutely divine. She groaned, relieved to be off the hard floor. Kathryn tugged her T-shirt down as far as possible, for added warmth as much as modesty.

"Get the hell out of my chair!" the metal voice screeched at her from a hidden intercom. The harsh mechanical tone accentuated the gruffness in his voice. Dylan was observing her from the other side of the mirrored wall. He had watched as she laid back in momentary luxury and was now cruelly snatching it away.

"Go to hell," she yelled back. The chair was too good to give up. It was such an inconsequential matter, she could not believe he was about to make a big deal out of this.   ·

What is he going to do? Run in and beat me up? She doubted it, or he would have done so without announcing it first.

"Rule Number Three: No sitting on any furniture. Ever," the intercom crackled.

"I am not your property! I am not an animal! You left it in here," she hollered, unwilling to move. Kathryn's eyes remained closed in stubborn resolve. Her fingers were laced together on her stomach in relaxed repose. Only the newly developed twitch at the corner of her right eye exposed her true fear.

"Talking back—three days. Sitting on furniture—seven days. Leaving food on the floor—three days. Attitude—five days. Total punishment—eighteen days solitary confinement. Now get the hell out of my chair!" crackled the mechanical voice.

"Solitary? Give me a break. Where am I? *The Hilton*?" Kathryn sat straight in the chair and put both feet flat on the floor. Perching her hands on the padded arms, she was ready to propel herself up and away should Dylan burst into the room unannounced.

A black silence fell.

Earlier, she had hated the room's lights. They hurt her eyes. She felt completely naked under their relentless blaze. They offered her nowhere to hide. But the blackness that smothered her now that they were off was terrifying. Unlike the hood, it was a darkness she could feel all over her body. It seemed to have a life of its own. She thought she could hear it laughing at her.

Kathryn hadn't realized she heard the faint whir of fans blowing air through the eight ceiling vents. They had been so quiet, but now that they were completely silent, she was stricken with an increased level of apprehension. She had never been in total soundlessness before. In the woods there was at least the chirping of crickets and the high-pitched whine of insects speeding by. Here, there was only the sound of her own shallow breathing.

No fans, she mourned. *No fans...wait! That means no air!* She grasped the extreme vulnerability of her position. The room was completely sealed except for the forced air sucked in through the vents.

How much air is there?

Kathryn couldn't help herself. She couldn't fight the response her body was making as she pushed herself up from the chair, careful to leave it in the exact same position she found it. Vigilant in not letting one wheel creak.

Air wasn't something she had ever had to think about. A case of asphyxiation had not come across her table in either Seattle or the Island. Thinking back, she struggled to remember some remote bit of information from first or second year med school. *A full-grown person needs...*but she couldn't remember.

Think, dammit. Think!

Kathryn felt her way to the closest wall and placed her heel flat against the smooth surface. Placing the heel of one foot directly in front of the toes of her other, she measured the distance to the opposite wall. *Twelve feet.*

Repeating her efforts, she measured the distance from the mirrored door to the wall behind the sink. *Twelve feet. Twelve by twelve by probably ten is around fourteen hundred cubic feet. Okay. Now what? How many cubic feet of air does one person need to breathe in one hour?*

Kathryn crouched in the tight corner between the wall and sink. It was small consolation, but at least he couldn't sneak up on her.

Hours? One cubic foot lasts less than two minutes. Fifteen hundred feet gives me...uh...less than two days to live. If I remember correctly...which I doubt...let's say, four at the most. That's all I have.

Kathryn had no idea how long she had stayed in that one position. Her legs were cramped and achy. She stretched out the stiffness, massaging the circulation back into her limbs.

The air was already stale. The room was hot and stuffy. Suspecting that she must have dozed off, Kathryn woke with an incredible, urgent thirst.

For a minute, she couldn't remember where she was. She wondered why she couldn't hear David's snoring.

Oh, God. Dylan. Prison. Solitary. The memory broadsided her.

Reaching up and over the sink, Kathryn turned on the faucet. The heavy air-dried her throat. Her nose was crusted with blood and her lips were too swollen to stay closed, forcing her to breathe through her mouth. The handle stopped twisting. The darkness smothered Kathryn's gasp.

He's turned off the water!

"I can't live without air and water," she screamed to the silence. "I'll die! Is that what you want? I can't give you what you need if I'm dead." Kathryn hoped he didn't want her dead.

"Rule Number Four: No talking while in punishment—three more days solitary confinement," crackled the intercom.

She had no idea how many days had passed. Or if any. It could just as easily have been twelve hours as five days. Her stomach was not complaining to any great extent. Kathryn assumed that meant it could not have been more than one or two days at the most.

Thirst nagged at her dry, scratchy throat. Her thick tongue licked at cracked lips. She winced at the taste of dried blood coating her lips.

Cushioning her head on folded arms, she turned to lie on her back. It was not any more comfortable than lying on her side—just a different position and a new set of bones to bruise.

Kathryn passed her waking hours envisioning the faces and memories of family and friends, remembering the last time she saw them. In her memories, Meaghan could again be held on a rocking lap while listening to a favorite story; special dinners could be tasted; conversation could be replayed and enjoyed; hikes on the beach and through the forest could be revisited...as often as she wished.

Kathryn told them how much she loved and missed each one, and tried to send them images and messages mentally, accepting that it was a silly idea. *You never know.* She was glad to at least have her thoughts to keep occupied.

Meaghan grew up and matured a hundred different ways in her mind. Boys were created and then discarded—not good enough. Kathryn imagined every type of suitor possible, settling on a fine young man with a sense of adventure, responsibility, humor, love of life, seriousness, and artistic flair. He was very handsome—like David. The young man's name was Thomas and they enjoyed a long, happy life together. Like Kathryn, Meaghan grew up to be a doctor, while Thomas went into the family business with David.

Meaghan had four children—two girls and two boys. They were wonderful grandchildren, inheriting the freckles and love of life from their grandparents. David played with them when they visited him...and his new wife...every other weekend...

Kathryn hoped David would remarry. She was alone, and didn't want him to suffer her agony. *He should be happy*, she decided.

No one would ever find her body after she died. Dylan would see to that. Her mind tried to picture what kind of memorial service they would have. *How long would they wait? The law said seven years, but without a body, would they ever be able to put me to rest?* Kathryn didn't think so. There would always remain the unanswered questions in the back of their minds. They would never know what had actually happened to her.

A fitful sleep claimed her when she wasn't thinking of home and family. Dreams quickly changed into nightmares in the brutal blackness of her cell. Mini panic attacks accosted her, rendering her more helpless and weak with each bout. Fear gripped her most of the time while tears shamelessly buffeted her face with the burning reality of what it meant to be under someone else's control.

Kathryn had never before considered what it would be like to be in a hostage predicament. Now she was forced into a situation that required her to ask permission for the very air she breathed. It was a plight to which she would never become accustomed. She understood why POWs always maintained a freedom mentality throughout their imprisonment term, despite how long that period lasted. They would not accept their situation to be final.

The heinous conditions of her incarceration overwhelmed Kathryn in the isolating darkness of the Plexiglas cage. She listened for his coming; waited for the click of the lock, anticipated the hiss of the door. Her mind trembled at the imagined thought of his footsteps as he clipped across the floor toward her...but without him, she would die.

Dylan, please come back, she pleaded. It wasn't that she was interested in seeing *him* as much as she just wanted to see somebody...anybody. And if he were all there was...

Breathing became difficult. Her breaths were shallower than she imagined possible, unless lying on one's deathbed. After days of pleading with the mirror for Dylan to come back, she gave up any hope of his returning. Dylan was obviously cold-hearted and cruel enough to consider his rules more important than her life.

Kathryn heard the sudden soft hint of a motor whirring in the distance. *A fan! He's turned the fans back on,* she thought, almost blurting it out before remembering his precious rule about talking. It was a mixed blessing to have air pumped in again—it meant she was to live another day under his control. Regardless, she could not help but feel relieved by the unexpected yet welcome sound. Kathryn chewed her bottom lip with nervous excitement. Climbing to her feet, she stayed close to the edge of the wall to find what fans were working.

Only one, she discovered. He had turned on the fan nearest the door.

The sudden noise of splashing echoed in the small black room. She jumped at the unexpected sound, unable to control her fear and uneasiness. *He's turned the water back on!*

Kathryn cried with joy.

Skipping back to the sink, she dipped trembling fingers under the cold water and guzzled as much as her cupped palms could hold. Then, with sudden concern for the life-giving flow, she turned the tap off. *It's probably another rule: Thou shalt not waste water.*

The little metal box clicked. Pinning her back flat against the wall, she turned to see the door slip open. Light fell across the room, forcing her to turn her eyes from the visual assault. Before she could regain her composure, the light was gone and the door was again locked.

Are you in here with me? she asked, inclining her ear toward the door to listen for any movement. There was no other sound except her own slow breaths and the quiet whir of the single air vent fan.

After an unbearable period, Kathryn edged along the wall, stopping every other foot to again listen in the darkness for any strange sounds. Her hands became her eyes as they reached out into the blackness, purposely feeling around for *him.* He was nowhere to be found.

Near the door, the side of her foot brushed against a low, flat object lying on the floor. Squatting onto her haunches, she gently used her fingers to probe the item sitting beside her. Her fingers felt around the circular rim of a small Styrofoam bowl. Kathryn carefully lifted the container into the air. It was warm. Her heart began to pound in her chest. Controlled with a cautious suspicion, she removed the thin plastic lid and brought the bowl near her nose to smell the contents.

Broth, she thought with hungry, stomach-growling excitement threatening to explode within her. The thought of food, any kind of food, after such an indeterminate length of time drove her to a level of hysteria.

Kathryn dipped her finger into the lukewarm contents and swirled it around. There were no lumps. The bowl was simply beef broth. *He's not going to let me die after all.* She sighed and greedily drank the contents of the bowl in a matter of seconds.

There was no way to tell the passage of time, so Kathryn decided to count meals. *Nothing else mattered, anyway.* He wouldn't turn the lights on or come back until he was good and ready. She had no control over how many days that would be—twenty-one or two hundred and one. It was his choice.

She knew that a person isolated from everything could only maintain sanity for a certain period. However, she couldn't remember how long that was. Being a people person, she didn't think she could hold out very long.

Forcing herself to keep active, Kathryn paced the cell until she memorized every inch. Despite the dark, she had learned to run from any point to another, skirting the table and chair without touching them. Hours were filled by studying the furniture until she knew every bend, crevice and contour. When she wasn't doing laps around her prison cell, she did push-ups, sit-ups, and deep knee bends. The worst thing that could happen was becoming atrophied, making her already shaky position worse.

Kathryn refused to let the lack of food and light beat her. She fought back the only way she knew—she kept as active as possible.

During the time of her solitary punishment, Dylan had slipped her three bowls of chicken broth, fifteen bowls of beef broth, and two bowls of vegetable broth. Kathryn could feel the protrusion of her ribs to such an increased extent that she figured he was feeding her only once a day. The isolation and lack of nourishment forced her to fall into constant naps that made her lose all track of time. She would awake with a sudden start of anxiety that would throw her once again into this nightmare of reality that had been forced upon her.

The hunger had long since passed. She had gotten used to the meager fare. If her fevered calculations were correct, Kathryn estimated that today was the last meal of the punishment period. Tomorrow he would enter her prison and she would be able to talk again. The pain of not being able to communicate had been unexpectedly unbearable. Perhaps it was the hardest part of the penalty.

Except for the lack of food, she added as an afterthought.

The door clicked open. The blinding light filled her room for only a brief moment. A hand scooped the bowl from the previous day and left another in its place. The light decreased as the door clicked shut. Kathryn no longer had to edge against the wall to get to the door. She knew exactly where the bowl was, where it was every day he had left one. She strolled over, squatted down and picked up the familiar Styrofoam container.

As was her habit, she lifted the lid to smell the contents. There was no odor. She dipped in a finger and swirled it around. The contents were cold and lumpy. There were wriggling legs beating against her finger. The contents moved on its own. One of the bowl's items climbed up her finger. He had given her a bowl of...*bugs*!

Screaming in one long, shrill shriek, Kathryn hurled the bowl across the room. She detested insects. She couldn't stand them in her house, her car, or even in her front yard, let alone in her bowl.

"Rule Number Five: No throwing food—twelve days. Rule Number Four: No talking while in penalty—ten days," cracked the intercom.

Chapter Eight

Dylan increased her meager fare. The menu now boasted of tasteless, watered-down stews and unsalted crackers. From the tinny taste of the diluted gravy, she suspected that he heated the meals from cans. Kathryn learned to stretch her food into several smaller meals throughout the day to shorten the long waiting periods between the filling of the bowls. The stews he offered were equally unappetizing hot or cold, so it didn't matter how long she saved them as long as the bowl was empty and in place when he exchanged it for a full one.

Although it was a far cry from her level of fitness before she became his guest, Kathryn could feel her strength slowly returning. Apathy had taken over her motives until she no longer cared about the pretense of keeping busy. A degree of lethargy set into her movements, leaving her unable to find the energy to move for any reason other than satisfying necessary body needs.

As a precaution against further penalty, Kathryn decided not to investigate the food. Her hunger was now great enough that it didn't matter if there were surprises in her bowl. Instead, as long as the contents did not move, Kathryn swallowed everything whole, afraid her teeth might crunch into something unidentified.

She had no idea how long it took her to clean the cell. On hands and knees, Kathryn searched the blackness for every insect and, wrapping them in tissue, flushed the dwindling infestation down the toilet. Afraid he would punish her by forever locking her alone in the dark, she scraped and washed the breakfast off the floor and wall as best she could without being able to see it, using her chipped fingernails as a scrubber.

With great effort, Kathryn kept track of the number of meals until the time finally arrived which she estimated to be the lifting of her banishment. On the day in question, she washed and prepared herself, hoping everything was acceptable. She had her fill of dark, silent aloneness, and longed to see a human face and hear a human voice—even if they did belong to a lunatic.

Waiting in the darkness, Kathryn crouched on the floor by the wall, staring into the solid black shadows. Her eyes played tricks on her, creating shapes that were not there, and making them dance in the silence. The minutes ticked by, each taking an eternity before moving to the next endless moment. Unable to deny her fragile emotions, Kathryn hugged her knees into her chest as spastic hands wiped at frustrated tears.

Lights flooded the room unannounced, revealing her hiding place in the far corner. Startled, Kathryn covered her eyes to shield them from the piercing pain of the sudden burst of brilliance.

Thank God, it's over, she sighed, not really certain if she were relieved or not.

After another lengthy wait, she finally heard the anticipated click of the door. Crouching in the opposite corner, Kathryn shivered from a sudden chill of fright at the thought of him. He had grown in her mind, becoming larger than life and posing a greater threat than she remembered. The darkness had fed her fear until she thought she would go mad from its poison. Afraid to move from her position, she was terrified of accidentally breaking another unknown rule.

The door was slow to open. As her eyes adjusted to the light, Kathryn searched the floor and wall for missed food residue, but could see nothing. A nervous panic pummeled her mind as she analyzed all the things that could be wrong in Dylan's sight. It was a hopeless task since she didn't know enough about him to help her understand how he would react.

"Good morning, Katie. How are you feeling this morning?" Dylan asked as he sauntered through the door. Bubbling with enthusiasm, he looked crisp and clean in cords and plaid shirt. His immaculate appearance made her feel even dirtier than she was.

Stunned by his cordial familiarity, Kathryn was unable to respond. The lack of food in his hands worried her, making her wonder about his intentions to feed her. For days, she had envisioned a plate of meatballs, whole potatoes, kernel corn, and mushroom soup gravy. It was a personal favorite since childhood. For some reason, she hoped he might come in with a steaming tray in his hands, set it on the table, and lift the metal cover to reveal endless helpings of her favorite foods.

Instead, he moved to the table and stared down at her cowering in the corner where she waited for instructions.

"Come here and turn around," he ordered through a broad grin, his words more commanding than he himself appeared. His eyes were not as cold and hollow as she remembered, and his voice had lost some of its rough quality.

Kathryn hesitated, uncertain what he wanted to do to her. She was not willing to step into an unknown position like a lamb for the slaughter. Her situation was precarious enough without being an agreeable participant in her own death.

The grin from Dylan's face transformed into a grimace of seething rage. His lips curled back to reveal gritted teeth, contorting his features into a scowling mask.

Fear escalated up her spine. The instant she saw his transformation, Kathryn knew she had broken another rule. *Oh God, no,* her mind moaned. *What will it be this time? Solitary? Starvation? Something worse?*

Dylan turned to leave as abruptly as he had come. The fury in his eyes revealed that his mind was in high gear, contemplating her next appropriate punishment.

A shock of terror shot through. The last penalty was unbearable. She had no idea what he could subject her to, but Kathryn knew she didn't want to find out.

"No, please. I'm sorry. I didn't mean it. Please, don't go. Don't punish me. I'll be good. I won't disobey again," she promised, desperation coating her words. Kathryn hated herself for begging and telling him that she was wrong, but it was better than being alone again. The thought of facing the silence and total blackness of her cell was intolerable. Besides, she was just plain hungry.

Dylan stopped, still facing the mirrored door with his hands clenched into tight balls by his sides, and glared at her image. Remaining immobile, he waited for her to make the next move.

Hesitating for the briefest of moments, Kathryn shoved one foot ahead of the other, pushing herself toward him. Images of a dozen possible scenarios of what he might do rampaged through her mind. With each step closer, her terror grew, knowing she would find out all too soon which one he would choose.

Dylan turned to face her as she approached. His eyes were lifeless blue pools. His lips curled into an unnerving grin of triumph as the tip of his tongue caressed the edge of his teeth.

Kathryn shivered against the commanding control of his unblinking stare. Pausing a few feet from him, she obediently turned to face the table and gripped her hands firmly around the stainless steel edge for support. Her knees weakened and she thought she would faint from the tense pressure of expectation. She braced herself for his touch as, from the corner of her eye, she saw his reflection move toward her.

This is it...don't resist, she reminded herself. *It'll only make things worse if you fight back.*

His hand clamped around her right wrist and yanked her arm backward. A soft click echoed off the Plexiglas walls as he secured her wrist into a metal handcuff.

Kathryn's skin trembled in the wake of his touch. Fighting the growing need and urgency to vomit, she started to sob instead. Dread overwhelmed her as he grabbed her other hand and slapped that wrist into the empty cuff, snatching away her choices.

The mirrored image of Dylan pulled a black bag from his back pocket. His eyes traveled up and down her body with sick appreciation of how the soiled T-shirt clung to her.

She watched as he shook the sack open. The noise of it snapping in the air behind her made her jump. Her heart pounded in her chest. A clammy perspiration popped out of every one of her pores. Unable to bear the sight of his movements one second longer, Kathryn shut her eyes, preferring not to know what he was doing.

He plopped the bag over her head and bound the cord into a tight knot around her neck, again throwing her into a choked world of darkness, cutting off the scream that lodged in her throat. Taking her elbow, he shoved and pulled her from the cell.

The plush feel of the carpet beneath her stumbling feet was a welcome change. The thickness of the fibers reinforced her belief of his wealth. Kathryn briefly took the time to think that being on carpet possibly meant they were in his home, since an institution or warehouse would not be carpeted with this kind of quality.

She tripped along beside him, unsure of her footing, afraid of tripping over or walking into something unseen. Her knees buckled, but he pulled her up before she fell. She bumped into a wall before he dragged her through another doorway. He continued to guide her across a more open area. At least the claustrophobic feeling disappeared when Kathryn bounced off a half-wall constructed from something hard and round.

A hallway, maybe a second floor railing, she reasoned, thinking it must be a banister. Kathryn tried to find some concrete point of reference along the way.

He jerked her through the different areas at a fast clip, leaving her little time to think about anything except where her feet were landing. Twice she stepped on his shoes; once he stomped her bare foot; several times he stopped her from falling to the floor.

In the event she ever had the opportunity to travel the same route unhooded, her mind counted the steps from her cell to wherever he was taking her. Hoping it might some day prove a help, she planned a blind escape route, picturing the surroundings in her mind.

Dylan yanked her arm around yet another corner, causing the cuffs to dig into her wrists. The click of his heels struck against the barrenness of tile.

Another cell? she panicked, not sure she really wanted to know. *Could there be a room worse than the one I've been in?* Visions of dingy interrogation rooms from past movies filtered through her thoughts and she again began to cry, her body heaving with great sobs.

He let her elbow drop. With a hand on both shoulders, he turned her around to face him. Kathryn wondered if she were in a small, desolate room housing a filthy cot used for prostitution. The answer was finally going to be revealed, and she didn't know if she were ready, but not knowing was worse.

Dylan stepped away from her. The heels of his shoes tapped the tiles in a slow rhythmic sweep as he moved around her, studying her from every direction. He dragged his hand along her body as he walked, not minding the touch of her cold sweat and clammy smell.

Kathryn's skin began to crawl under the pressure of his touch. The need to scream consumed her, but she knew it would be a fatal mistake, so crushed the urge before it became irrepressible.

His fingers ran down the length of her arm and stopped at her wrist, fondling the metal manacle in an almost loving way. Kathryn's hand fell from the handcuff and she let it drop unhindered to her side. He caressed her right arm and released it from the remaining cuff. She could hear the metal clang as he tossed the cuffs before moving around to face her.

Kathryn reminded herself to breathe. She attempted to calm her pounding heart. Her fingers began to quiver. A gulp lodged itself in her throat. She braced herself for the obvious.

Dylan's fingers fumbled with the knot at her neck, his touch impatient and urgent. He untied the hood, yanked it off her head, and tossed it on top of the handcuffs on the counter behind him.

Kathryn blinked in the unexpected light of the room. Staring into his vacant blue eyes, she was surprised by their nearness. She knew he was standing in front of her, but hadn't sensed his being so close. Smelling the mint toothpaste on his breath made her want to turn and run as far and fast as she could. Instead, frozen with fear, she stood a motionless victim before him.

Dylan stepped aside, closed the door, and locked them into the new room.

Kathryn dared to turn her head and scan the area. To her surprise, he had brought her to a lavish bathroom. The entire room was covered in a white and black marble with heavily decorated, silver Elizabethan accents. Two hanging pots were overflowing with lush ferns, giving her the first sight of life she had seen in over a month. Grateful for their presence, she consumed the small sense of reality they offered in this nightmare.

"Take off your clothes," he instructed from the door, his voice low and commanding.

She turned to face him, not wanting to be any more naked and vulnerable than she already was, afraid to move and even more terrified not to.

His raised eyebrows clearly said that he expected her to comply at once. His face was flushed with excitement. A sickening smile slid across his lips as he already undressed her with roaming eyes.

"I said, take your clothes off. Be warned, I will not keep saying things more than once," he whispered. A frown of anger crept over his brow as his eyes narrowed into slits. Dylan's hands bunched into fists.

"What are you going to do to me?" she asked, stalling.

"That doesn't matter. If I tell you to do something, your job is to do it right away. Nothing more. Nothing less. Is that understood? Or do you need another crash course?" he hissed, the artery in his left temple throbbing with angry anticipation.

Kathryn shook her head, hesitated for another brief second, and finally submitted to his demand. She draped the dirty T-shirt in front of her, trying to cover herself with its hanging limpness, unwilling to discard it totally. Returning his heartless gaze, she followed his eyes as they traveled down her body. Horrified with her new vulnerability, the panic caught in her throat, threatening to hyperventilation. With every ounce of effort she could muster, Kathryn forced herself to calm down—not wanting to add to his domination over her by becoming an emotional cripple.

Dylan stepped around her, snatching the T-shirt from her hands as he went. He tossed the soiled clothing into a laundry hamper. Sauntering over to the toilet, he sat down, using it as a chair.

Kathryn stood frozen, afraid to even breathe.

"You may not care about your appearance, but I'm the one who has to look at you. And you look awful. So, you're going to take a bath and get cleaned up," he announced as if she had chosen to be in this condition.

She hated him for that spiteful affront and though his words hurt, the mere thought of a bath thrilled her. The concern about his being in the same room passed, outweighed by the delight of soaking in a hot sudsy bath. She looked over her shoulder at the ebony marbled...inviting...wonderfully   oversized...Jacuzzi-equipped bathtub where she could wash away the ordeal of the past month. For however long he permitted, she would be allowed to feel almost human again.

"There are different bottles of bubblebath in the basket there. I'm sure you can find one you like. You'll find some shampoo and conditioner in there," he said, pointing to the black wicker basket in front of the fern at the far corner of the tub.

Kathryn edged toward the raised tub, still unsure of him, and flipped the lever to lower the plug into the drain. Steam soon billowed upward as the water cascaded into the bathtub. Choosing a floral scented bubble bath, she liberally poured it into the water. Bubbles immediately filled the tub, beckoning her to come in and play. Unable to resist any longer, Kathryn climbed into the scented heat and soon forgot he was even in the room.

Taking one of the sponges forming a decorative pattern around the basket, she began to scrub at her skin, threatening to scrape it off her body. The bruises had long since disappeared. The visible evidence attesting to the length of time she had been in solitary was an unsettling shock. Her skin had lost its glow, taking on an unhealthy pallor from her stay in the dark without proper nutrition. Kathryn decided to confront Dylan with her needs later, but right now, she didn't want anything to interrupt her bath.

Dylan didn't take his eyes from her the entire time she soaked. The only sound in the steamy room was the water splashing from her sponge as she squeezed the warm luxury over her grateful body. He didn't try to approach her, but instead, studied her like she was a bug under a microscope.

Kathryn thought of David and Meaghan, wondering how they were taking her disappearance. *Meaghan is probably still at Mom and Dad Breslin's. Dad must be beside himself with worry. David must be going crazy.*

Speculating on Wendy and Bill's reaction, she knew Wendy would blame herself for not waking up in time to help her. *Had you been there, Dylan would probably have hurt you. But there was nothing you could have done, Wendy. He had everything planned. He played us all for fools. Don't be angry with yourself. I'm all right,* she thought, hoping her feelings would reach out to Wendy from wherever she was.

The police would be following every possible lead, but she doubted one would steer them here. *If they had anything concrete, they'd have been here by now,* she realized, thinking Dylan might just be correct about his self-proclaimed cleverness. *And if they can't come to me, then I have to find a way to get to them.*

A chill began to settle into the water and Kathryn was compelled to leave its once warm embrace to face the colder reality of Dylan's world. The only rack with towels was beside Dylan on the other side of the room. The distance obliged her to walk naked far longer than she appreciated. Sighing, no other option at hand, Kathryn stepped as quickly and modestly as she could to grab a towel off the bar by Dylan's head.

Dylan snatched up the large black bath towel before she got there. He stood up and held it out to her, his eyes suggesting she let him dry her off.

Kathryn froze. She didn't know if she should try to reach for the towel, or let Dylan hand it to her. Weighing the two options, she waited for some further indication from him regarding her next move.

Dylan stepped forward and draped the towel over her shoulders, rubbing them with gentle, broad strokes, letting the thick, soft cloth soak up all the moisture. He proceeded down her arms, drying each individual finger almost lovingly. With lingering, sensual sweeps, he slid the towel round her back, buttocks and breasts before continuing down her legs.   .

Kathryn chewed her bottom lip hard to keep from crying. She could feel his escalating excitement through the luxurious material as he worked his way around her body. His fingers trembled with the proximity of her flesh. Kathryn suppressed the nagging desire to kick him in the groin with her knee and run away through the...*what? The locked door?*

Cursing his foresight, she knew she wouldn't have time to grab the key from his pocket before he regained control of the situation. All she would successfully accomplish would be to infuriate him, and that would only result in another vicious beating.

Dylan dropped the wet towel to the floor and strolled to the vanity. Reaching for the silver canister of dusting powder, he brought it back to where she stood. With painstaking patience, Dylan dabbed her paralyzed body with the large powdered puff.

Kathryn wept softly from his forced attentions, hating herself for allowing him to do whatever he wanted. She could do nothing except stand as still as possible until he finished the task, covering her again with a clean white T-shirt.

He must have a supply of them, she thought, annoyed by the lack of color he afforded her. *Probably to strip me of any identity.*

Dylan pulled the hood from the counter and tugged it over her head, this time leaving it untied at her neck. Pulling her arms back, he again clamped the handcuffs around her wrists. Then he yanked her back to the cell the same way they had come.

She heard the click of the door as he abandoned her again, still bound and hooded, to the silence of her prison. Kathryn moved to her corner by the sink and sat on the floor with her legs outstretched before her. She didn't know how long he would be and settled into the endless waiting game he seemed so fond of.

Her skin felt cleaner than it had for a long time. It might have been a small concession for him, but for her, it was like he had given her the world. Kathryn wanted to tell David all that had happened to her since she became Dylan's prisoner, but couldn't. If David was standing right before her, she wouldn't know where to begin. There were so many thoughts and feelings. There were so many tears that needed to be shed.

Kathryn's mind wandered aimlessly, refusing to settle into one consistent train of thought. She knew she would have to focus and control her emotions if she ever hoped to escape his power.

The soft click of the door sounded as it popped open.

"Breakfast is ready, madam," he announced with an outlandish British accent, as if he were bringing food to his master instead of his hostage.

She heard him plop the tray onto the table and walk over to where she sat. Kathryn pushed herself to her feet as he tugged on her arm. Wincing with pain because of the odd angle at which he pulled her arm, she stifled a bellow of protest.

He whipped off the hood and ushered her to the table, leaving her to stand at quasi-attention on one side. Moving to the opposite side, Dylan collapsed into the chair and looked very pleased with himself.

"I've outdone myself today. I hope you like poached eggs on toast and porridge. I made some for both of us. I figured you might be hungry," he prattled, stirring the milk and sugar into one of the bowls of pale brown mush.

"My hands...Could you please undo my hands so I can eat properly?" she begged in her sweetest voice.

Dylan stopped stirring his porridge and stared at her through a vacant glare. She gulped as his eyes told her she had done another unthinkable thing—she had spoken without permission.

"I'm sorry," she apologized, hoping her repentance diffused his anger in time.

She hadn't paid attention to him in the bathroom. Now, as she studied his face, she could see his hair had grown long enough to stand up in tufts of thick curls that gave his appearance a European flavor. The dark circles were gone from under his eyes and the color of his skin had become more swarthy than jaundiced. His baggy clothes draped loosely over a lean body without affording him any definition. A red bandanna was tied neatly around his neck to accent the black shirt and cords. He was not an ugly man, or even homely, yet she couldn't say he was attractive either.

Normal looking, not the kind of face that would jump out at you in a crowd.

Dylan's ears stuck out a bit and were longer than usual, making them rather unappealing. They made his head look larger than it was, while at the same time Kathryn appreciated that if he allowed his hair to grow, he could effectively conceal them. *Probably got teased as a dumbo or radar in school.*

"Are you hungry?" he asked, intruding into her thoughts.

"What...? Yes. Yes, I am. It smells good," she added quickly, hoping to appease the god of wrath sitting before her.

"Do you promise to be good? Do you promise to eat like a person this time?" he asked, filling his mouth with a scoop of milk-sodden porridge. "I don't want my meal ruined again with your nonsense. Understand?"

"Yes. Anything you want, just please remove the cuffs. They're hurting my wrists," she pleaded, keeping her tone level and her voice sweet. Kathryn managed a half-smile. Her stomach growled in anticipation of the food she could smell.

Dylan gave her an imperceptible nod, shoveled another spoonful of the mush into his mouth, stood, and beckoned her closer. Reaching around her, he unlocked the handcuffs and let them drop to the floor.

Kathryn stooped and picked them up, placing them on the table in front of Dylan. He was smiling, pleased at her thoughtfulness, and she knew she had passed a test. *Dylan: ten thousand; Kathryn: one.*

Returning to her side of the table, she stood while digging hungrily into the food before her. Each of her movements was calculated so as not to encroach on anything that might be his. She watched closely, waiting for any change in his temperament, guiding her movements strictly by what was and was not approved by his body language.

"Mmmm. Wonderful," she complimented, savoring the steaming brown coffee through tiny sips. During solitary, she had dreamed of sipping cappuccino in a specialty café overlooking the ocean. It seemed like forever since she had anything hot to drink. The coffee was strong and she couldn't remember ever tasting anything so delicious.

Dylan watched her as she held the Styrofoam cup between her hands. Unwilling to take his eyes off her, he pushed himself up from his chair with great effort and rounded the table. Kathryn continued to sip from the cup in a futile attempt to ignore the approaching threat and remain calm. Dylan stood beside her, and hesitantly, he reached out his hand and rolled her damp hair between his finger and thumb.

Kathryn closed her eyes, hoping to shut out the onslaught of his touch. Gritting her teeth, she braced herself against the storm she could sense raging inside him. It was painfully obvious what his intentions were, and somehow, she found herself wanting him to get on with it so at last that would be over. The hardest part was the waiting. Kathryn did little else. She waited eternities for food, light, drink...

Now that the moment was here, she found herself almost relieved. The unknown was always more frightening and horrible than the reality. As long as he didn't beat her, she decided that she could bear the ordeal...that she would endure it and survive.

Kathryn had tended to many victims of violent crimes while in Seattle. She had seen their tears and heard their whispered secrets through the agony of their bitter silence. She had bandaged wounds and treated patients with all the warmth and caring she knew. Kathryn thought she understood the trauma these women had gone through. When they were brought to the hospital for medical attention, she thought her compassion made a difference to their suffering. But now, in the light of her own treacherous situation, she knew she could never have imagined one moment of the unfathomable fear that accompanied such an act of aggression. In all her attempts to soothe and comfort those women, she had no clue how they truly felt...or why.

Circumstances had changed her in the last month. *Maybe it'll make me a better doctor,* she hoped, struggling to keep focused on any good thing that could come from this experience.

"I want to know everything there is to know about you. I want to know how you feel; why you feel; when you feel; where you feel. I have to know what makes you the way you are. I want to know everything you think when you think it. What makes you so different from everyone else, so different from me? Why you make me feel the way I do?" he whispered.

Dylan brushed her thick auburn hair back from her ear, and caressed her skin, engrossed in the unfathomable discovery of her body. He followed the line down her neck and shoulders, lifting her arm in his hand, examining the texture of her flesh. Touching each finger, he scrutinized the bones beneath, attempting to inspect their outline. He poked at the soft tissue on the palm of her hand, excited with the fleshiness; tracing the lines with his finger; bending and straightening her hands with all the intensity of a scientist.

She watched his growing amazement. He was like a little boy discovering his first frog. She wondered if he had ever seen a human being before, besides himself. He seemed captivated with her body, exploring how everything moved. He bent her joints backward to see what prevented their full rotation.

Minutes ticked by into what she thought had to be hours as he soberly examined every inch of her body. Dylan spoke to the air as if there was someone else in the room she could not see. He reported his findings, dictated things he wanted to look into further, made verbal evaluations... He ordered Kathryn to sit, stand, and finally lie down on the cold steel table to endure his exhaustive examination.

Without ceremony or notice, Dylan abruptly turned on his heel and clicked out of the cell, leaving her alone under the blaze of lights. Kathryn wept bitterly, unable to withhold the flood of pent-up emotion that gushed forth. She bit her lip, and, sliding off the table, collapsed into her corner by the sink.

Rule Number Three: No sitting on furniture, she remembered.

She wondered why he did not force himself on her. Nothing was over. It had only begun. Again she was subjected to the endless waiting game. Exhausted by the stress of the morning, Kathryn fell into a fitful sleep and dreamed about being chased by wild animals and being carved up in an autopsy.

Chapter Nine

"Have you ever been afraid, Katie?" Dylan asked from behind her. He looked off to a distant horizon. His feet were perched on the far end of the table. Leaning back in his chair had become a favorite position, and he'd sit for hours contemplating some philosophical mystery.

Kathryn felt stiff from sitting cross-legged on the floor. The thin metal table leg dug into her back. Lifting her head, she glared at their images in the mirror. She was tired of the mirror. The sight of him. The sound of him. The smell of him. This room. His chair. Him.

Kathryn was weary of herself...and her life...the life he gave her.

She had long ago lost count of meals and baths—they came too erratically to be an accurate gauge of time. The stress and poor nutrition had slowly stopped her menstrual cycle so its use as a calendar was also stripped away. Hours grew into weeks and months. She had no way of telling, and had long since given up caring.

Every day was the same, like a monotonous ritual. She found herself put through the motions of a routine she didn't understand. He came into her small Plexiglas prison and, after locking the door, headed straight for the chair that stood sentry between the table and the sink. Sitting motionless for hours, he would simply stare at her without saying a word.

Dylan watched her sleep, eat, and pace. He studied her as she performed each move; everything from sponge bathing to running fingers through her hair. The only semblance of privacy he afforded her was when she used the toilet—Dylan would at least turn his head pretending not to watch...but she could see his eyes in the mirror.

Kathryn would let him scrutinize her until she couldn't bear it one second longer. Then, sighing loudly, she would pace, circling the table endlessly. In an attempt to relax, she counted each step, making the habit a daily chant. She would continue the mindless dirge until Dylan, after studying her awhile longer, would get up and leave. The distracting disturbance of her counting annoyed him and that alone made it a worthwhile practice.

Sometimes he would gaze at her with such intensity that she felt as if his eyes were boring holes right through her. There was no escaping him. If he left her alone, she knew he was on the other side of the mirror, watching. She had seen the tip of his cigarette too often to think he had lost interest in voyeurism.

The only breaks in the mundane routine of their shared existence were the occasional meals, rare baths, and frequent and undeniably ridiculous periods of endless questions. She had tried to answer him the first few times, mistakenly thinking that was what he wanted. But she discovered the only right answers were his answers and so she stopped, letting him vent himself until he too got tired of his own voice.

Kathryn sighed...again. After days of studying her every move, he asked this question that had absolutely no connection with her reality. It was as if he lived on another plane of existence and she had been sucked through a knothole into the vortex of his insanity.

Duh! Of course I've been afraid, you asshole. She scowled, wishing she had the nerve to say it aloud. She was tired of being afraid of him, of dying, of living...it had been too intense for far too long.

"How long have I been here?" she asked, knowing he wouldn't answer. He never did. She would ask him how long she had been his *guest*, or what possible reason he had for taking her, or anything else that could possibly pertain to her present situation, and he would either leave the room or continue with his own meaningless banter. Sometimes she would ask him these questions hoping it would force him to leave.

"I mean really afraid. Afraid you would live and never be permitted to die. Afraid that if you did die, it would only be worse than being alive," he continued. His eyes were fixed on the back of her head. He had chosen to ignore her.

Kathryn stretched her back, and, rolling her shoulders, got up from the floor. Her movements were no longer fluid. Her skin no longer had a healthy glow, but instead, had adopted a gray pallor from the lack of sunshine and fresh air. Her eyes, glazed from long nights without sleep, were circled with a dark purple color. Dry and unkempt, her hair was inches longer than she liked to keep it. Her fingernails were jagged and broken from drumming them on the Plexiglas to hear any sound other than her own breathing...or his.

She had asked him for a few necessities: hairbrush, toothbrush, toothpaste, deodorant, soap, towel, tampons, and clothes. But he refused her requests, remaining adamant that anything for her personal care remained the exclusive property of his bathroom. He did not allow her to keep anything in her cell, making it abundantly clear that the use of such items, and his bathroom, were at his discretion alone. It was simply another method of control he exerted over her every minute of every day.

She walked over to his chair and stopped just in front of him. Returning his gaze long enough to feel an unpleasant mixture of disgust and pity for the creature seated before her, Kathryn shook her head and moved to the far corner. It was another of his endless rules that she not barricade herself between the sink and wall when he was in the room. He wanted free access to her always.

"Afraid you're the only one who sees the truth? Afraid of being the only one in the entire universe left when the end comes?" he continued. Consumed by his thoughts, his voice became flat and his eyes glazed over with a vacancy. At times he would intone words with the same monotonous attitude of a sci-fi talking computer, as if he had descended into a deep trance.

She had long since discovered that her sole purpose for being here, locked in this room, was to wait and listen for the great philosophical words and foolish wisdom that spilled forth from the mouth of a raving lunatic. His mind analyzed things and ideas until they no longer resembled the original and she had forgotten what his point was initially.

Since that awful day when he had examined her so intently, he rarely came nearer than the chair. Much to her surprise and relief, sex was not his main focal point or even on his mind. He hadn't touched her in that way. His meticulous examination of her was more curiosity than sexual. Now, from a distance, he studied how she ate, swallowed, walked, stood, sat, and breathed. There was no end to the ordinary occurrences that would captivate and fascinate him for hours. He mentally probed the throb of the tiny veins in her hand; the twitch in her eye; the color of her hair; the freckles on her skin.

"Will you shut up!" she screamed, unable to listen to another word. "Punish me. Torture me. Kill me. Do whatever you want! I don't care! Just shut up! I can't stand it anymore. Why can't you just leave me alone?"

Kathryn cradled her head in arms that hugged trembling knees close to her chest. Rocking back and forth, her shoulders slapped against the wall in a subconscious attempt to keep time with her mounting tension. The rhythm dragged her down into a numb trance. She wished he would do something other than talk. Anything other than the tone of his monotonous voice would break the depressing hold.

Dylan had not made any demands that would lead to her eventual release. In the back of Kathryn's mind, she entertained the idea that if he got what he wanted, he would be forced to let her go. However, he hadn't told her what he wanted. That one clue remained a mystery, and she suspected it was because he didn't know himself.

She had gone over plans of escape a million times in her mind. But he always kept her on a short leash, either by blinding her with the hood or locking her in this room.

Kathryn had tried to overtake him during one desperate, foolhardy moment. In the feeble overthrow attempt, she pushed him over before he had locked the bathroom door. Running to the hallway, she had one hand on the banister by the time he lunged at her, pushing her down the stairs. Landing on the floor at the bottom with a dizzy grunt, she lay dazed and confused. Dylan was on her before she could lift her head and hauled her back up the stairs by her hair. Later, in the quiet of the cell, he had given her such a harsh beating she feared for her life.

She learned that Dylan was two different people. He had an uncontrollable, volatile anger that exploded with such an intensity of rage she was afraid for her life. During those times, he was completely self-absorbed with the fury that possessed him. He no longer noticed she was in the same room. Dylan would rant and scream at unseen things, refusing to cave into whatever they were demanding. He would flail futile fists in the air while squatting on the floor in the corner, cowering and trembling in utter fear...just as she had done.

His torment knew no limit. Dylan screamed from horrors that raged within his darkened heart. Fighting against *them* as long as he could, he would resort to inflicting physical injuries on himself. She could only stand by, struck with helpless awe, as he sliced open his foot or hand with a knife. He caused himself a high level of physical pain in an attempt to overpower the mental and emotional agony *they* wreaked on him. It was an incomprehensible response, but one he whispered as she tended to his gaping wounds after he again came to his right mind.

The other side of Dylan was completely contrite. He apologized for breathing too loud, walking too fast, speaking too often...He seemed to consider her needs first in all his thoughts and actions. During these times, he would let her take a bath and change her T-shirt. Meals were better prepared and delivered more often. He was quieter, waiting for her to speak instead of asking so many meaningless questions.

There was no balance within him, and she didn't know from day to day what the fuse would be to set him off on another tirade of abuse. Sometimes, she could tell it was going to happen by the look in his eyes—they became the eyes of someone who had no life within; cold, distant, hopeless eyes. His glazed look was that of someone who hated not only her, but also especially himself and the unseen *things* that haunted his life.

When she was mirrored in those eyes Kathryn was most afraid for her life.

"Get up," he snapped, pushing himself from the chair. He grimaced.

Kathryn rose to her feet. Hesitation had indeed given way to resigned, learned obedience, and she pushed herself over to where he stood. Stopping the obligatory two steps in front of him, she placed her hands behind her back and waited for him to restrain her. The echo of metal handcuffs clanging against the table made her back bristle. In the mirror, she saw his reflection fluff a hood in the air directly behind her. It was a very predictable part of the normal procedure followed by thirty steps, turn left, thirty-five steps, turn left, four steps, and stop. It was the ritual that ended in his bathroom.

When he had bound her, he tugged on her elbow. She fell into pace beside and slightly behind him, ticking off the steps in her mind as she went: thirty steps, miss the wall, turn left, thirty-five steps...thirty-six, thirty-seven...

They were not heading to the Jacuzzi tub. A fresh shot of fear coursed through her. She thought all her feelings had been smothered so very long ago, but now fear, anxiety, and excitement caused the sound of her heart to pound in her ears.

Maybe he's letting me go, her mind suggested. Kathryn stumbled as her foot missed the first step downward.

Dylan caught her before she fell. He curtailed their pace so she could regain her footing.

Yeah, right, she answered herself. Her heart skipped a beat as he ushered her down a staircase, one slow step after another.

Don't be a fool, Kate! she argued, feeling smug as her belief of being on a second floor was confirmed.

At the bottom of the staircase, Dylan directed her left through another carpeted room and around several pieces of furniture. The sweet odor of cedar drifted through the air. It was a pleasant change from the antiseptic smell of her room. Walking through another doorway, they stopped when the cool, hard surface of tile was beneath her feet. She remained still and waited patiently as he slowly removed the hood.

Kathryn blinked in the bright light of the room. It took a few seconds for her eyes to adjust before being able to take in her new surroundings.

They were standing just inside the doorway of a very impressive kitchen. The floor was covered with okra tiles, complimented by one accent wall of rich burnt okra brick trimmed with yellow cedar. The island in the middle of the kitchen area held a black designer stovetop. A built-in spice rack covered one end of the island while the other housed several shelves of cookbooks. The large stained-glass ceiling was trimmed with a copper rod and lit up the island. From the rod hung very expensive imported culinary pans and utensils.

At the opposite end of the room was a raised eating area nestled in the center of a windowed atrium. It overlooked a vast wooded area just beyond a clearing.

A tear of familiarity found its way to the corner of her eye. It had been so long since she had seen a room like this. She was overwhelmed with the honor of being able to stand in a kitchen again.

"Why have you brought me here?" she whispered.

He looked at her through dead eyes that failed in their attempt to smile. His upper lip curled into a broad grin, giving him a demonic appearance even in the daylight. "I thought you could make lunch and then, maybe...we...uh...could go out for a walk," he said, sweeping his hand toward the woods just beyond the house. Dylan was obviously pleased with himself. He had planned to surprise her and succeeded.

Surprised and thrilled, Kathryn looked through the window, her mouth falling open from the sight of the woods just beyond the glass. A heavy blanket of snow covered everything. Tree limbs bowed low under the weight of their added burden. The shock of snow stunned her.

What month is it? she asked incredulously. David had taken her on the sailing trip in May. Flowers were blooming. Everything was green. The weather was cool but pleasant. It had been a late spring when Dylan had taken her prisoner.

She blinked at him, obvious loathing for Dylan seething through her glare. "How long have I been here?" she pleaded. The sadness of her voice cracked under the strain of realization.

"Not long," he smiled.

"How long?" she screamed, turning to confront Dylan. She pushed herself at him and stepped right up to his face. His hot breath on her forehead activated her hands into potent fists.

Dylan became visibly uncomfortable by her threatening closeness. He couldn't look at her. Averting his eyes, he stepped back to a more acceptable distance.

"I don't know. I haven't really paid that much attention. It's so peaceful here, I actually hadn't noticed," he said through a defensive swallow that lodged in his throat.

"How...bloody...long...have...I...been...here . . .?" she screeched, hysteria overwhelming any self-control. Her hands balled into tight fists. Pounding his chest, she tried to solicit an answer from him.

"Well, let's see. It's February, so I guess that makes it a little over nine months," he replied.

"N...i...n...e...months!"

Kathryn darted to the table and frantically gaped at the whiteness blanketing the forest all around them. When she could no longer bear the mute witness to the length of time she'd been locked away, she turned and slumped to the floor. Tears gushed from her eyes as she sobbed, totally possessed by the utter despair of her plight.

It was some time before Kathryn pulled herself together enough to move. Her tears slowly stopped, and when they did, Dylan approached her. He had given her the necessary space to overcome the trauma of her discovery. He was hungry and wanted to eat. To camouflage his discomfort, Dylan urgently pulled her up from the floor and ushered her to the fridge.

Kathryn found it difficult to think about cooking. He gave her free run of the kitchen with the liberty to make whatever she wanted. Stews, soups, cooked cereals, and breads had been her only fare for months. She fancied a Chinese stir-fry, but because of the lack of fresh food, she selected a small pot roast—he at least had most of the ingredients for that, even though they were frozen.

Dylan had equipped his kitchen with every conceivable convenience except fresh food. All his food was either frozen, packaged or canned. There was no range of ingredients to speak of, so Kathryn had to make do with what little she found. Despite the handicap, the meal was delicious. She dug into it hungrily, scooping a small second helping onto her plate.

Dylan enjoyed the gravy and meat, devouring each piece with a large bite of bread. He nodded as he chewed, filling his mouth with more food before he finished the last. Through overstuffed mouthfuls, Dylan agreed that she was a far better cook than he.

Kathryn decided to seize the opening. Placing her fork down carefully beside her plate, she dared to look up at him, swallowing her disgust. His sociable habits were barbaric at best, and she always had trouble stomaching them while eating.

"If I make a grocery list, would you go shopping?" she asked. "Then I could make more interesting meals, like a Greek salad, maybe...or pepper steak...even bake something like an apple pie."

"I'll think about it," he conceded, complimenting her again on her meal, giving her a faint hope. The rest of the dinner was eaten in silence. He filled his mouth, allowing almost as much food to fall out as he shoveled in.

Kathryn stared out the window as she chewed absently and picked at the food left on her plate. Snow began to drift down from the overcast sky. The large, fluffy flakes reminded her of a time when she was a child. It had snowed on Christmas Day that year. After breakfast and gift opening, she had run out to play with her sisters. The snow had lasted until early next morning, every trace disappearing with the usual winter drizzle before noon.

She was mesmerized by the gentle beauty of a forest of trees transformed into soft geometrical designs of frozen elegance. Finding herself lost in more pleasant memories, she allowed herself that time of escape until he pulled her back.

After lunch, Kathryn offered to clear the table and do the dishes. It was a welcome relief to do something that even remotely resembled life before Dylan. Kathryn cleared the table with a certain degree of peace. Dylan leaned back in his chair, propped his feet on the seat of another, and lit a cigarette. While dishes clanked in the sink, he blew sloppy circles of smoke into the air, never quite able to perfect the smoke rings he was trying so hard to make.

Kathryn started to hum a song from a bygone memory. Unaware of making any sound, it still nevertheless generated a warm feeling inside. As her hands moved through the subconscious motion of dishwashing, she kept her eyes fastened on the winter scene framed by the window behind the sink.

A deer emerged from the heavily wooded area behind the house. Kathryn gasped with delight. She had almost forgotten that there was life outside the cell. Her hands froze in mid-motion, afraid that the slightest movement would scare the doe away. A bird swooped down from the sky. The deer pricked its ear upward to discern the reason for the crow's cry. Satisfied that it was nothing, the deer jumped through the deep snow until she crossed the corner of the clearing and disappeared into the dense forest again.

Overcome with joy, Kathryn began to cry, suddenly displaced from her actual surroundings. Her mind carried her to another place and time where she was waiting for David to come home with Meaghan. Wondering what she should make them for supper, she thought a cake would be nice to welcome them home. Meaghan had been away so long at David's parents...What a surprise Meaghan would have when, after spending so much time in the desert of New Mexico, she could play in the winter wonderland surrounding their home. She was only three and as yet hadn't had a chance to play in the snow. It was a rare occurrence on the Island.

"Katie?" cooed an unexpected voice from behind her.

"David, you're back," she smiled, pleased he was early. Her hands held a plate in midair as she waited for him to come up and kiss her.

A loud crash sounded behind her, exploding her fantasy and returning the dreadful reality. The plate fell from her hands and toppled back into the sink where it landed on a glass as it fell. The shattering sound was muffled by a sink full of soapy water. Startled by the thunderous racket, she turned to find the cause.

Dylan's face was purple with rage. He pounded his white knuckled fists on the table in a seething rhythm. The chair toppled over as he jumped up and shoved the table away. Turning, he bent down and picked up the chair, smashing it on the table until it was little more than kindling.

Kathryn cowered by the sink, watching his fury devour him.

Dylan stormed toward the island. He grabbed for canisters, jars, hanging pans, anything within reach, and heaved them at the wall to appease his wrath. His eyes became black pits as he ranted in such guttural tones that Kathryn couldn't make out what he was saying.

He banged frustrated hands on his head. He pushed on his temples as if he were afraid they would explode. Covering his ears, he winced with a sudden, great pain. Crying out, Dylan's hands leapt to his abdomen as he doubled over.

Perplexed, Kathryn could see no physical reason for his apparent agony. Feeling useless, she didn't know what to do. The doctor part of her argued with the victim part, but neither seemed to be winning the battle as she remained frozen by the sink.

He crumpled onto the floor, unable to stand the invisible pressures being exerted on his mind. Reaching his hand to the ceiling in a futile attempt to hold back something that seemed just beyond his grasp, Dylan's face wove a pattern of bizarre contortions as he fought unseen enemies.

She knew if she stayed in the same room he might kill her. Desperate but afraid to move, she prayed for an opening that would offer her a chance to escape.

Dylan screamed in torment as he held his head and covered his ears. Scratching and smacking himself, he thrashed around as if he were in a cloud of insects. He swore, ranting in guttural tones of a language she could not understand. He beat his thighs as if he were trying to encourage his legs to either move at his command or stop crawling from within.

Her mind raced as she watched the self-absorbed madman explode with refreshed fury as he rolled on the floor.

Digging fingernails into his hands, he cut through the soft flesh of his palms. Blood oozed from the punctures as he slammed his hands repeatedly onto the tiles. The impact of his blows left bloodied palm print patterns on the plain squares. The force he used to beat the unseen *enemy* terrified her. The savagery of his self-abuse sliced through her paralyzing panic.

Kathryn knew what she had to do. It was the sign she had waited for. She had to grab this one chance and run for her life. Without further deliberation, she edged along the counter to the doorway of the living room.

Unfamiliar with the layout of the house, she didn't know how to get to the garage or if there even was one. Remembering the time of year, she knew she couldn't survive in the snowy cold forest clad only in a T-shirt. She had to take a car—his car. It was her only chance, because, without it, she would either remain his prisoner or freeze to death.

Kathryn decided that a plan wasn't necessary. If she were going to escape, it had to be now, while he was preoccupied with his present delusion.

Lunging through the door into the living room, she dashed around the couch. Running past the fireplace, Kathryn grabbed a poker from the stand before entering the front hall across the room. The sounds of his thrashing and cursing in the kitchen still rang in her ears.

Dylan had not noticed she was gone yet. He was still occupied with increasing his fight against the unseen *adversary*.

Running into the hall, she could see the staircase they had come down earlier. The sound of silverware crashing onto tiles echoed through the house. Dashing through another doorway opposite the stairs, she entered the foyer at the front door.

A coat and scarf draped from a coat rack. Kathryn grabbed them and dressed as quickly as she could. Unlocking the front door, she yanked it open and raced barefoot into the snow, breathing in the first breath of fresh air she'd had in nine months.

She ran along the front walk far enough so she could survey the layout of the house. The garage was on her left. It was a free standing building joined to the house by a breezeway. Without further thought, she bolted toward it, praying it was unlocked as she ran.

Reaching the garage door, she stopped dead in her tracks. There was no handle. There was no lock. It was operated by an electronic garage door opener or by the numeric keypad attached to the front panel. She threw the poker at the door in frustrated anger. Punching numbers as quickly as she could, Kathryn hoped to hit upon the code that would free the vehicle. After many frantic attempts, she finally spied a small key lock below the numeric pad.

"Damn," she cried. "I forgot about keys."

The chill of the snowy night suddenly hit her. She had few options left. If Dylan did not come out to find her, she would either have to return to the house or die outside. The struggle of decision offered her neither warmth nor solution.

Shivering, she danced in the snow to get the circulation moving in her feet. Kathryn slammed her fists into the pockets of his coat to keep them from frostbite. The knuckles of her right hand scraped against a metal ring of keys that scuffed the skin off two knuckles. Gasping, relief washing over her, Kathryn whipped them from the pocket and held them in cold, trembling fingers.

Oh, God, let the key be on this ring, she prayed, succumbing to the bitter cold.

Seconds ticked by as she fumbled through the ring of keys to find a match that would open the only chance to freedom she might have. Frantically looking back at the house to see if there was any sign of Dylan, she continued trying to shove each key into the lock.

One...two...three...The fourth key unlocked the garage door. The electronic mechanism began to automatically pull the heavy door upward. She could hear the motor grind away, but the door stayed closed. It was caught on the frozen barricade of snow at its base.

Kathryn scooped up the poker and began to smash the ice holding the door, hoping to free it before the mechanism broke. With the last effort of her fading strength, she dug her hands into the barricade and helped heave the door up, freeing it from the frozen obstruction at its base.

A green minivan was parked in the garage. She couldn't remember ever being so relieved or happy to see anything in her life. In the dim light from the house windows, she searched through the keys until she found the one with the Dodge symbol and shoved it into the minivan's keyhole. The lock snapped. She yanked the door open, climbed into the driver's seat, threw the poker in the passenger seat, and slammed the door shut behind her. As she struggled to push the key into the ignition, missing twice before getting it in straight, she could hear him bellow her name.

Dylan sounded as if he were close.

The motor didn't turn over. *Damn!*

She gave the gas petal three quick jabs with her foot and turned the key in the ignition again. The Dodge Caravan roared into action as she floored the gas. Slamming the gearshift into reverse, Kathryn floored the gas again to push the tires through the barricade of ice and snow. She could see Dylan running along the front yard, following her trail of footsteps. She pushed the petal to the floor, begging the van to fly to safety, but only achieved to spin it around in the freshly fallen snow covering the sheet of ice that used to be a driveway. Panic speared her ability to think clearly, and before she could straighten the wheels, they were buried past the axles in snow.

She tried to rock the van from its prison, but it didn't budge.

Dylan charged the Caravan, cursing and screaming, shouting for her to get out.

Kathryn locked the doors, revving the engine with increased efforts to free herself.

He ranted in front of the van, pacing back and forth between pregnant threats as the wheels spun, digging themselves deeper into the snow. Something black stuck out of his fist as he banged on the driver's window, screaming for her to unlock the door.

Refusing, Kathryn impotently threatened him with the poker if he didn't go away.

Dylan only laughed and lifted the revolver he clutched in one hand and pointed it at her, screaming again for her to get out.

"Go ahead. Shoot me. I'm not going back with you. I'd rather be dead," she hollered back at him.

"I mean it, Katie. Get out or I'll shoot!"

"Go ahead. I want you to," she shouted. Kathryn's eyes pleaded with him to put her out of her misery.

Dylan lowered his revolver and stared deep into her eyes.

"Go ahead. Shoot! Shoot!" she cried, slamming her fists down onto the steering wheel.

The horn blasted, making him jump.

"Shoot! Shoot!" she shouted hysterically.

So he did...three times.

Part Two

The Winter

Chapter Ten

Kathryn stretched and groaned with the effort. She was stiff and sore. The bed was soft and comfortable. A thick, feather-light comforter wrapped round her as she wriggled deeper under its warmth, vaguely aware of daylight. She didn't care. She wanted to sleep late this morning. It had been a very busy night, one filled with countless nightmares. Kathryn rolled over on her side. The sudden pain in her shoulder and arm yanked her awake.

"What's that?" she mumbled, not wanting to wake anyone else up. Her left hand instinctively cradled the injured right arm to protect it from any further trauma or movement.

Kathryn opened her eyes and eased herself up in the bed, trying not to disturb the blankets or her now throbbing shoulder. She didn't know if David was up yet, but thought she would let him sleep if he wasn't. Through the shadowy haze of light in the bedroom, she looked down at her arm and shoulder and saw that they were heavily padded in bloodied gauze and tape.

The fog in her mind lifted with the evidence of the incident. The memory of last night crashed down on her, crushing her again into painful reality.

"He shot me. The bastard shot me," she said, a sense of shocked disbelief in her voice. "Oh, God, why didn't he just do it right and kill me?"

Leaning back on the pillows, she was careful not to jar her right arm and shoulder any further. The pain from the wounds mounted with an intenseness that tethered her unwilling mind to the growing beat of its aching rhythm. She tried to relax, hoping the pangs would dull or at least lessen enough to allow her to bear it.

Looking around, she realized she was not in her cell but in a New England Shaker bed. Heavy drapes were pulled across the window, allowing only a slit of sunlight to filter into the room. There was not enough light to see proper color, but she could tell the walls were dark and the furnishings were a contrasting lightness. On her left, between the bed and an entire wall of shelving, was a small table and large recliner chair.

He likes comfort, she realized again, glad that he was finally sharing it with her. *Probably feels guilty.*

The room was comfortable. The bed was luxurious. Despite her situation, Kathryn was pleased she was not on the floor in her cold, barren cell.

Dylan was nowhere to be seen. She thought it odd that he would leave her unguarded with the door on the opposite side of the room ajar. Concentrating on the damage caused by the gunshots, she concluded that it was more painful than debilitating.

Probing the wounds with careful fingers, she tried to tell if the bullets were still lodged in her muscles or whether Dylan had taken them out. However, the vision of Dylan fishing around, practicing backstreet medicine on her body, made her pray that they were still inside. She suspected it would be healthier.

Kathryn pushed the comforter away and began to climb off the bed, only to be stopped by a padded chain around her ankle. *I should have known,* she thought in disgust, settling back under the covers, and wondering where Dylan was hiding. *He's most certainly watching me from somewhere.*

Lying back, Kathryn concentrated on relaxing. She was rewarded for her effort to ease the pain by dozing off into a light sleep between thoughts.

"Katie," a soft voice whispered, pulling her from her sleep. "Katie."

"Uhmm?" she mumbled, still trapped in a foggy mind.

"I brought you some breakfast," he said almost sweetly.

"Da . . ." she began to say, catching herself just in time. The last time she said David's name, Dylan exploded into a fit in the kitchen and she was shot three times in the arm. ". . . ylan. Thank you." Kathryn pushed herself up in bed with her good arm, cradling the hand of her wounded arm in her lap.

"Be careful or you'll start the bleeding again. I had a helluva time getting it stopped," he cautioned.

"My arm...how bad is it?" she asked, unable to discern the extent of damage done from just the internal feel of it. She knew there had to be torn ligaments and severe tissue damage, but wasn't sure just what else had been blown out of the way.

"Well, I think it's all right. The bullet went right through your shoulder, near your armpit. There's a hole in your back, so I assume that's the exit wound. But it's your arm I'm worried about. You took two shots there. One was only a flesh wound. About half an inch of flesh was ripped off the side of your arm as the bullet passed through. The other one, lower down, still has the bullet in it. At least, I don't see any exit wound so I figure it must be in the bone or something.

There might even be some glass from the shattered windshield in the other cuts and scratches," he added, averting his eyes to hide the nakedness of his guilt.

His voice told her he was genuinely concerned about her condition, and that confused her. She couldn't understand how he could be concerned and still do the things he did. She wondered if he bought his own lie.

"Did you clean them?" she asked, not remembering much of anything after the second bullet entered her body.

"Sort of. I wasn't sure what to do, so I poured alcohol on them. I didn't know what else to do, so I thought I'd wait until you were awake. If you tell me what to do, I'll look after it," he offered. His tone sounded truly penitent. There was a new humbleness in his voice.

The thought of his probing into her arm with a pair of tweezers or a knife did not excite her, but she doubted she could do it herself. He was her only option since she knew he was not about to take her to a hospital. "What kind of first aid supplies do you have?" she asked.

"Nothing to speak of. Some small Band-Aids and half a bottle of peroxide. I used all the gauze and alcohol already," he said, setting down the bed table over her lap. He fluffed the pillows behind her back so she could sit up straighter to eat, then eased himself into the recliner beside the bed.

Kathryn winced as she repositioned herself in the bed, gasping aloud when a fresh stab of pain shot through her. She was hungry, sore, and still exhausted. She didn't know if she had the energy to survive any more of this life he had chosen for her. "If I make a list of things, can you get to a pharmacy?" she asked, unsure if the minivan was still stuck or could make it through the heavily packed snow...or whether he would even be willing to go.

"Sure. I can go on the snowmobile." He grinned, cocking his head to one side like a small boy caught in a little white lie.

She grimaced at the conspicuous irony and flagrant authority he held over her simply by his knowledge of the inventory and physical storage place of everything. If she had thought of snowmobiles, she might have been safe in town instead of wounded in bed. But it wasn't an obvious choice considering she lived on an island where the little bit of snow that fell once or twice a year lasted a day or two at the most. Besides, she had never driven one.

Dylan opened the night table drawer, pulled out a pen and paper, then sat, one leg flopped over the other, mimicking a secretary awaiting dictation.

Kathryn munched on the now cooled toast and peanut butter as she dictated the list of medical supplies they would need to fix her wounds, knowing he would have to go to a hospital for most of them.

She hoped it would be enough to alert either the pharmacist or hospital security. She knew the hospital staff would not simply hand the surgical equipment over the counter. He would have to find where they were stored and steal them without being detected. She hoped he was unraveled enough by the urgent need of the supplies and lack of planning to slip up and get caught.

Dylan finished writing the list, double-checking the spelling and pronunciation of the unfamiliar medical items. "Don't want to make a mistake and bring back the wrong stuff," he said as he crossed out a wrongly spelled word and replaced it with her corrected version.

He offered to take her to the bathroom and refill her coffee. After helping her to his bathroom and back, Dylan poured her another cup of coffee from the carafe. While she sipped the hot liquid, he chained her ankle to the bed, then closed the bedroom door gently behind him.

The small click of the lock sealed her into the darkened bedroom. She settled back to get some rest until Dylan came back from town, knowing she would need all her strength for the ordeal ahead.

There was little else she could do except dream that Dylan was in police custody. Dylan would be brought back to the house in an armored paddy wagon and forced to show them where she was hidden. Kathryn fell asleep with visions of him dressed in a bright orange jump suit. Five guards stood over him, beating him with billy clubs, while both his hands and feet were manacled.

The light sifting into the bedroom had turned dark by the time Dylan walked into the room. In his rush to check on her, he hadn't taken time to change. He was still wearing a dark navy ski suit. Snow still clung to his boots and hood. Four satchels of supplies dangled from his gloved hands. She had no idea how long he had been gone, but decided, considering winter hours, that the entire trip must have taken at least ten hours. Kathryn assumed town was no more than four hours away by snowmobile.

Although he was not in chains, Kathryn was relieved to see him. Her bladder was more than ready to burst and she would have been lying in a wet bed had he taken any longer.

Dylan unmanacled her ankle and helped her from the bed, offering himself for physical support as they walked across the room and down the hall to the marble bathroom. Kathryn made her way to the toilet while Dylan put the newly purchased medical supplies on the counter top. She was surprised to see a doctor's medical bag and several surgical trays among the collection. Eyeing him in disbelief, she vowed to never again underestimate his ability.

Joining him by the sinks, Kathryn stripped off the bandages and personally examined the wounds with the aid of a mirror. Her skin was inflamed and tender.

Following her instructions, he removed the lid from the peroxide and poured the chilled liquid into the bloodied holes. Together they watched the peroxide bubble and froth before Dylan prepared to stitch the more obvious wounds. The bullet was indeed still in her upper arm. He would have to pull it out before attempting to dress it.

"Do you have any drugs left?" she asked, hoping he did. She didn't want him poking around and then sewing things together without something to take the edge off. There was no need to put herself through that torture if there was an option.

"Yeah," he hesitated. Knowing he would need her not only conscious but aware to instruct him during the operation.

"Well, before you go probing for bullets and glass, I'd like something to help me through it. Go get it and I'll administer it," she ordered. Kathryn planned to give herself a sufficient enough dose to ease the agony of the operation while keeping it low enough to allow herself the ability to think.

Dylan gaped at her, surprised at her usurped authority. He hesitated for only a few seconds before heading out the door and down the hall. In his determination, he forgot to lock the door behind him.

Kathryn was acutely aware of the unlocked door leading to freedom. She knew if she could just get out and find the snowmobile he had used, she could follow his tracks to town. However, she also knew that she would not get very far trapped with the inability to control the skidoo's steering and without proper clothing. The memory of pain when her body was jolted was enough to dissuade her from any attempt to escape.

Cursing the cruel temptation he put before her, she settled back to examine the other cuts caused by the force of flying glass. They were scattered over her torso, upper arms and legs. From the sheer number and pattern of them, she thought Dylan must have pulled her out through the front window of the minivan after he shot her. She knew he didn't think straight when he was in one of his *states.*

Kathryn picked up the tweezers and started to probe the cuts for obvious chunks of glass and removed three small pieces herself before Dylan returned with a syringe full of morphine. She gave herself a hefty dose to tame the already annoyed and screaming agony of her injuries.

Chapter Eleven

The drapes were drawn back to reveal a beautiful, bright winter morning. Birds twittered and called others to come and join them. They pecked at a suspended suet ball and the abundant seeds filling a birdfeeder he had placed just outside the window especially for her.

Frozen ice and snow glistened like jewels on the maze of branches in the forest just beyond the clearing. The beauty and stillness of the winter filled her with wonder, and she longed to be outside enjoying it first hand.

A titillating toastiness gently spread through her body as she snuggled deeper under the feather tick. Its light comfort wooed her and promised that today would be a special day. She smiled from the warmth inside. It was a feeling she had only experienced a few times in her life, and, although she was curious why it would come to her here, in his house, she was nevertheless grateful for the pleasant sensation.

It was a feeling she always associated with childhood. The day was warm and pleasant. Her parents were at work. It was a Monday morning. The sheets were crisp and clean, heated by her small body curled under the covers. A special feeling of warmth, security, safety and happiness had flooded her that morning, as it did today.

It's a good way to wake up, she thought, hardly noticing the bars across the window anymore. The rare, exquisite awareness passed too soon, leaving her alone in Dylan's world.

It bothered her that for the first few minutes after waking, she still did not know where she was. She wondered how long this displaced feeling would continue to assault her, deciding that if at home, she'd probably wake up thinking she was still in the cell.

"Well, sleepyhead, how are you feeling this morning?" asked the voice she had grown to hate. Turning her head, she jumped at his closeness, his face pushed so close to hers that she could smell the mint mouthwash and flowery aftershave.

She fought against the nausea his presence gave her. Suddenly agitated and uncomfortable, she turned back to face the window. He was the last thing she wanted to see...or smell...on such a glorious morning. Kathryn wished she could go skiing or take a walk outside, even build a snowman. It had been years since she had built a snowman or made an angel in the white mantle of winter.

Her arm was healing satisfactorily, although the deeper injuries would take at least another couple of months. Dylan had to pack two of the wounds every day to let them heal from the inside out. Cleaning them with savlon, they then rinsed them with peroxide before stuffing the packing material into the fleshy holes. To her relief, the bullet thought to be lodged in the humerus bone was only trapped beside it. Kathryn could have lost her arm, and even her life, if the bullet had lodged in the bone. Bone infection was one of the most deadly to deal with, and without the lifesaving efforts of a hospital, her chances of survival were low.

Dylan had a tough time finding the little slug of metal. The hole was larger than it should have been. The bullet had deflected off the steering wheel, and the force of the impact caused it to flatten out before it hit her arm. She kept a close eye on its progress, bathing her arm in savlon and the topical antibiotic creams Dylan had picked up.

It had taken Dylan three hours to do an operation she could have done in less than a quarter of the time. The morphine wore off before he was finished, but she refused another dose until after the operation was completed.

His stitches were sloppy and he had difficulty tying them. Kathryn finally insisted he sew a wire in one continuous loop instead of trying to tie off each thread. It would make an ugly scar, but right now that was the least of her worries.

Dylan was forced to cut away the flesh around the bone to find the slug imbedded beside the humerus. She had been grateful that the bullet missed the two places where the artery intersected the bone. Without a measure of skill, it was difficult to stop an artery from bleeding and she could have easily lost her arm.

He made each cut with slow, meticulous care, as if he were examining every microscopic movement he made. She didn't know whether to scream at him to hurry up, getting the intense pain over, or have him keep going at that agonizing speed to insure there would be fewer mistakes. As it was, he had to do unnecessary cuts to make up for his lack of training and knowledge.

That was fifteen days ago. Since then, she had spent her time staring out the window to watch what little nature she could see, and counting the days of her recovery. She cherished the red and orange tinges edging the clouds at sunrise; they reminded her of the splendid views of the ocean she enjoyed so long ago, when she was free. She was grateful for anything she could see through the bedroom window. It offered her a welcome contrast to the last nine months of watching her own deteriorating reflection stare back at her from the mirrored wall.

Kathryn had asked Dylan if she could read one of the hundreds of books stuffed into the shelves of the bookcase along the wall, but he refused her that escape. She was allowed to read only the titles, and if she couldn't make them out, she guessed at what the letters said. It became a game used to pass the time.

Kathryn longed for any words or sights of the world she once knew, the world she knew still existed beyond her bars and forest. Rationalizing that the news of her disappearance must have long since ceased making headlines, she couldn't understand Dylan's adamant refusal to allow her to listen to a radio or cassette. He seemed to need her totally isolated from the world outside this locked room; her only existence was the one he offered.

"I hope you slept well," he continued, oblivious to her growing despondency.

"Yes I did, thank you. Dylan, why can't I read a book or listen to the radio?" she asked, her voice quivering with fear, knowing she was possibly treading on dangerous ground by bringing the subject up again.

He didn't answer. That worried her more than his shouting.

"I have to do something, Dylan. If you keep me here like this much longer, you'll end up owning only the empty shell of a body. I'll be an insane prisoner instead of the person you say you need so much. I can't just stay in confinement tied to a bed or locked in a room all the time. You have to let me do something before I go absolutely mad. Even prisoners in jail get to do something to keep their minds and bodies active," she continued, unwilling to let the matter drop this time. It didn't matter the cost he might exact. She could feel her tenuous hold on sanity slipping from her grasp.

Dylan flopped onto the end of the bed, pensively giving her words great deliberation. He stroked his chin, played with his ear lobe, ran his fingers through his now unruly hair, and stared at the ceiling lost in deep thought. "All right," he said finally, with a real smile. "What is it you want to do?"

She wasn't sure how to react. He so rarely smiled at anything, but perhaps that was because in the last nine and a half months there hadn't been anything worth smiling at. He was making her an offer and she didn't want to ruin the opportunity—there might not be another one.

"What are my choices?" she asked, deciding to be very careful and test the waters first.

"Anything. Anything at all. Just let me know and I'll decide whether or not it's acceptable," he answered.

"A walk. Outside. Can we go for a walk? First, I'll cook breakfast, if you like, and then we could get ready and go for a walk through the woods. I won't try to run away. You have my word on that. I promise to be good," she whispered, bracing herself for yet another refusal.

"All right," he said, not giving it a second thought.

Kathryn could hardly believe her ears. She expected it to be another of the many cruel tricks he so enjoyed. In the past nine months he had pulled too many mean gags on her, touting his cleverness over the following weeks.

Dylan unshackled her ankle and helped her out of bed, retrieving the sling for her arm from the back of his chair. She slipped her arm into the material, and although it was much better, her shoulder was still intolerably painful when left loose. She hoped it would not hinder her in the kitchen. If she didn't keep her side of the bargain, he might not feel obligated to keep his.

She headed to the bathroom, leaning on Dylan's arm only because he insisted on supporting her. He left the door open and headed down the hallway and steps, leaving her alone on the upper floor of the house unguarded.

She didn't waste any time, making absolutely certain to do nothing questionable in case he was watching. She headed down the staircase. The front door loomed in the foyer before her. His snowsuit hung on the coat rack, inviting her to take it and run. It was a test. Fighting the insatiable urge to flee, she pushed herself into the kitchen, knowing he wouldn't let her get as far as the front door again. Kathryn was somewhat concerned about the strangely generous mood he had exhibited. She did not trust this side of him any more than his dark ugly one.

Dylan was sitting at the table, taking in the scenery. A coyote padded through the snow, crossing the clearing diagonally. She joined him, standing the obligatory two paces behind his chair. Dylan didn't seem to be aware that she was there until Kathryn cleared her voice to give him warning of her presence. He turned and looked at her, smiling again.

"Well, what shall I make for breakfast?" she asked, still testing his mood.

"Anything you feel like making," he answered through a grin that made her believe that he was actually happy.

"What about pancakes? I haven't had pancakes for a long time. I love them," she said, trying to keep the mood light. Before realizing it, she had offered to make him the last meal she'd ever had at home, and prayed he would not make the connection with the phone call he'd made about Meaghan. It was almost ten months ago, but it could be just the sort of thing to set him off.

"Sounds like a fine plan. I'd like an egg or two, scrambled, to go with it. And maybe some potatoes on the side. What do you think?" he asked, interlacing his fingers on the table.

"No problem. I'll put the coffee on while you're waiting," she smiled. A sudden lightness captured her thoughts, making her feel almost giddy. His pretense of humanity was grating her nerves, but she seized on the hope of going out, concentrating on whatever it would take to make that happen. This was a new side to him that she hadn't seen before, and she wasn't sure just how to handle it.

Kathryn turned and headed to the counter, looking through the cupboards and drawers to find the necessary ingredients to brew coffee. As she worked, she began to hum absently as the smell of coffee filled the room. It was good to be cooking again. It offered her a sense of normalcy she'd missed for so very long. Perhaps the pancakes were a sign that her life was going to be better in the days to come.

Dylan stared out the window, seemingly unaware of Kathryn as she prepared breakfast, set the table and poured his coffee. His inattentiveness helped to shake off her nervous anxiety and let her almost relax. It took several trips to carry the food to the table before she too could sit down, but he waited for her like a gentleman. She was even allowed a place at the table as though she belonged there and had assumed her rightful position.

Kathryn was terrified of saying a wrong word. Her entire life was like walking on eggshells. They ate with strained conversation. She found herself performing the perfect lady role in an effort to be without flaw. Her exaggerated motions and tiny forkfuls of food extended the uncomfortable length of breakfast until she could not bear it another second. Begging leave, she rose from her chair and began to clear the table while Dylan still sipped at another cup of coffee.

While she finished putting the dishes away, Dylan brought out two snowsuits.

Snow crunched under her boot. It was a delicious sound. The earth was blanketed with a deep, clean white covering, creating a stillness in the air. It was different from the forced silence of the room. This quiet was alive. She could sense the very life of every living tree and animal. The whole world waited for the dawning of spring so they could once again lift their heads toward the long days of warmth. She breathed softly so as not to disturb the serenity of the woods around her, but deeply, trying to reabsorb all the life she had lost.

Dylan had given her a soft fleece-lined suit and lightweight boots to wear. She felt warm despite being able to see her breath crystallize with each exhalation. The hood kept her ears comfortable. The mitts protected her fingers against the cold. She felt wonderful despite the fact that the moisture in her nostrils chilled and they almost froze together with each inhalation. She might have succeeded in her attempt to escape had she known about this outfit and the snowmobile the night she tried to breakout.

Dylan walked behind her and let her wander freely. Neither spoke a word; she was afraid to break the enchanting spell of the forest. He let her examine the bark on trees, smell handfuls of cedar needles, follow the different bunny and coyote trails to their fruitless end... It had been so long since she had been outside with the glory of nature that she could not get enough of the wonders she had once taken for granted.

A peace she had forgotten existed permeated her. It was as if she were sitting on a beach listening to the song of waves courting the sands, gently caressing the land with rhythmic affection. She didn't miss the ocean as much as she thought she might have. This was a different ocean...a sea of trees as far as she could see. If she stopped and held her breath long enough, she thought she could hear the ebb and tide of the forest's life force swaying ever so slowly in the windy horizon beyond.

The sky grew a dusty gray in color and the warmth of the earlier hours dissipated, giving way to a chill that promised a crisp night ahead. Dylan tugged on her sleeve and she understood that it was time to return. He pointed in the direction they should head and Dylan lead the way back to the house. It took another two hours of trekking through the snow and over hills to reach the house. They had to stop and rest a good deal of the time since her weakened condition hindered their progress. By the time Dylan opened the front door, Kathryn was exhausted and famished.

While she took off the snowsuit, Dylan headed to the living room and started the fire, tending it until the logs crackled into a bright, warm blaze. She hung up her suit and walked into the living room, stopping just behind him, not knowing what she should do next. Dylan poked the fire another couple of times before turning to face her.

"I put some clothes out that I thought you might like to' wear. I picked them up when I went grocery shopping in town the other day," he said, pointing his chin toward the sofa on the opposite side of the room.

Kathryn could see a pair of blue jeans and a plaid flannel shirt lying on the cushion. Overjoyed, she ran to the sofa and hurriedly dressed, afraid he might change his mind. The material hugging her body transported her into a world of complete ecstasy. It had been almost a year since she had been fully dressed, or, in fact, worn more than a simple T-shirt. Life had taken a sudden, pleasant change, and she wasn't sure what to make of it...but she didn't want to ask in case the bubble might burst.

"You look wonderful," Dylan offered as he admired her from head to foot.

Kathryn blushed. It had been a long time since she looked good to anyone, a long time since she felt good. It had been just as long since she felt a real physical tiredness from being active and adventurous. Kathryn felt grateful enough to give him a hug—and that frightened her. Feeling uncomfortable and a little awkward by his appreciative gaze, she asked if he were hungry. She thought a nice steak, salad, and baked potato would be perfect, hoping that he would be just as hungry.

Dylan thought it was a wonderful idea and offered to get a bottle of wine as she started cooking, saying he'd like to finish the day off with a special treat. He left Kathryn alone in the kitchen to prepare the meal, acting more like a date wanting to keep out of her way.

Kathryn appreciated the time alone in the kitchen. She concentrated on cooking, not letting her mind entertain thoughts of escape. She decided that this was perhaps a better way. He would eventually drop his guard if his comfort zone were to continually increase with more days like this one ending with dinner and wine. If she could get him to relax his vigilance enough, she might be able to successfully escape. It was a chance she did not want to ruin with spur of the moment action. She could not afford to make the same mistakes again.

She hummed while the dinner cooked, enjoying the freedom he allotted her. Careful not to take advantage of it, she decided not to take any possible weapons from the kitchen. That could wait for a time when he was more trusting of her, and when her plans were more concrete with a good chance of success.

Dinner went extraordinarily well. Dylan had set up a special table in front of the fireplace. The meal was delicious. Wine flowed freely. Conversation was easy and comfortable. They talked about safe subjects, Dylan listening to her endless stories about her childhood and the years at the university. She could see the unbelief written on his face as she explained simple things that every child experiences while growing up. He had no comprehension of the world she was from, and she was totally baffled about his.

Dylan's attempt at small talk was awkward and shocking. He spoke of horrors that she had no idea really existed, and yet they were as much a part of his life as going skating with friends was part of hers.

Kathryn drank more wine while he talked because it made her more relaxed and gave her a distant removed feeling, somehow making it become less personal—like watching a movie. She needed to wash away the influence of his nightmares and lies from her mind.

The sensation of eyes boring into her soul woke her up. Labored breathing vibrated the bed. She tried to move, careful not to jostle her arm, but her hips were wedged beneath a heavy weight. The nauseating smell of sweat suffocated her. Fear erupted in her confused mind.

Things had been going well in the last two weeks. Dylan was pleasant and sociable, lavishing her with unexpected treats and presents. At night she was still manacled to the bed, but in the daytime he allowed her to walk around the bedroom, take daily baths, cook, look out the windows, clean and, best of all, wear clothes. He had allowed her to be almost human, and she was grateful for his generosity and apparent change of character.

Everything had changed.

Curiosity forced Kathryn to open her eyes despite the fear screaming at her to lie perfectly still and pretend to be asleep. The light from the hallway dressed the room in a shadowy haze. The faded glint reflecting off a blade startled her. Dylan was sitting on her pelvis, brandishing a knife less than two inches from her face. Gasping in shock, she was paralyzed as terror bludgeoned her into reluctant silence.

The blackness of his eyes convinced her that tonight was the night she would finally meet with death. The reality of his madness crushed the breath out of her.

The struggle slashed across his features. Dylan's dark, hollow eyes darted from side to side as if he watched a panoramic movie that wasn't there. His tongue licked at dry lips as his rasping breath fouled the air around him.

The knife clutched in his quivering fingers was suspended in the air as two forces fought for control of its direction. Kathryn watched the war that raged within him with keen interest, praying the outcome would be favorable for her.

His crazed eyes wore the same glare of desolation that had veiled them the night he shot her. She knew if she made one wrong move, the scales would be tipped against her, and she was sure that she couldn't survive such a point-blank attack. She knew once he started venting the pressure that the demons within put upon him, he could not stop until he had exhausted himself. She had been fortunate the other night because his energies were spent trashing the kitchen and then dragging her from the minivan and back to the house. If he stabbed her now, she doubted he would stop before she became unrecognizable.

Eternities passed during each nervous blink of her eyes. Dylan remained poised between two worlds, the knife ready to destroy the enemy in whichever side he momentarily vacillated towards. When the one that hated her had the upper hand, the knife moved close to her heart; when the sphere that hated him won, the knife moved close to his own heart. She studied the shadowed strain in his eyes for any clue about which way the battle lines would be drawn in the coming seconds, hoping to get out of the way enough so his stabbing would not be fatal.

His head glistened with sweat and she could see that his pajamas were stained a dark, wet gray. She wondered how long he had been battling this war above her and why she hadn't woken until now.

"I...won't...do...it..." he whispered through gritted teeth, the consequence of his words thumping in the veins of his neck.

Kathryn's body remained rigid as tried not to move or visibly breathe. She gulped as the knife edged again toward her heart and she watched as it hung, suspended, and ready to plunge her life into the pits of his hell. She remembered the first time she heard his voice on the phone as it cascaded over her again. Her heart pounded. The palms of her hands became greasy with perspiration.

"Stop...breathing..." he fumed, trying to pull the knife from her heart with all his strength. The blade quivered in midair, trembling under the weight of its mission.

Kathryn held her breath, wanting to reach up and grab the blade from his grasp. But she knew that would be a mistake. Any movement would only encourage the direction it was already moving. She felt his muscles tense as if he were fighting against an unseen force pressing him down onto the bed. His visible muscles shuddered and flexed as he wrestled with the night. They told her that he was no nearer to the end of the battle than when he first climbed onto her bed.

"Go...away!" he muttered through pursed lips. The sweat dripping down his face annoyed him and he tried to clear the wetness from his eyes by wiping his face on his shirt. The unsuccessful attempt only fueled his anger, and he swore in a low, seething tone.

Kathryn didn't know how long she could stay in that vulnerable, mute position. Her muscles began to cramp. His bones ground into her as he struggled. Her arm ached with each movement he made. She hurt everywhere under the unbearable burden pinning her down.

"Leave...me...alone!" he screamed, barely able to spit the words out. He squirmed, trying to avoid the touch of something she could not see. Dylan screamed, ranting in words and gestures that were beyond her understanding. "Shut up!" he ordered, his voice reaching terrifying levels of hysteria.

He peeled his eyes from the knife and searched the floor for intruders. He leaned back on his knees, pulling his weight off her, screaming and slashing the knife into the air and bed. He stabbed at private visions clinging to the side of the bed; he sliced away personal nightmares that hung from the ceiling and walls.

Kathryn cried softly as each passing second further dissipated whatever thin connection he might have had to reality.

"I...WON'T...DO...IT!" he hollered. Dylan shot the knife into the air and perched its swaying blade above her breast. The polished silver glistened in the dim light, ready to plunge into her heart.

Tears ran down the corner of her eyes, wetting her pillow. She held her breath and closed her eyes against the inevitable. Kathryn wished she could have said good-bye to David and Wendy and held Meaghan one more time...seen them one more time...

"NO!" he yelled with an agonized grunt into the shadowy light. In a single, awkward move, he dove off the bed and stumbled out into the hallway, slamming the door behind him.

She opened her eyes with the reverberating sound of the slammed door echoing in her ears. He abandoned her in the bedroom, locked in the bitter darkness with her own visions and fears. She placed her arm carefully on the bed beside her and curled up into a fetal position, letting her tears flow freely. Kathryn waited in the quiet of the night, watching minutes grow into hours, waiting for him to return. Not knowing which Dylan would burst through the door, she prayed the evil one had somehow done the world a favor and was no more.

Chapter Twelve

"Time to get up," he said through a yawn as he pulled at her covers, prodding her awake.

Kathryn rolled over, keeping her arm close to her body. She had dozed off during her hours of vigil and so now had no idea how much time had passed. The curtains were still pulled closed from the night before, keeping the natural light outside. Afraid to see him, she willed her eyes to look his way. To read the mood he was in, she needed to look into his eyes.

Dylan unbound her and stomped out of the room before she had a chance to become fully awake.

She could smell the tantalizing odor of coffee drifting from the kitchen. Kathryn rubbed the sleep from her eyes, but the weariness was unwilling to leave after so few hours of sleep. Forcing herself to stay awake most of the night, she insisted on remaining vigilant in case he returned.

Kathryn pushed herself from the bed and stumbled to the bathroom where Dylan had laid out clean clothes for her to wear.

Sensing Dylan's mood was foul by the way he woke her up, Kathryn tiptoed into the kitchen. She found him already slumped in a chair at the table, rolling a cigarette between his fingers. He was lost in a world of contemplation and didn't seem to hear her come into the room. Kathryn poured herself a cup of coffee and joined him at the table, cautiously sitting across from him.

Sipping her coffee, she watched the dark cloud of despair settle over him. His stare was cold and hard. His lips were dry and cracked. She couldn't remember ever having seen him so drained of life and color. The cigarette spinning between his fingers burned slowly as the ashes dropped onto a little pile on the table.

The tension was heavy and uncomfortable. Not knowing what to do, she was reluctant to intrude on his world and risk brutal retaliation. *On the other hand, if he didn't want me to make breakfast, then why did he get me up?* Kathryn decided to say nothing and wait until he came round himself. It was the safest course of action.

"It's my toes. They're growing together. I can't stop them from growing together. They do that. It's part of the punishment. I didn't hurt you. I couldn't. So...*they* hurt me. *They* know this drives me crazy and that's why it gives *them* so much pleasure," he whispered, finally breaking the silence.

The cigarette had long ago given way to the full pack. Each one lit off the end of the other. Each predecessor allowed to smolder and burn unattended. He apparently preferred the first fresh part of each cigarette.

The backdrop of a late morning sky gave way to one of early dusk. Kathryn had sipped eight mugs of black coffee, helping him drain two pots in an attempt to quiet her grumbling stomach. She made no other move to disturb his thoughts, but kept a safe distance.

"I can't stand it when *they* do that. I have to stop the skin from webbing. The skin itches and crawls, tickling deep down in the fleshy part. Several times *they* have tried to web my toes, like my father's foot, but I've stopped *them*. Each time, I've managed to stop *them*. But it gets more difficult because *they* try harder. *They* always try harder," he whispered, reaching for a handful of napkins from the holder in the middle of the table.

Kathryn watched, feeling helpless, unable to understand his actions. She wanted to laugh at his desperate mania, but knew better.

Dylan shredded the napkins into eight rolls of compacted paper and shoved them between his toes, pushing the paper as far between his toes as he could. Unable to keep his feet still, he stomped them up and down on the floor, between periods of lifting them and repositioning the paper. He squirmed on the chair as discomfort from the webbing torture plagued him with increased fury. Unable to withstand the torment, he screamed and ran from the kitchen, making a mad dash through each of the many rooms before escaping outdoors to ram his bare feet into the freezing snow.

Kathryn searched the house as she followed him from room to room, examining every corner of the lower floor of the house. When he dashed outside, she headed back into the kitchen to retrieve a knife from the drawer. He had forgotten he left the drawer unlocked in anticipation of breakfast. She hurried up the stairs to hide the blade in a pillowcase where she could easily reach it if necessary. Then, returning to the kitchen to make something to eat, she hoped Dylan would be settled down and ready to eat when he returned.

Tired of waiting for him, and not knowing what else to do, Kathryn headed up the stairs and laid down on the bed. Still too weak to make a run for it, she decided it would be safer to wait until conditions were more favorable—she would have to be healed and it would be better to wait for spring.

She left the hall light on. Placing the pillow concealing the knife stacked beneath a second one, Kathryn slipped into a troubled sleep with her hand close to the blade's handle in case he should come into the room even more menacing than last night.

The sound of his muffled footfalls pounding up the stairs pulled her awake. She sat up in the bed and grabbed the knife with her good hand, keeping it safe in its hiding place.

Dylan burst into the room. A wild look danced in his blackened eyes. His wet hair was glued to his head. Snow coated his pajamas. His hands trembled from the chill of winter. His teeth chattered as he wrapped his arms around himself in an attempt to keep what little warmth he had left.

A shock of fear shot through Kathryn at the sight of him. She cowered closer to the headboard as he approached her. Her hand gripped the knife tighter, ready to pull it out and thrust it into his heart.

Dylan stopped halfway to the bed. "You...have...to go back...into the...room...now. It...isn't...safe...for you...out here...with me," he panted with a strained voice.

She was unsure what to do.

"Hurry! You must hurry. *They're*...coming. It...won't...be safe...for you...out here. *They'll* get you...like *they* got me," he mumbled, struggling with the words.

Kathryn didn't want to go back into the isolated cell. She wanted to retain this degree of dignity. She didn't want to be locked away. *What if he dies? What if he doesn't come back?* She hesitated, staying where she was under the covers.

"You...must...go...now! Before *they*...get here. Hurry! Get up!" he ordered through panicked breaths. As the snow on his clothes melted, damp pajamas limply draped his body. Little rivulets of water flowed down his face from the disappearing snow on top of his head. He looked back at the hallway and glanced at the floor, searching for signs of *their* imminent coming.

Without wasting another moment, he pushed himself over to the end of the bookcase and pushed a button near the back wall under the fifth shelf. To her surprise, the bookcase began to open, exposing a window into the world in which she had been imprisoned for nine months. The glare from the four banks of lights blinded her as they lit up the dark bedroom.

Panic churned her stomach into knots. She was overwhelmed with a company of emotions. Fear. Hatred. Anger. Shock. They all joined to make a bitter soup of bile in her stomach. She was appalled that he had sat in this recliner chair, slept in this bed, while she suffered in there, only a few feet away from his comfort. Anger raged within her as her hiding place was revealed.

Dread swept over her as she realized why he was so confident in the security of the cell. No one would think of looking behind the bookcase for her. She was horrified at the thought of going back to the world that she had hoped was now behind her forever.

As she sat rigidly in the bed, staring at the room on the other side of the see-through mirror, Kathryn couldn't shake the feeling that she was looking at an elaborate coffin. And he was going to bury her again. Only this time, neither knew for how long.

Her body refused to move from the bed. She couldn't leave her knife behind, but she could see no way of taking it with her. She was still too weak to overtake him in a skirmish. *Damn*, she swore, as conflict and confusion took possession of her will.

"Come! Now!" he huffed, walking toward her.

Reluctantly, Kathryn let go of the handle. From her time on the psych ward in Seattle, she had learned that people in an unbalanced mental state were stronger and more determined than normal. It often took several orderlies to restrain a patient while she administered the meds required to calm them down. She knew she was in no shape to wrestle with Dylan. It might open the tentative healing of her wounds and that would only complicate her condition. She would have to leave the knife and pray he didn't find it.

Dylan helped her rise from the bed, and pulling the card-key from its pocket taped on the back of the bookcase, he slipped it through the slit and opened the door.

Kathryn limped into the blazing lights. She turned to face the silver wall as he closed the door behind her, and then headed to her corner by the sink. *At least in here, I'm safe from his madness*, she told herself in a futile attempt at comfort.

Squatting on the floor, she faced the mirror. Her image glared back at her, spitting out the words of the defeated. *Yeah, but for how long?*

Chapter Thirteen

She sensed that he was watching from the comfort of her bed, lying under that warm, lightweight comforter she had so enjoyed. In her mind, she could see him snuggle under the covers, fluff his pillow to just the right position, pause, and find the knife she had buried. She knew he would seethe with anger and want to punish her for the betrayal. Betrayal would be exactly how he would see it and not as a natural self-defense response.

Damn! she swore, knowing it was just a matter of time before he found the knife. *That had to be the worst spot I could find! Why didn't I think?* she asked too late. But where else was there to hide it? *Under the bed? In the bookcase?* she asked herself. *Neither would be accessible when I need it...like now! And any other time he has me chained to the damned bedpost!*

I could have hidden it anywhere but in the pillow! She berated her panic and lack of experience with such things. It was a reaction...a poor one...but a reaction nonetheless.

Kathryn had no idea what she planned to do. *Escape? Kill him?* It was probably the most logical thing to do. *But how?* She knew it would come down to either him or her. He got to her once. He had just walked in passed police protection and took her. What would prevent him from doing it again?

Prison? *No, he would eventually get out.*

Police? *No, they knew he was coming and were right outside guarding me that fateful night.*

Moving? *How did he find me in the first place? Even if I changed my name, he would locate me through the family. He seems to know everything about me.*

She didn't think she could live with even the remotest possibility of him walking into her life at any time. Her mind quickly flashed through a lifetime of frightening scenarios: she's just turned forty and Dylan forces her at gunpoint to sneak out the back door of her office; after turning sixty and feeling safe from him, Dylan yanks her from her bed and takes her away again; David throws her a party on her eightieth birthday when Dylan strolls in uninvited and pulls her kicking and screaming from the gathering. No matter how old she was, Dylan could come anytime he wanted and take her again.

She knew, without a doubt, however long it took, he would never leave her alone as long as it was in his power to take her.

No, it's either me or him, she decided. *There is no other way. He will never let me have a life without him. I have to be at least that strong. I must not let him have a life with me.*

To be the winner, she would have to get into his head and understand him. She would have to learn his strengths and his weaknesses and use them against him. Kathryn would have to learn to think like he does and become him to beat Dylan at his own game.

During the time of her internment as his *guest,* Kathryn had learned very little about Dylan. She knew he didn't like different foods touching on his plate; he wore the same clothes and ate the same food for days on end; he avoided accidental human touch; he liked plaids and bright colors; he was obsessive about trivial matters; and he didn't seem to comprehend the simplest human responses or needs.

Most of the time Dylan stared into space and spoke of distant things that held no meaning for her or anyone. He treated her as if she were a pet he had purchased from a store. In his mind, she was his personal property secured by right of some obscure law that exists only in his mind.

A goldfish, perhaps. She almost laughed, except the irony was far too real and painful.

His moods were unpredictable as he bounced between two distasteful extremes. On one hand he was varying degrees of caring and thoughtfulness; ten seconds later he flipped to descending depths of mean to terrible. There was no consistency or middle ground. She never knew what triggered the transformation from one side to the other.

The tone of her voice, the twitch of her dimple, the way she would look at something...these, all involuntary triggers, seemed to fling him into moods of a warmth that passed dangerously close to affection. The inflections in her voice, her lack of appreciation for the battles he fought with invisible *adversaries,* her inability to understand the things he spoke about...these prods, which also remained beyond her comprehension, were the very ones that pushed the buttons that plunged him into moods of terrorizing meanness.

He changed so suddenly from one to the other she sometimes could not see it coming. It was like sitting beside a ticking bomb twenty-four hours a day without the knowledge of how to diffuse it or even how to read the clock attached to it.

She tried to manufacture the triggers to learn precise cause and effect, but nothing worked consistently. What she thought would have set him off on am angry rampage might have no effect, or what should have appeased his wrath only pushed him further over the precipice. It kept her unbalanced and vulnerable. Kathryn never knew from one minute to the next what was going to happen or how to prepare for it.

No matter what disposition he wallowed in, he injected such heaviness into the surrounding atmosphere that it was unbearable to be near him. He had no easy pleasantness or natural emotion. Every nuance and mood seemed to adhere to some rule or law he was forced to follow. Both their lives had to followed a form that did not allow the slightest compromise for any reason.

When he talked, which was not often, his words were dramatic and shocking, each one designed to keep her broken and shrouded in fear. He seemed incapable of just socializing, making small talk, or doing anything she could relate to; while at the same time he expected her to fit in and enjoy life here in total recluse. For Dylan, life was an unendurable task and an unconditional mission. He hated everything and everyone with a consuming passion. He believed no one to be the equal of his intelligence, his aspiring ambition, or God-ordained calling. Dylan declared that he alone was the elite of the human race and proclaimed that everyone else was created for his amusement. He was like an emotionless automaton, more a visitor to this world than an involved member.

Dylan was a complete riddle to her. One she would have to work a lot harder at solving if she was to survive.

Everything was just a matter of time, she groaned. *Life hangs by a thread...and he has the damn knife to cut it.* She was furious with herself for leaving it behind. *But how could I have brought it with me? There was no time, no warning.*

Kathryn found it harder to remember David's face, his touch, and his smell. The life she had before was slowly withering from her thoughts, living only in the rare pleasant dream. The nightmare she was daily submerged in was becoming her reality, replacing everything she once knew with something horrible and distasteful. She was wearied with trying to keep her past alive, leaving no strength to pour into the futile battle at hand. It was easier to simply live in Dylan's world and become part of Dylan's life.

Perhaps what disgusted her most was the growing compassion she felt for Dylan.

Her thoughts floated back to Dylan's distorted face of fear as he whisked her into the room as absolute panic possessed him. He was terrified of the *visitors*. He was afraid that *they* would find her. She wondered who *they* were.

Maybe he has partners he has to answer to, she thought. *Maybe they finance him for some reason. Once he mentioned someone named George.*

Dylan obviously had money. That was evident by this house, although she could see no visible means of income. He did not leave the house enough to hold down a job and, as far as she knew, he didn't work at home. He spent far too much time with her to be able to run a business. He rarely left the house to go to town—she was aware of only twice. Of course, she didn't know what he did when they weren't together.

There are people who don't have to work. Inheritance? Hmm. Maybe.

But who are they, then? she thought. *And why would I be in danger from them? Surely they can't be any worse.*

He offered her no answers to her troubling questions. He was as much an enigma now as he was in their first encountered.

Perhaps it's not me who would be in danger. He can't afford for them to find me because they don't know about his kinky sickness. Maybe if they found me in his house, they would let me go. Has it happened before? Perhaps they are family. Then they could easily investigate his house and find me in the bedroom. An ex-wife? She could come in and claim her belongings if they were separated. Maybe these are her clothes. They fit quite well. His clothes are always so baggy. These must be her jeans. Surely she would notice her clothes missing. How on earth is he ever going to explain that?

She felt as if she were one of the king's men and he was Humpty Dumpty. He dropped little clues, but she couldn't piece him together. Kathryn sighed, tired of trying to figure things out with so little available information.

Kathryn curled up on the floor and dropped off to sleep while listening for any sound coming from the other side of Alice's mirror.

Her stomach was growling nonstop by the time he returned and let her out of prison. He informed her it was the fourth day since *they* had come and harassed him. Apologizing for the incident and subsequent imprisonment, he led her to the bathroom before heading downstairs to begin breakfast. Dylan suggested it was the least he could do, and she wholeheartedly agreed, but thought it wise to refrain from saying so.

Kathryn melted into the lusciousness of the steaming Jacuzzi. She carefully tended her arm, checking for any sign of infection. During the days in lockup, she hadn't been allowed to give it the attention she felt necessary. Cleaning and packing the larger wounds, Kathryn rebandaged her arm, which felt now better from the care.

An hour passed before Kathryn walked into the kitchen. Dylan ushered her to the table where he had set a hot cup of coffee when he heard her coming down the stairs. While sipping the black brew, she watched as he stirred his favorite "scrambled omelet" in the pan. Dishing it out onto two plates, Dylan carried the meal to the table with a broad grin of proud accomplishment.

Kathryn waited until he was seated and had taken the first bite before she lunged at her eggs, scooping them up like a starving child. She had forgotten what hunger was like...and a full stomach. Afterward, she leaned back in her chair and sipped the hot, delicious coffee. The soothing warmth was a welcome relief after the starvation diet of only the cold water of solitary lockup.

Dylan stared at her before stumbling over irrational words. "Do you want to do anything special today?" he asked.

Kathryn glared at him in disbelief. *How can you act like nothing happened after you were such a complete jerk?* she asked, not daring to speak it aloud, but wishing she could. Dylan was master of unbelievable reactions.

"Go for a walk? Sit in front of the fire?" he continued, oblivious to her wide-eyed scrutiny.

Kathryn decided to put her plan into action. "What would you like to do? We can sit and talk in front of the fire, if you like," she suggested, hoping to begin her investigation. She knew it was going to be a long slow process, but it didn't matter. She'd be here anyway.

"Well, we could do both, if you feel up to it," he smiled, almost genuinely. Dylan never seemed able to extend the basic emotion beyond his lips to his eyes.

God, I hate that smile. She grinned back.

"Good. We'll put the dishes in the sink, get dressed and be on our way then," he said, rising from the table with hands full of plates and cups.

Kathryn helped him clean the kitchen while trying to muster a bubbling enthusiasm for his company. She wanted him to feel as comfortable as possible so she could proceed with her investigation of what went on inside her captor.

The walk was short. Fresh, cool air filled her lungs. The sunshine was wonderful. Kathryn started to shiver as the cold temperatures pushed through her weakened condition. She had trouble walking in the snow. Dylan offered to pull her along on a sled, but she refused, wanting the exercise. Kathryn didn't feel like staying out too long in the winter weather.

By early afternoon, the snow began falling again. Dylan looked up at the clouds, thought for a minute, and then agreed that they should head back.

Once inside, he worked the fire into a roaring inferno that took away the chill in a matter of minutes. It was a large, cut-stone fireplace that allowed Dylan to build a tremendous flame that crackled, spit, and sang an inviting song of warmth.

Kathryn sat close to the blaze, and let it soothe her growing anxiety. While in the cell, she had contemplated the ramifications of having sex with Dylan. He was a good-looking man. It might not be a physical hardship, and she was growing fond of him...in a curious, unnatural way. She was beginning to convince herself that his touch would not be as repulsive as she had once thought.

Dylan brought her a glass of red wine and joined her on the black bear rug before the hearth. She sipped the dry, full-bodied liquid with a certain measure of gratitude, waiting for the effects of its heat to permeate her insides.

"Tell me about yourself. I don't know anything about you," she whispered, her words barely discernible.

"Not much to tell. What do you want to know? Ask me anything," he said, taking a big swallow from his glass.

"Well, what do you do for a living?" she asked, feeling a little braver at his lack of rebuff.

"Nothing. I do only what I want when I want," he answered smugly. His eyes glistened with pride at his cherished independence.

"Oh, I see," she said, unsatisfied with his answer. "But how can you afford all this?" Kathryn's eyes roamed the living room pointing beyond the visible boundaries of the room.

"I have money," he replied, maintaining a degree of allusive mystery.

"What about your family?" she asked, realizing she had to change the line of questioning since she was getting nowhere on this track.

"They're dead for the most part. I have uncles and aunts that live back east, but my parents and sister are dead. They died when I was fairly young. I'm not close to the rest of them at all. I haven't seen them for years. I don't go out of my way for them, and they certainly don't go out of their way for me," he said through a clenched jaw. There was obvious animosity between Dylan and his relatives, a feeling that ran deep and strong within him. His eyes were tortured and dark at the thought of them.

"I'm sorry to hear that. You must have had an unhappy childhood," she prodded, trying to get him to open up. It wasn't easy. She could see his discomfort increase. It was difficult for her to picture a terrible family life. Her childhood had been classic America. Her family and siblings were loving and happy, and they were encouraged to live up to their dreams and full potential.

"Who cares? They don't. I brought myself up. Since I was seven. They had no idea who I was and what was happening to me. But that's fair. I have no idea what happened with them. When I was seven, I did whatever I wanted. It was as if I were an adult then. I suddenly became British. George and I were together always. We had become one, joined in a very personal and intimate way. I packed my bags back then and have never found a reason to unpacked them," he whispered. The memories were painful for him. The strain of remembering showed on his face, creating deep crevices of pain on his smooth features. He looked weary of life and the struggle embroiled with being Dylan. Things were not easy for him.

His agony tugged at her heart. An irresistible urge to hold him and comfort him pushed through her awareness, forcing her to struggle with the unnatural feeling.

"Were you molested as a child?" she asked, hesitating to be personal so quickly. But it seemed obvious by his tone.

"No. Nothing like that. They just ignored me. What they couldn't figure out, they thought would simply go away if they turned a blind eye to it," he mumbled without emotion. His voice became flat and dry, cracking under the tension of his words.

There was a bitter coldness in his eyes. She shuddered under their intensity, cringing from the seething hate they portrayed. His face set into a concrete mask. The mounting fear confused her resolve until she didn't know whether to continue to probe him for answers or just change the subject to something more pleasant.

But what else is there to talk about? He can't comprehend anything remotely normal like chit chat, she rationalized, struggling for direction, *not to mention what reservoirs of recent experience do I have.*

The air was becoming increasingly uncomfortable. Dylan riveted his gaze to her every move. Kathryn swallowed nervously, sensing that he was ready to erupt. She couldn't pin point what it was about his family that changed his mood, or what she could do to pull him back from the elevating summit of his anger. The day had been good. She didn't want to lose that now.

"Do you want any more wine?" he asked, rising from the rug.

"Yes, that would be very nice," she agreed.

His movements were stiff and exaggerated, giving him a marionette appearance as he stomped across the room to the wet bar to retrieve a new bottle of Bordeaux. "Listen, Dylan. I didn't realize that talking about your family would upset you. I shouldn't have brought it up."

He struggled with the cork, which finally popped with a muffled sound as he pulled it out of the bottleneck. He carried it back to the rug, sat down, and poured it into their glasses, ignoring her last comment.

"Really, I'm sorry. I just thought it would be good to get to know you better. After all, we're going to be spending a long time together, and we shouldn't be strangers. It's just that...we're like husband and wife now." she added, trying to pull him back to a level where they could communicate.

Dylan sipped his wine in silence as he watched the crackling flame caress the scorched logs. The fire was cozy, but he didn't seem to notice. He stared into a world beyond the blaze, his eyes flinching from the pain of what he saw. His face grew darker as a scowl set into his features, hardening with each passing second.

Kathryn was afraid of the depth of the pit he was plummeting into. She would remember not to bring the subject up of family again, but right now, she concentrated on getting out of the situation before he was unreachable.

"Did you want anything to eat? If you're hungry, I can whip up a snack. We can eat right here, where it's cozy," she offered with an almost cheery voice.

Dylan continued to stare blankly into the fire. She wasn't even sure he heard her.

"Well, I'd like some cheese and crackers. It would be nice with the Bordeaux," she continued, trying to reach him. "How about a few veggies with dip?"

He turned to her, his eyes wet and glazed. Without saying a word, he nodded.

"All right, then. I'll go and make up a tray. Be right back," she said as she raised herself up from the rug.

His eyes followed her into the kitchen.

Kathryn gathered three different cheeses, the fancy crackers, and the bottle of green olives she had asked him to purchase on his last trip to town. As she opened the package of sharp white cheese, a vision of the knife flashed through her mind. *I might have put it in my pants to be better hidden later.* She opened the drawer and rummaged through the silverware looking for a paring knife. Opening a second drawer, she scoured the contents.

Serving spoons, spatulas, flippers, ladles...nothing of use.

Intent on her search, she didn't hear him come up behind her.

"Looking for this?" he asked with a lifeless chill to his voice as he held the familiar butcher knife in the air before her eyes.

Her hand stopped in mid-motion as she froze, recognizing the chilling tone. It was too late. He had jumped of the cliff of decency and plummeted down into the depths of savagery.

Chapter Fourteen

Kathryn woke up after a few hours of anxious sleep. She wanted to get breakfast on the table by the time he was up and ready to eat. Awake most of the night, she planned and replanned the menu for the entire week. It was part of the contract they made last night. Negotiations were difficult, but they had come to an agreement he could live with and she could accept.

He wanted to kill her last night in the kitchen. The deadness in his voice as he hovered behind her told her that, at the very least, he would make her life a complete hell for as long as it took to deplete his store of wrath. But, to her dread, Dylan kept his anger controlled.

As she suspected, he had found the knife the first night. However, *they* had demanded too much of Dylan's time for him to be able to respond immediately. By the time he did react, four days later, he had settled into controlled revenge.

His glare pierced her soul with a terrifying chill that paralyzed her. He had snuck up behind her without a sound. In his hand he brandished the knife, but refused to hand it over to her so she could slice the cheese. Instead, he helped her prepare the snack tray. They returned to the fire only after he locked the knife away in the drawer with the other utensils he considered too dangerous to be accessible.

The disjointed discussion had been surprising. Kathryn braced herself, expecting him to make impossible demands and strip away what few privileges she had won. Dylan held all the cards and could do whatever he wanted, and there wasn't one thing she could do about it.

Dylan was silent for the longest time. As he stared into the fire, the inner struggle to remain calm showed on his twisted features. His eyes were hard and unfeeling. He clenched his jaw tightly. He suspended a piece of cheese in one hand and a cracker in the other, but the two refused to come together. Redness crawled up his face, stopping briefly at his cheeks before growing past his ears and disappearing into his hairline.

Turning back to the fire, Kathryn nibbled at a piece of cheese to distance him from her thoughts and separate her fears from his words. When he finally did say something, the words were shocking and unexpected.

"What do you want?" he finally asked in a flat tone. Turning his bloodshot eyes toward her, their stare searched her features for any sign of what she might be thinking.

"Want? I only... want... to... live," she said, keeping her gaze glued to the flames, not daring to return his look lest she break down in tears. She hated when he toyed with her. *Why don't you do what you have to and get it over with?* she wanted to snap, but bit her lip instead of agitating him any further.

"What will it take?" he whispered, ignoring her words.

She couldn't stand the increasing pressure growing inside him. In response, a cracker snapped into pieces in her fingers. The crumbs rained down onto her knees and the rug. Kathryn let the cheese fall from her fingers as she stared at him, uncertain what he was asking. She had the feeling that it would be disastrous to give a wrong answer.

His eyes were pained with the struggle to maintain control of his turbulent emotions. Desperation and stress were chiseled deeply into his wounded features. He was hurt. The depth of his anguish was revealed by the bottomless pit of his sorrow, and she was afraid of being sucked in.

"What will it take for what?" she asked hesitantly, unable to see into his thoughts. Biting her lower lip, she fingered the crumbs on her lap before flicking them one by one onto the rug. It was an action she would never have done at home, but she wasn't at home. She was here, in his house, and no matter how hard Kathryn tried, sometimes she just couldn't forget that.

A flash of anger sparked in his eyes before he again took command of himself. "What will it take for this to work?"

"For what to work?" she asked, perplexed.

"Stop acting so dense. This isn't easy for me to talk about. I want to know what I have to give you for you to give me what I want." he barked, balling his hands into white knuckled fists. The struggle clouded his piercing gaze as he resisted the urge to hit her. His countenance darkened as the inner storm settled over his mind.

"What is it that you want from me?" she asked, exasperation covering her fearful confusion. In the months she had been his prisoner, he had not yet made his intentions clear.

Dylan clicked his tongue in angry disgust. He jumped from his chair and lunged across the room to where Kathryn was sitting. His impatience with her was mounting. "Why do you insist on playing these ridiculous games? Just tell me what it will take," he snarled, bringing his fist up to her face. For a moment, he suspended it in the air in front of her eyes before smashing it into his own thigh as if releasing a pressure valve.

Kathryn scrambled to decide what she should answer, grasping at any plausible thought that skipped through her mind. She didn't understand what it was that he was saying to her, but she had to come up with an acceptable reply before he exploded, wounding her with the shrapnel of his hate.

"God, why do you force me to say it? You know what I want. I want you to love me," he hissed, angry with the words he spoke and furious at her for making him say them. "I want you to let me love you. It's what I've always wanted." Dylan's voice sank to a barely audible low whisper. He turned away from her and stormed to the hearth. Frustration compelled him to pound his fist on the stones in a pulsating beat.

Kathryn was numbed by his answer.

Dylan had made neither physical advance nor suggestion toward her. Instead, he had treated her with sexual kid gloves. Initially, the possibility of rape had been one of her greatest fears. Sometimes his desire would be so self-consuming that the air between them would become frightfully tense. The inner battle raged in his every move and colored his moods to a dark black depression. Despite the physical war that tore through him, and his place of obvious authority, he still managed not to make any physical overture toward her.

The lack of physical contact did not give her any relief. She knew it must only be a matter of time. And that time, it seemed, was now here.

"You can physically take me any time you want. I can't stop you. I can't even fight you. I am, after all, your prisoner." Kathryn's eyes stared at her trembling finger riding round the lip of her wine glass as it created a soft, high-pitched hum.

"No, I can't take you. You have to love me. In the way I need to be loved. You have to become like me. I want you to love me the way I love you, talk to me the way I talk to you," he whispered to the flames. The fingers of his left hand tightened around the stone mantle piece as his other fist slammed into the rocks below. Intense shame and embarrassment spilled over his self-control. He raised one foot onto the brick hearth as if, for a moment, he contemplated jumping into the flames himself.

"God, Dylan. I just don't understand," she said tearfully. His riddles were beyond her.

Dylan grabbed his glass from the mantle, sucked back the last few mouthfuls of wine, and then threw his empty glass into the fireplace, watching the sudden explosion of flames lap up the alcohol residue. Annoyance sliced through the taut air. He pursed his lips ready to say something but changed his mind, trapping the words on pouting lips. Instead, he hissed a loud sigh and spoke to her as if she were a child. He stumbled to couch and knelt on the carpet before her. Reaching out, he took her hand, pulled it to his lap, and laid it between his own two hands.

"When I touch you like this, when my palm touches yours, I can see into your soul. I can see everything you are, everything that you were, and everything you will become. I am inside you. Can't you feel me?" he asked urgently. Dylan's eyes descended into terrified reflections of the bewilderment and desperation within him. It was the first time he had ever honestly opened his heart to her and it made him dangerously vulnerable.

Kathryn could feel the warmth of his hands. They were not as disgusting as she had thought they would be. Instead, to her surprise, they were surprisingly human. His fingers trembled ever so slightly as he cupped her hand between his. It had been a very long time since someone touched her for any reason. Even though they were his hands, it felt good to be held again. For one brief moment, she was grateful that he touched her so gently, like David used to so very long ago.

"I'm sorry, but I don't understand what you're talking about. I'm trying, but I just don't feel anything," she muttered, truly not comprehending what he was saying. There was no sensation going through her body except the nervousness with which she was well familiar. He was not *inside her* as he said. *No, he must be madder than I had thought.*

"I need someone to be like me. That potential is in you. I recognized it the instant I saw you in the restaurant with that other woman. There is a special quality about you. If you try, you can do it. So what will it take? What do you want in trade?" He gazed deep into her eyes. He let her hand drop and crossed his arms across his chest in a protective gesture.

His hopelessness tugged at Kathryn's heart. Before her huddled the only person she had ever hated in her entire life and he was begging her to love him. The anger she felt shifted from Dylan to herself. He was simply pathetic, but she was turning traitor as she began to feel something for this man. The change in her own heart toward him enraged her. For one passing moment, she wanted to sleep with him to comfort not only his internal suffering, but hers as well.

His hands...they felt so warm and nice.

She didn't have the slightest idea what he was talking about. Kathryn stared at the pitiful man at her feet. The firelight danced off the sheen of his burgundy silk shirt. She wondered when his features had become so familiar to her. It was the same familiarity she had with David's face, like that of an old friend. She knew the contours and blemishes.

Her eyes searched his to find the subtle meaning hidden behind his words. Deciding to play it safe, she asked the least offensive question. "What are you offering?"

"Anything within reason," he said, gulping nervously.

Kathryn sipped her wine in deep deliberation. She knew he wouldn't arbitrarily give her freedom, but she did question what might be within his acceptable limits of reason. She didn't know if she should press him as far as she could and risk making him angry, or if she should ask for little only to find out afterward that he was willing to offer much more.

In no great hurry to commit herself, Kathryn finished her glass of wine before speaking. "My freedom. It will cost you my freedom." She decided to go for the whole nine yards.

Dylan grunted his response.

They then labored through the negotiations for several hours.

By the end of the evening, Dylan had promised to allow her free run of the house. She was to be allowed the use of his house as her own. Kathryn could do whatever she pleased, of course, within the confines of the building. She was given the privilege to clean, cook, listen to music, watch movies, do needlework, play games. Dylan would relinquish complete control of the meals and household. He would, of course, continue with all the shopping, but it would be done according to her specifications. As a precaution, she would be locked away for safety while he was in town. Otherwise, she was unrestricted, except the rooms and drawers locking her out. There would be no television or radio, but she could watch video movies and listen to favorite CDs. He did not want her to learn their location. All the windows and doors would remain locked and the alarm would be on at all times to prevent a repeat of her escape attempt. There would be no potential weapons allowed. If she needed a knife or scissors, it would be checked in and out under his supervision.

In payment, she would talk to him, become a friend, and teach him about herself and the life he had missed. Kathryn would teach him social graces, and she would show him how to share human emotions.

He sealed the contract with something he called "joining," which consisted of holding the palm of her hand against his and "bonding with her on a spiritual level." His expression was filled with such an earnest seriousness that it lent a certain mystical, and very comical, eeriness to the procedure.

Watching him intently, she found it difficult to keep a straight face as he worked. The entire thing was ridiculous and held absolutely nothing for her. Deciding against telling him her thoughts,

Kathryn instead chose to play his game with the hopes that he would soften. If he began to· trust her enough, it might just provide the much-needed opening for escape.

During the night, while tossing and turning, she tried to formulate a plan of attack. Kathryn promised herself that she would act normally regardless of how difficult it proved to be or how long it took. She would simply have to wait until he dropped his guard and left open a door of opportunity.

Dylan kept his word. He let her go to bed unfettered. He slept in a separate room, leaving her alone all night long. For the first time she felt almost free and didn't want to miss upholding her end of the bargain. When the clock struck 8:00 A.M., Kathryn jumped out of bed and raced to the bathroom for a quick bath. Dylan didn't usually rise until an hour later, and she wanted to have everything ready when he came down.

After slipping into jeans and shirt, the only type of clothes he allowed her to have, she rushed downstairs into the kitchen.

Dylan stumbled into the kitchen just after 9:00, following the rich smell of brewing coffee to the table. He smiled a broad, happy grin as she dished out his favorite creation onto two plates. She had made his own scrambled omelet recipe, along with sausages and hash browns. Sitting at the table, he waited for her to join him. As Kathryn sat in the chair opposite him, she fluffed her napkin and spread it over her lap. It was a level of etiquette he chose to ignore, and instead shoved his napkin to the side of his plate.

Kathryn struggled to find some light conversation. She had gone over several choices last night, but they all seemed so phony and pretentious in the light of day. Each topic was cast aside for fear that they might scare him off or make him angry, and that would definitely not be a good start so soon after last night's agreement. Breakfast was emotionally painful and draining, and Kathryn realized that she would have to work very hard at this relationship. But she was determined to succeed.

Dylan attacked his breakfast with gusto, not noticing Kathryn staring at him between her own petite bites. He seemed oblivious to the finer points offered to him so far this morning. Shoveling one spoonful of food after another into his mouth, he remained, as usual, consumed by the very act of eating. Each occasion for eating was like an Indy race with Dylan. He swallowed his food almost whole, which led to an unfortunate chronic attack of stomach upset and acid regurgitation.

Kathryn was amazed at Dylan's uncanny ability to completely separate one moment from another. He didn't connect cause and effect, and could not relate to time in a chronological or sequential manner. Instead, each minute was attached only to the current situation with no awareness to what period in his life it actually occurred. He spoke not in terms of hours and days, but specified events as "in the time of Syracuse," or "in the time of Karen." This made it very difficult for her to have a discussion with him because Kathryn equated each relational time reference to an approximate date. She taught Dylan to calculate his present age and count backwards to the approximate date of the incident he was relating, but this method was only marginally consistent.

The other problem was with his communication. Dylan's views of life, the world, conceptual ideas, and words were completely visual. When he plummeted into one of his states, he struggled with grammar and language, turning every sentence inside out or leaving them altogether incomplete. His mind watched an internal television and halfway through an obscure scene, he would attempt to either share or finish the thought verbally—without the benefit of filling in the blanks or introducing the new topic. Dylan's mind jumped from one topic to another at a little less than the speed of light, and Kathryn had learned to either ignore what he was saying or try to go along.

As he devoured his breakfast with gusto, Kathryn attempted to find a topic to which they could both contribute. *Don't bring up family,* she reminded herself, wishing Dylan would come up with something. He remained quiet, except for the sound of his gorging.

While Dylan ate, he didn't talk. At times he would bury his anger in chewing, as if he were capable of doing only one thing at a time. He hid his embarrassment, confusion, and emotions with the process of eating, hoping that a mouth full of food could avoid exposing conversation. It was a wall she would have to break down.

"What do you feel like doing today?" she asked, finally breaking the suffocating silence.

Dylan just looked at her with a mouthful of food and nodded. "Anything you want," he mumbled before shoving another piece of toast into his already full mouth.

"Well, I could do some house cleaning, and write a grocery list for you, and later tonight, we could make some popcorn and watch a movie. I'd love to see a movie. There must be a lot of new ones out that I haven't seen," she bubbled, excited at the prospect of eating popcorn in front of a television again. She and David often curled up on the sofa together to watch a couple of videos on the weekend.

Dylan nodded his consent. "What do you want to watch? What kind of movies do you like?" he asked between swallows.

Kathryn leaned back, nursing a mug of coffee between cupped hands. It was a question she hadn't thought about for a very long time. *It was a good day, so maybe a comedy or something exciting. It would have to be something without sex so he won't be stimulated into thinking of areas he has hopefully put on the shelf. Maybe I should avoid violence as well. And sentiment, for my sake.*

As she mulled it over—what was left?—she hadn't realized what a difficult task it would be to pick something that was interesting to her without being inspiring to him, something safe. It would be easier to pass on the idea of a movie, but she desperately needed a connection to the outside world.

"Oh, I don't know. Something funny. Something light. Have you seen *The Gods Must Be Crazy?*" she asked cheerfully, struggling with titles that would fall within the parameters of safety she had determined.

"No. Is it good?" he asked, a shade of distaste tinting his voice. "I like thrillers and science fiction. Movies with lots of blood, gore, and violence. Sure you don't like action movies? The heroes may not be able to act, but who notices through all the violence? I want to see one of those. What about you?" he suggested, his tone suggesting that she should choose from his list rather than her own.

Kathryn didn't know what to do, so she agreed to leave the choice up to him.

The hours rushed by unnoticed. She had almost hoped Dylan would have to go to town to rent movies. However, Dylan had an extensive library, and since he didn't want to disrupt her first free day, they would take their choices from there.

They ate a light supper, leaving the popcorn for dessert. They headed to his television room, and to her surprise, Dylan had a large screen television in a room that was set up like a movie theater. He had over three hundred movies ranging from musicals to horror. It was an odd assortment of choices that seemed to belong to several people instead of just one man.

Kathryn chose a light comedy, surprised to find such a movie in his collection, while Dylan picked a mafia trilogy. Together, sitting side by side in a recliner love seat with a bucket of popcorn in each of their laps, Kathryn and Dylan had their first date.

Part Three

The First Anniversary

Chapter Fifteen

Kathryn was excited. The sun, which now rose before 7:00 A.M., was already warm and inviting. The forest was alive with the song and dance of a variety of colored birds. Red squirrels flew from one branch to another, scampering through the forest in a lively game of tag. Tiny red-cheeked hummingbirds darted around several special feeders, dodging possessive wasps that were also attracted to the sugary water. A small breeze carried the heavy aroma of cedar and undergrowth through the barred but open windows.

Jumping out of bed earlier than usual, she wanted to make certain everything was prepared. It was important that nothing go wrong, giving him reason to retrogress from keeping his word. Kathryn was so ecstatic she hardly slept all night. Dylan had promised to take her to his favorite quiet place—a waterfall on the east side of the mountain.

For the journey, Dylan had purchased two pairs of walking boots at her request. After being badly blistered from wearing new boots on a field trip, Kathryn vowed not to make the same mistake twice. To break them in, they had worn the boots around the house and yard for the last month.

The trip to the waterfall and back was an anticipated full-day hike through the forest. He didn't expect to get home before dark, and so entertained the thought of staying overnight. The waterfall was in an isolated area of government land and was only accessible by foot, which gave the area a degree of safety.

It was Kathryn's first adventure since the sailing trip she and David had taken over a year ago. The thought of camping was exhilarating. Anything that would get her away from this house was thrilling. She was more than ready for an adventure outside, even if it meant hiking through the wilderness with *him* for two days. Dylan had occasionally let her walk around the property, but he was always careful to keep her on a short leash. When they weren't in the house, he was nervous of any sound that might mean someone uninvited had come for a visit.

She had worked hard to be on her best behavior since the agreement was reached. What at one time was considered drudgery, she now embraced as privilege. Each task was accomplished with an overabundance of appreciation and cheerfulness, and now Dylan decided to present her with the reward of the hike.

Kathryn planned the menu two weeks in advance, sending Dylan to town to purchase special foods, nut mixes, and dried fruit to nibble on the way. Added to the list were backpacks, a tent, canteens, a first aid kit, camping equipment, tarps, sleeping bags, and two outdoor hats—a navy blue one for him, while she stayed with the original unbleached white. Kathryn wore her hat in the fashion of an Australian design, while Dylan snapped both sides up and wrapped the string over the front and back in a Western style.

He purchased two additional outfits that belonged more to a forty's German mountaineer than a nineties' American hiker, but she received hers with an acceptable amount of enthusiastic gratitude. He had been so pleased with the matching outfits that he pranced into her room, too excited to keep his surprise a secret.

In the last three months, unlike before, Dylan had begun to spend a good deal of his time thinking of things he could do for Kathryn. He would serve her coffee in bed every other morning, expecting her to reciprocate the thoughtfulness. Instead, Kathryn avoided the suggestion of intimacy by creating other things she knew he would appreciate—apple pie, chocolate cake, and pumpkin tarts. While keeping his culinary appetites satisfied, she hoped to keep his intimate appetites at bay from a safe distance. The time had passed quickly and she could almost say that there were some occasional good moments. Eventually, a day did not go by that he didn't give some gift to her—flowers, boxes, jewelry, clothes, or chocolate treats. He'd even purchased movies and music geared to her taste rather than his.

Kathryn prepared enough food for four days, just in case he decided they could stay longer. Packing the food into the new backpacks, along with the other supplies, she evenly distributed the weight so each bag was relatively equal and well balanced. She and David had camped often during their marriage, and he had taught her well.

Along with the needed supplies, she packed a swimsuit that he had picked up according to her specifications and his tastes. He said she might be able to go swimming later, although he himself would not go near the water. Dylan emphasized his fear of water, repeating the chant that he swam like a rock.

Things had gone well in the last two-and-a-half months since they had struck their agreement. He had allowed her to rearrange furniture, and bring a more feminine touch to the house with potpourris and flowers. She organized their eating habits to make the food more varied and nutritious, adding supplements as part of the morning regime.

Pushing her family and home from her mind during waking hours, her heart dared to let them drift back only in her dreams. Kathryn concentrated on her current predicament, determined to make the best of the situation while watching that no opportunity escape her notice. She worked toward regaining her strength and health in preparation for any opening to run for freedom.

Each morning she woke up knowing what her fully scheduled day held. In order not to slip into the depression that hovered in the back of her mind, Kathryn kept every minute filled with activity. Pushing herself to act normally, she kept alert and watchful, not letting his moods or her circumstances overwhelm her.

To her surprise, Dylan was capable of laughing when the situation was right. He had a strange dark humor, roaring at things few others would notice. He loved slapstick comedy and offbeat British humor draped in innuendo and subtleties that were more ridiculous than funny. No matter how hard Kathryn tried, she could not find the different hair colors or the absurdities of spaceship mining ship crew humorous. Yet Dylan would slap his thigh and laugh repeatedly, mimicking every British joke with renewed laughter for days following. Kathryn, who didn't see any humor the first time, saw it even less with each retelling, and had to remind herself of the necessity of a good attitude.

Much to her distress, his second passion was science fiction, but she endured the endless hours of imagination for the cause. They would watch sci-fi marathons as well as the many "B" movies he had in his collection. Dylan was quite proud of his extensive library of hard-to-find titles and considered himself an accomplished collector. She was, unfortunately, learning more about the history and fantasies of science fiction than she cared to know.

Her apparent interest in his life made him happy, and that mood was a very essential element of her long-term plan. He remained blissfully ignorant of the great effort she put forth to remain cordial toward him, and that, too, suited her undercover plan.

Dylan's moods were unstable and unpredictable. He was either fun and happy, or dark and haunted by *things* she could neither see nor hear. Nighttime was the worst for him and often his screams would catapult through the house, filling the darkness with his own private hell. There were nights when his raving shouts were so disturbing that Kathryn would feel compelled to go to his room.

At first, she would stand by the door, staring into the room at his shadowed figure huddling in the corner of the bed. At times, her presence was enough to allay his fears. However, most of the time, she was required to enter the asylum of his battlefield and sit on the side of his bed. Kathryn would reach out her hand and he would grasp the precious offering, clutching her hand between his and close to his throat. Dylan would then rock himself to sleep with the security of her touch while clenching his eyes shut against the horrors that assaulted him.

She had often thought about escaping while Dylan was asleep, but he had the house completely sealed with bars, deadbolts, and alarms to immediately announce any such possibility. Motion detectors prevented her from even going downstairs between certain hours. Dylan had taken every precaution, being especially aware of the degree of vulnerability his own condition sometimes placed around him.

Kathryn had entertained visions of killing or rendering Dylan unconscious so it wouldn't matter if she set off the alarms, but he had already taken that into account. Dylan hid every key and numeric code to the locks in a safe she had not been able to find. The house was completely isolated from the outside world, even to the extent of not having a telephone or a mail service. He had arranged that, if anything should happen to him, she would die and forever remain a prisoner of the house, whether or not she was locked in the Plexiglas cell.

After much consideration, Kathryn decided that her sole chance of escape would only be presented when already outside. *Like on a two-day camping trip.* She smiled as she started the morning coffee.

Dylan rarely left her alone during daylight hours. Sitting close by to observe Kathryn performing even the simplest tasks, he would pressure her to explain each step with an endless stream of questions. Insisting she fill in every detail, Dylan was fascinated by things she took for granted—why she brushed her hair in a certain way; why she cooked this way or that; how she planted a garden...

After purchasing a rototiller as a surprise, Dylan marked off a sizable plot of land in the clearing south of the house for Kathryn. She worked from early morning to late afternoon planning and planting her garden, tending to every detail a little more enthusiastically than necessary. Efforts put into growing an award-winning garden were used as a smokescreen to keep herself out of Dylan's way. The allowable half-acre vegetable patch was enlarged to include several flowerbeds all around the yard and house. Grateful for the privilege, Kathryn found that working in the dirt was therapeutic—at night, she fell into bed, physically tired from a full and productive day.

Dylan didn't believe Kathryn concerning the promised harvest. Having never paid attention to anything green, either in the yard or on a plate, he had no concept of reproduction of plant life. He was stunned as she explained what each seed would produce, disbelieving the explanation of how potatoes grew. What she said didn't make sense to him, and, to make it interesting, he wagered a hefty stake that she was wrong.

Laughing at his honest ignorance, she could not resist the sure gamble when he made the stakes so very attractive. If the potatoes grew as she predicted, he would take her for a twelve-hour daytime ride in the van; if they did not, she would allow him to "join" with her hand at will for an entire day while making an attempt to comprehend the communication process.

In her heart, Kathryn hid the hope that this bet might just be the possible opening she had been praying for. The chance filled her dreams and gave her the incentive needed to produce a top-notch garden that would be the envy of any state fair contestant.

During the summer months, Dylan traveled to town at least once a week to fill her many lists that ranged from supplies to entertainment. Kathryn had him stock up on jars and ingredients needed to preserve the produce after harvest that would fill the pantry she asked him to build. Every attempt was made to encourage him to believe that she had accepted that her life was here with him for however long he decided.

While he was gone, Kathryn was locked in the glass room until he returned. It was a tense, uncomfortable time. The more freedom he allowed her, the more she detested the confined lockup of her cell. Her imagination would run amuck in the claustrophobic cage. She'd see him in a head-on collision; his dead body would be sprawled across the road; the police would wrap his body in a black plastic bag... Although this image had been appealing in the past, the fear of his not returning increased with each lockup. At times, the unwanted visions drew her into an hysterical crisis in the room's brilliant solitude.

When he was home, hours were spent learning the subtle complexities of new games. She taught Dylan the strategies of chess and backgammon while he reciprocated with how to gamble with a poker hand and the point spread of crib, using chores and treats for collateral. Movies, in-depth talks, games, wine, and duties made her time with Dylan almost palatable.

Their talks followed the same ritualistic pattern each time. Unaccounted tension would mount within Dylan and stifle the air around him. His movements would become stiff as he began to pace through the house, stare out windows, and clench his hands into tight fists while nibbling on his lower lip. He would then clench his jaw and strut around like an unfeeling android before the edginess settled in. The next step was anger and an argumentative nature before he'd finally get to the point of avoiding mirrors and reacting with an intense terror every time his feet touched the floor.

These visible signs of his needing to talk escaped his notice every time. Dylan was always amazed that she knew when there was a problem. He seemed to believe that he acted no differently from one moment to the next and prided himself on his consistent nature. But Kathryn was very aware and, unlike Dylan, was willing to admit his roller-coaster moods and unnatural reactions.

At first she was uncertain how to approach him when he was lost in one of his moods. Not knowing what he so desperately needed to talk about, she struggled with what subjects to address or avoid. Many difficult evenings passed before she developed a system of steps designed to get him to talk. Learning to take note of what his words did and didn't say, she listened to his disjointed stories wide-eyed and open-mouthed. The blatantly obvious omissions often said more than his version of the facts remembered.

In the sessions she could make sense of, Kathryn learned that his life was bizarre, even after weighing in the "Dylan" factor, through which she filtered all his words. Consumed by where he was going, he ignored the past that had shaped him. Although always working toward an elusive goal in *The Grey Land*, he would, for the most part, avoid talking about the hopes and dreams that loomed paramount in his thoughts. Sweat would begin to form on his forehead at the mere thought of the mysterious land.

Kathryn heard the faint whistle as Dylan hopped down the stairs and strolled into the kitchen, pulling her from her thoughts. Jumping instinctively, she braced herself for the anticipated battle over the planned camping trip. It was his habit to regret his offer and try to find any excuse he could to forbid it. With breakfast ready and on the table, she was determined not to give him any.

"Good morning," she smiled. "You sound chipper this morning. Breakfast is ready. There's a cup of coffee on the table for you. Hope you're hungry. I made your favorite."

"I feel great. I had a really good sleep last night. No nightmares. No visitors. Just a really good sleep," he said, giving her a passing peck on the cheek on his way to the table.

Kathryn froze. Dylan usually avoided physical contact. Not knowing how to respond, she was not willing to let him set her up for a fall and ruin the day. She had worked far too hard for far too long to earn this treat. Watching him saunter to the table, she pushed down a growing apprehension, wondering what he was planning.

"Great!" She smiled. *Keep your cool, Katie,* she cautioned herself. Seized with a sudden fear, she bit her bottom lip, trying to concentrate on serving the food in a pleasing appearance onto the plates.

"So, everything ready?" he asked, glancing at the two backpacks by the door.

"Yes, everything's packed. I even made a special picnic for when we arrive at the waterfall. I checked the list twice just in case I forgot something," she said, placing the plates on the table before taking her place across from him.

Dylan leaned back and put his feet on the chair at the end of the table. He picked up his fork and stabbed at the scrambled eggs. "I really don't feel like this right now. It's too good a morning to have something this boring. You don't mind, do you? How about some crepes? I have such a craving for crepes."

"No problem. Coming right up. You've got a few minutes. Why don't you go and get dressed while I make them?" she suggested with a smile. Picking up the plates, she carried them over to the counter and tossed the contents into the garberator before pulling down the crepe pan. Kathryn forced herself to stay in an amicable mood and ignore each of his games while trying to push him gently. She wanted to get out on the trail as soon as possible. He would be less likely to change his mind if they were already on their way.

Dylan looked down at his pajamas, hesitating to move before his coffee was finished.

She watched him struggle with the decision and tried to figure out the best way to prod him into moving without making him angry. "I can have a plate full of crepes for you by the time you get back."

He pushed himself from the table with an audible grunt and shuffled out of the kitchen like a chastised child, heading back upstairs to get dressed.

Kathryn put two pans on the stove so she could make the crepes quickly. By the time Dylan returned, she had a dozen crepes smothered with strawberry purée ready for him.

An hour later, they were on their way to the east side of the mountain.

Chapter Sixteen

Crows flew through the trees, cawing warnings to the smaller birds that were chasing them out over the water away from their territory. An eagle screeched triumphantly, soaring high above the forest, flying into the setting sun with a snake dangling helplessly from its talons. Crickets, beginning their songs of early dusk, chirped in chorus with the throng of frogs hiding by the water's edge. The breeze was warm; shimmering leaves fluttered in the light air. The river above rushed over the rocky face in a race to jump into the basin below forming a small, cold lake. A rainbow adorned the mist hovering over the base of the thirty foot cliff. Lush green ferns were gilded with a thin, glittering layer of dampness rising from the plunging water.

Setting up their tent on the shore opposite the waterfall, Kathryn unpacked their gear for an early night while Dylan built a fire in a well-used fire pit. The site, one he'd often used before, was clear and fairly flat. She made a pot of coffee and placed it on the rocks around the fire to keep hot. Dylan always liked a cup or two before going to bed. Spreading out a red blanket on a large grassy area, she began to lay out their evening meal.

Famished after the long trek through the challenging terrain of the forested mountain, they dug into the long awaited spicy fried chicken. The hike had taken longer than expected. Kathryn found that she was still a long way from being in shape for such an expedition. Despite the added activity she was now permitted, the time in the cell had drained more of her health than she had realized.

The serenity of the clearing infused them with a warm peacefulness. The river sang an exquisite symphony as it cascaded over the rocks and down the cliff into the basin below. Overcome by the majestic beauty of the area, Kathryn could almost forget whom she was with and the circumstance of their being together here in this Eden.

They arrived too late for Kathryn to swim in the cold mountain water. The damp coolness of the evening was approaching with haste. After supper, they leisurely roasted marshmallows over the open fire until the sun had fully set. Exhausted but exhilarated with the day's journey, an early night was an inviting prospect.

Once in the tent, Dylan zipped Kathryn into her cocoon sleeping bag, leaving only her face exposed. He slipped the cords of the tightened hood through the zipper, tying it so she could not work the zipper down from the inside and escape. It was a system he concocted to ensure himself a good night's sleep, while at the same time it would be easier on her than tying her hands and feet together for the night.

Kathryn had promised not to make any attempt to escape in trade for the minimum two days, but Dylan still wanted the added reassurance. Although freedom was still very much an issue, the urgency of it had diminished over the months. She controlled herself so as not to make any move that could be misconstrued by Dylan, and he, in turn, relaxed his vigilance and mistrust of her.

They fell into a quick, well-earned sleep. Awakened after only a short while later by the horrendous bedlam of Dylan's snoring, Kathryn tossed in futile agitation, unable to get away from the annoyance. The unbearable racket of grinding teeth was soon added to the snoring cacophony of his deep slumber. Although his combined noises robbed her of sleep, it could not steal the precious joy she felt from just being away from his house and his environment.

Dawn came early. The clearing was damp from the heavy dew combined with the waterfall mist. A pleasant coolness hung in the air, waiting for the sun to chase it away. Squirrels squeaked as they jumped through the branches all around, raining down the water droplets from the trees overhead. In the early hours, as Dylan started to wake, his sounds ceased and a stillness returned to the camp, broken only by the delicate songs of birds.

Patiently counting the endless minutes for Dylan to rise and release her from the bag, she reorganized her thoughts and plans for the day. Deciding to get Dylan his breakfast first, Kathryn wanted to go for an early swim. Kathryn longed for the chilly reminder of the ocean she missed so very much. After the swim, she intended to tell Dylan that she brought enough food for another two days if he wanted to stay.

Dylan began to stir in his bag, stretching and yawning with a great bluster of noise. He scratched his backside and leg with unusual gusto. Starting to thrash around, swearing and unzipping the sleeping bag as fast as he could, Dylan scrambled out and jumped to his feet.

Kathryn chuckled at the scene of a grown man stomping on the discarded sleeping bag in fervor while insisting that a gigantic spider had snuck into bed with him.

"Damn bugs! I hate them!" he exclaimed in a panic. Searching frantically for the culprit that had used him for its morning meal, Dylan's eyes swept the floor of the tent.

"Company?" she said, stifling a laugh that wanted to erupt into the cool air.

Dylan snorted as he knelt down on an insect-free spot of the floor and untied Kathryn's zipper, releasing her from the quilted prison. He hacked morning smoker's phlegm, straightened his clothes, and headed outside to relieve himself.

Kathryn, still chuckling, rolled up the bags and shoved them to the back of the tent. Yawning with an exaggerated stretch at the door of the tent, she then also headed outside for her morning regime before starting breakfast.

While breakfast was being prepared, Dylan wandered around the edge of the clearing. He heaved stones across the basin, challenging himself to a distance contest. Before each throw, he glanced back at the campsite, checking to make certain she was not abusing her freedom.

Kathryn called to him and he waved an exuberant acknowledgment. The smell of coffee floated over the camp, enticing his taste buds. It was his practice to eat immediately after waking. She had put him on a blood sugar-regulating diet since she discovered he had hypoglycemia. He was easier to live with if she regulated what he ate and drank, having experienced firsthand the unpleasant results of when his glucose level dropped too low. He was most unstable during these times, and the most dangerous.

On the blanket, Kathryn laid out poppyseed bagels, cheese, and fresh fruit. Everything was prepared. Dylan had insisted that nothing that she might use as a weapon be brought on the trip. It seemed that Dylan had gone out of his way to make the preparations for the trip as difficult as possible, hoping she would decide that it was too much trouble and want to stay home.

Spending weeks envisioning every possible scenario and detail, Dylan had insisted that every precaution be taken to prevent her escape. He kept a hatchet and knife attached to his belt and a rifle slung over his shoulder at all times to encourage her cooperation. Promising to kill anyone who happened along, he assured Kathryn that he would not let her go under any circumstance.

Running around the basin, Dylan trotted into camp wearing a large grin. His mood was light and pleasant. There was a twinkle in his eyes that too often was hidden by dark despairing shadows. He made a small protest of the healthful array of food she had chosen, but settled down and ate with zeal.

Wearing an emerald green bikini, Kathryn plunged into the chilly water. She swam hard, managing four laps across the small lake before climbing from its refreshing grasp. Goosebumps dappled her dripping flesh as she scampered onto the grass and into the tent to dry off and change into warm dry clothes. The temperature was pleasant, and when she emerged from the canvas bedroom, Kathryn was ready for hot coffee and breakfast.

"What do you think about staying another day or two?" she asked, sauntering toward him and drying her hair in a towel. Crossing her ankles, she eased herself onto the blanket beside his reclining body. Ignoring the slight frown resting over his closed eyes, Kathryn poured herself a cup of coffee and sipped at its welcome warmth.

"Don't know. It's a possibility I guess," Dylan mumbled. He stretched his interlaced fingers pillowing his head. "Why do you like the water so much? How come you don't sink when your feet don't reach the bottom?"

"I don't know, I've always loved the water. Swimming, diving, and boating... I love it. If I wasn't human, I think I would have liked to be a porpoise. You know, we could stay and explore the area. There's easily enough food for two more days. That way, we wouldn't have to rush back first thing this morning. It'd be like a holiday," she added, trying to convince him.

"Sure, I guess it wouldn't matter. We're pretty isolated here," he agreed, smiling, his eyes still closed. "And I guess there's no rush to get home. Sure. Sounds good."

Kathryn was overjoyed. She picked at her bagel and cheese and washed it down with another hot cup of coffee, contented to soak in as much of this paradise as she could.

The day was bright and hot from the noon sun. Kathryn spent the morning examining pinecones, fallen trees, and the tiny tracks of life at the water's edge. Wandering where she pleased, she kept within view of Dylan at all times. If she roamed a little further than he thought appropriate, he'd call her back as if he were training a dog not to stray.

Despite his constant vigilance, Kathryn enjoyed the water as she attempted to make up for the last year away from the ocean. As she swam leisurely on her back, the water was a refreshing contrast to the sunny day, and she was grateful for the special treat. Considering repaying him for his kindness, Kathryn decided to get him to talk. He appreciated having someone take an interest in him and his dark secrets.

Dylan needed to unburden his soul, piece by awful piece, hoping she understood what no one else could. To prove he was beginning to trust her, he seemed overcome with desperation to expose the demons that plagued him. He longed to be free of *their* strangulating hold and end *their* decades of tyranny in exchange for being held securely by Kathryn. Terror prevented him from talking about *them* at night, as *they* seemed far too large and numerous in the dark.

Kathryn returned to the campsite and poured two cups of wine from the five-liter keg, then checked supper. Earlier, she had placed two prepared foiled pouches of steak, potatoes, onions, and carrots into the ashes under the smoldering flames, letting them cook in the low heat for several hours. By the time she had finished her walk around the basin, the meat was tender and the pouches were ready to be served.

Dylan was surprised by the caliber of meal, commending her ingenuity and talents with each garlic-laden mouthful. After the early supper, Dylan laid more wood on the campfire, working it into a blaze ready to roast marshmallows—a personal favorite. He relaxed into a good attitude.

The smudge pot to keep away mosquitoes died down, inviting a myriad of insects to again plague Dylan. He was terrified of insects, and Dylan was prone to brutal insect harassment. They seemed to come out of nowhere to feed off him without mercy. Kathryn worked hard to convince him she could look after the problem and prevent the attack, and he hesitantly agreed to allow them to stay longer.

Dylan also had an unreasonable fear of large animals due to a vicious attack from a large shepherd chained up in his family's backyard. Kathryn labored tirelessly to calm his fears with each new snapping twig or rustling leaf. She was determined to enjoy as much time outside the house as possible.

First she allayed his fears about the actual size of wildlife skulking through the forest, making the giant bears shrink to chipmunks. Second, she pulled the food into the branches to convince raccoons and bears that there wasn't one thing worth eating where they slept. Third, she kept the fire going during the day, leaving the night shift to him, because he believed it was the only protection they had to keep the animals away.

However, doubting the validity of their safety, he kept his hand on the rifle every moment.

Two more cups of wine followed supper and Dylan felt pleasantly talkative. The days were longer this time of year, and that gave him more hours free from the battles of the night in which to talk about the only things that mattered. They laughed and talked while roasting marshmallows. The subject stayed light and meaningless. Tiring of the senseless nonsense he couldn't quite get a handle on, like the name of the little purple flowers around the edge of the basin or the different types of plant life filling the forest floor, he switched the topic to the ethereal value of life.

Kathryn agreed or disagreed as his features indicated the appropriate response. Taking a deep breath, she plunged into the taboo topic. "Tell me about the things that frighten you so badly," she whispered, her voice gentle and soothing.

His eyes searched her face for the reasons behind her words. Trust hesitantly replaced suspicion in response to a smile that slid onto her lips. He began to nibble his cheek, revealing his fear of where these words might take him. The nervous twitch of the tiniest muscles around his eyes and lips exposed the internal agitation beginning to rage inside.

"Help me comprehend what makes you so afraid. I want to understand, but you have to help me. Tell me what *they're* like," she said, hoping her sincerity would encourage him to open up.

Kathryn knew he hungered to talk, but the need only frustrated him as he proved unable to effectually express himself. Sometimes, he managed to stutter through his thoughts, but more often his fear of repercussion was stronger, forcing him into angry silence. Repercussions from what, she could neither fathom nor recognize. His uncontrollable outbursts had given her valuable snatches of insight, but he would never explain what was going on inside his head. She had no way of dealing with something she couldn't grasp, and there was still so many pieces of the puzzle she did not have.

Regretting now that she hadn't given more time to psychology, Kathryn was grateful that she at least understood layman concepts. Watching him twitch and stammer before her now, she realized that it was nothing close to the true depth of his insanity. The voices that plagued him indicated the possibility of a bipolar condition; his mood swings were as extreme as a manic-depressive; and he had the volatile instability of a bipolar problem. She didn't need to label it, but she did need to understand his particular illness.

Experienced analysis was a hopeless cause, and she decided that the only thing left to rely on was gut instinct. Praying she possessed enough natural instinct, Kathryn first needed to eliminate any physical cause for his problems.

"*Them*? You want to know what *they're* like? You have no idea what *they're* capable of. Sometimes *they* hurt me with such intense pain...the pain explodes inside me...like a volley of knives slicing through my guts...or a fire raging inside my head. *They* hurt me. *They* constantly prattle at me. Sometimes it's all I can hear. If you can imagine all the people in New York City shouting at the same time— that's what I hear." He sighed, remembering the pressure *they* exerted on him. "I get so tired of the pain...the noise that I finally give into *their* deal. But it's always a hard deal. *They* want me to find others to take my place. As long as someone is hurting, it's okay. If I hurt the innocent victim, *they* stop hurting me. *They* force me to do horrible things to others. *They* demand pain, feeding on it, like it's food. *They're* a sadistic bunch of bastards," he whispered, his voice growing distant and quiet.

"How often do you see *them*?" she asked, nursing the enamel-covered metal cup.

"All the time. *They're* always around. Since I was four, I would see *them* staring at me from the dresser mirror and the bedroom windows, always as a reflection. *Their* black eyes were hollow; translucent green skin was pulled tight over angular bones; scraggly white hair stuck out like a halo; *they* didn't have a neck or body, just faces. *They'd* watch me sleeping until sunrise. Translucent green hands would search for me. *They* crawl along the floor, raised up like giant spiders, feeling out every inch of the floor...looking for me...to hurt me." He started to tremble ever so slightly.

"Are *they* all green?" she prodded, pouring more wine into his cup, hoping to reduce his growing distress.

"Yeah, all of them. I've only ever seen two full-bodied ones— James and George. When *they're* whole, *they're* shades of gray. You can see color, but it's a gray color, like gray with a hint of red or blue. I don't know, it's hard to explain unless you've seen it. Sometimes, *they* look so normal *they* trick me. I remember once when was on a bus going to Syracuse—I lived in Rochester then—and a man came and sat beside me. I talked to him the entire way. We talked about everything. He was such an interesting man. He wore brown cords and a plaid vest. When the bus was pulling into the station, I looked out the window for just a minute to see the other buses. By the time I turned my head back to say something, he had disappeared. Poof! Gone! He was nowhere to be found on the bus, and they didn't have bathrooms in those days. I felt like an absolute fool. I learned afterward that it was one of *their* endless streams of mean and nasty jokes," he continued. As he talked, Dylan looked around uneasily, his eyes searching out every detail of the growing shadows surrounding their camp.

Kathryn stared into her cup, not wanting to see the dark, haunted glare that was taking root in his eyes. When he talked about *them,* his features became shrouded with terror. She could feel the tension growing inside him until it choked the air around him. Feeling uncomfortable, she again wished she were anywhere other than here. However, this mood swing was the next natural step in the process of his thinking, and she was getting used to the explosive depressions that attacked him. She had learned to stay quiet and out of his way when he was caught in their suffocating grip.

"It's gotten worse since I was a kid. There're more of *them* now. *They* terrorize me all night and all day *they* yell at me. Sometimes, *they* make rude jokes about the people around me, but most of the time *they* just threaten me. Always demanding pain, either from me or someone else. There's a price to pay for everything *they* give me. If I want to get *them* off my back for a while, I have to hurt someone else, you know, sacrifice them in my place." His voice became lower and fainter with each word, and his eyes grew more distant.

Kathryn felt sorry for him. She didn't understand what drove him to be the pathetic creature he was, but she did know there was something good buried somewhere under the ugliness he revealed. She could see the kinder side of him in the gifts he brought her. Each was chosen with special care, knowing exactly what she would like without asking. In a bizarre way, he did care for her very much.

"What I hate most are *their* hands. *They* crawl along the floor, then up the furniture, crawling...always crawling...ever so slowly. *They* come like a relentless legions of army ants and I want to run, to escape and hide where *they* can't find me. But I'm too afraid to go past *them*. So I sit on the bed, making sure to keep away from the edge, and I watch *them* come for me. *They* find me no matter how long it takes...and touch me...severed hands roaming over my body...horrible bony fingers examining me...." His tongue flicked in and out, dampening lips dried from panicked breathing. His eyes glanced wildly at shadows that loomed in the light of the campfire and exaggerated every bush and tree into a sinister creature.

Knowing how it felt, Kathryn shuddered at the remembrance of how he had examined her. She found it difficult to picture the horrors his words portrayed or understand the level of fear he experienced. *Can any of this be real or is it all imagined?* she questioned. It was a question she would have to find the answer to if she were to survive.

"I can't stand the hands. I have to keep off the floor so *they* won't get me...because if *they* get me...if all of *them* reach me...then *they'll* be strong enough to kill me." Dylan gulped loudly, the noise drawing her attention away from her own thoughts.

"How on earth did you ever function in the real world?" Kathryn asked, unable to see him in any type of normal situation or relationship. At times, he could manage to speak rationally, but she knew his sanity swung like a pendulum, and the string on which it hung was so taut it was ready to snap.

Dylan glared at her through strained, distant eyes. It was the look that said she was calling him crazy.

"I mean, it must have been difficult for you to see those things knowing others didn't. It must have been hard on you. People must have treated you differently because they couldn't understand," she stumbled.

Dylan hacked a dry cough. Reaching a hand for his rifle, he laid the weapon across his lap. One finger twitched perilously close to the trigger. The level of his paranoia increased as the fire died out and the shadows grew. Agitation clamped his jaw as he searched the ground for his enemies. His nervous, panted breathing said he was ready to give the order for her to jump out of the way at a moment's notice.

Pretending not to notice, Kathryn stretched and pushed herself from the ground. She sauntered to the piled firewood, grabbed a bundle, and headed back to the fire. Tossing a few logs onto the dying fire, she rubbed her arms as if chilled, and sat back on the ground beside Dylan. The flames licked at the dry wood and soon blazed into a comfortable fire. From the corner of her eye, she could see his finger relax its vigil near the trigger and his breathing slow to a more regular rhythm.

Everything between them was a contest. She could not afford to let Dylan discover that she was aware of his turmoil inside. He considered himself far too complex for any one person to understand. It was a great source of pride with him, and she did not want to strip him of that confidence. So she played the game, and he was either not aware of her deception or he chose to play as well.

"I had no friends. People avoided me. They treated me like I had a contagious disease or something. No one ever took the time to get to know me, or ask me how I was. No one ever wanted to be bothered with me. I tried everything to get attention. Once, when I was just a kid, I pulled out four of my own teeth to get my mother to hold me. But she wouldn't leave her card game with her friends. She told me to rinse my mouth with salt water and get back to bed. All I ever wanted was for someone to listen to me...someone to care about me and let me care about them," he whispered. His eyes became vacant, black pools as if he were in another time and place.

Dylan's hand wrapped around the rifle; he gripped it with all his strength. The barrel swung in a slow sweep, stopping only when it was aimed under his chin. Internal agony seared his features with a hopeless desperation. It was a look he often wore. Suicide loomed in his mind. This too was simply a natural step in the progression of his sharing himself. He had an unreasonable terror of exposure and momentarily preferred death over vulnerability.

"Well, now you have someone to talk to. You have me and I want to help you," she answered, reaching out a hand toward him, laying it gently over his quivering hand. Slowly, she cupped his hand and lifted it from the rifle. Kathryn clamped her palm to his, giving him the opportunity to *bond* with her.

Dylan looked down at her fingers and smiled at the comfort she offered. He raised his gaze and looked deep into her eyes, examining the contours and shadows of her face. Firelight danced on the thin film of moisture spreading over his eyes. A fleeting smile threaded across his lips before disappearing into the sadness that took final possession of his heart.

The forlorn little-boy look about him tugged at her sympathy. She couldn't help feeling sorry for him, couldn't help forgetting how she came to be here with him. The wine, the fire, the beauty of nature complete with fresh air, the croaking frogs...they all played with her thoughts until she no longer coveted the life she had so very long ago.

"I'm here for you, Dylan. You're not alone anymore," she added, squeezing his hand in hers. This wretched man sitting before her, fingering his rifle, was the only person she had known for over a year. Dylan was her whole life, because he had made *her* his entire life. In a way, they were committed to each other. There were things about him that were detestable, but there were also many things about him that were likable. They had grown together in a bizarre fashion over the past thirteen months, and it was that inexplicable bond that grieved her to see him suffer.

"You wouldn't be here for me if I didn't keep you here. You wouldn't give me the time of day if you weren't forced. If I didn't keep you away from everyone else, you wouldn't even notice me. I'm not stupid. I know you don't really care about me. No one ever has, except George. He's the only one. It's worth all the pain I go through, because I know no matter what happens, he'll always be there," he snapped, yanking his hand away from her. His eyes squinted as hate shot out toward her from the cold pit within his heart.

Kathryn didn't know what to say as his words jerked her back to cold reality. He was right. The reason for her concern was to play the game and survive. The game was in the web of insanity he wove. She would have to learn what dark shadows plagued him, memorize their intricacies, and convince him that she believed. Pouring more wine for them both, she decided on a more honest approach.

"It's true, if I had a choice I wouldn't be here. But I didn't have that choice. How I got here does not change the fact that, over the past year, I've grown...well, I've come to like you. You haven't raped me. You've given me more and more privileges, like taking me on this trip. You've done many things for me that you didn't have to. I can only respond to your kindness with concern for you. And I wouldn't ask if I didn't care," she rebutted, knowing the tone of her voice was important if he were going to believe her. She wanted to convey that she was hurt by his honesty. Drawing her eyes away from him slowly, she emphasized her hurt by staring at her fingers as they wrung her shirttail into a knot.

"You must think I am an idiot," he snapped in disgust. "You don't give a rat's ass about me. It's getting dark. We can't stay out here. Time to go to bed. We're going to leave first thing in the morning," he ordered with a curt tone. Fresh anger blazed in his eyes as Dylan tossed the contents of his cup into the fire. He sneered at the sudden splash of flame that brightened the night.

Kathryn stared at him with wide eyes and open mouth, shocked at herself. She actually was hurt by his words. Not knowing how or when it happened, she discovered that she had become fond of him and it upset her to be rejected.

Dylan rose, motioning her to do likewise. He insisted that she see to her last minute bathroom needs and get into her sleeping bag. As Kathryn walked by him toward the tent, Dylan snatched the toilet paper from her hands. He stomped off into the bushes himself, holding his rifle close to his chest.

For light, Kathryn lit a candle and adhered it to a rock. She climbed into her sleeping bag, zipped it up and laid back. Tired and ready for sleep, Kathryn drifted off before Dylan returned. It had been a good day, although she didn't get very far with Dylan. *But, there was always tomorrow, and then the day after that...*

Dylan stomped through the tent's opening. Screaming in a fit of uncontrolled fury, he kicked at the candle and the rock. The flame flickered as they flew through the air, extinguishing just before bouncing off the back wall of the tent.

"Are you crazy? You want to call every bloody ghost around? I told you about candles. *They're* drawn to the flame. *They* can see it a hundred miles away. I told you, everything is gray where *they* live. If you light a candle, the flame cuts through this world into *theirs*, and *they* have to check it out. It's like a bloody beacon! White candles are the worst. *They* swarm to it like moths. Don't you ever light a candle again. Ever! You hear me? Not ever!" he hollered, groping in the dark, on his hands and knees, looking for the cord to *tuck her in*. Not finding them, he gave up and just yanked her zipper as far as it would go.

Kathryn cowered in the bag as his ranting yanked her from the first level of gentle slumber. The wonderful evening chorus by chirping crickets eased her distress. Tomorrow was another day, and he would be in a different mood by then. Morning was always a fresh start with Dylan. It was a peculiar quirk he had. Over coffee, he would take an objective look at what happened the day before, but he rarely recalled the emotion. To keep his anger fueled, he would again work himself up into what he believed was the correct rage since he could not remember how he felt.

"I'm sorry, I forgot," she mumbled. He hadn't told her about the candle. The occasion had never arisen. She had found a box of emergency candles in a kitchen drawer and packed them because he hadn't bought a lamp for the tent. It was a rule that they be asleep before dark, so he didn't see the need for a lantern. It was an innocent mistake. She couldn't know he would react so unreasonably to such a simple thing as a burning candle.

Dylan flopped onto the floor, afraid to climb into his bag. He mumbled indistinct words about the spider lying in wait for him. Unable to bear the stress another minute, he lunged at the tent flap, zippered it shut, and scrambled to the corner opposite her head.

She couldn't decide if it was a natural spider or a *green one*.

Kathryn could hear his teeth chatter in the warm night. His fists thudded into the tent floor and hard earth. Without seeing him, she knew he was spiraling into a whirlpool of despair. She had seen him like this many times before. The sweaty odor of his terror permeated the small canvas enclosure. Sitting up in the dark, she forced herself to remain calm. The heaviness of Dylan's uneven breathing echoed in her ears.

"Let me help you," she whispered, her voice overshadowed by the rapid panting of his fear.

"Go away!" he shouted. "Leave me alone!"

Kathryn climbed out of her bag, reached her hand into the darkness, and felt for him against the tent wall.

"Leave me alone!" he screamed louder. His voice cracked with hysteria.

The urgent scrambling sounds of his hands and shoes scratched the canvas floor as he hid as far into the corner as he could go. The tent wobbled with the force of his fear.

"Katie?" he muttered with a desperate and barely audible voice.

"Yes," she said softly.

"Hold me, Katie. Hold me," he begged.

Kathryn eased herself into the corner where he huddled. Her hands found his legs, and followed his body past the rifle to his shoulders. She gently coaxed his trembling body into her lap and cradled his head in her arms. She rocked back and forth, humming a tune her mother used to sing to her when she had bad dreams.

Kathryn drifted off to sleep with Dylan still trembling in her arms and the waterfall playing a symphony of peace beyond the canvas.

Part Four

❧The Autumn ☙

Chapter Seventeen

Kathryn stretched under the warmth of the covers, not really wanting to get up. Last night, Dylan had insisted on staying up late to watch his two favorite videos. She had already put in a full day preparing the garden for winter and wasn't in the least bit interested in seeing movies she had already seen at least thirty times in the past year and a half. But he was insistent. They were his *feel good* movies, and he watched them whenever he already felt good or wanted to feel good.

Still tired, she snuggled under the blankets to squeeze in just a few more precious minutes.

Yesterday had been a good day. After rototilling manure into the garden, she covered it with a thick layer of straw and a sheet of black poly. The land gave a better yield than she had hoped, and so now she wanted to ensure an even bigger crop next summer.

As usual, Dylan watched her work from the ease of a hammock slung on a metal frame. He had no desire to learn gardening. He wore a thick thermal plaid shirt and sheepskin vest to ward off the cooling late October days. Lying back in the swinging net, he thumbed through the pages of one of the most revolting books she had ever seen, a book that had once belonged to his grandfather. He had already read the book twice, but it was his habit when he enjoyed something to savor it repeatedly.

Almost eighteen months had passed since Kathryn saw her family. The pain of loss had lessened, but some nights, tears still streamed down her cheeks when a dream of David and Meaghan wakened her. Hugging a pillow, she would rock herself back into a sorrowed sleep.

She had learned to put thoughts of her old life, and of the futility of this one, behind her. Most of her deliberations were concentrated on remaining pleasant toward Dylan and actively working at keeping his attitude peaceful. Except for certain nights when the old dreams still haunted her, she was able to maintain the charade of well-being with reasonable believability. She could lose herself in her work and become so tired nothing else mattered, especially Dylan and his eccentricities.

Since the camping trip four months ago, Dylan became obsessed with rules. These dictates were found in a book he alone could see. Some twenty years earlier, he had apparently studied its meticulous details for a lengthy period before it again disappeared back to *Grey Land* from whence it had originated. Instructions, which were inked in blood on hundreds of pages, regulated everything from home decor to the few emotions he was allowed to display. The book contained thousands of decrees that had to be memorized to become an honorable member of the *Land* he coveted.

The rules were complex and tediously precise: silverware had to be of a specific weight and design before he would use it; mirrors were only located in the bathroom; red and yellow were predominant colors in his bedroom; the walls of his room with painted with dual symbols resembling a blood red "F" outlined with white; plastic must be a certain weight, texture, hardness, and color, or it would be instantly thrown out; flowers could not be of the evil variety; clothes had to be a *proper* style and texture, and were layered no matter the season or temperature; furniture was placed in a specific way to diminish the shadows and shapes of night; objects had to face a specific direction. The list was endless.

If she broke the same rule twice, he flew into a rage and screamed about the cost of such errors—a price he alone was required to pay since he was the disciple. Because they were "joined," Dylan paid the cost for each of her sins, past and present, making certain she knew it was a burden he gladly claimed.

With each passing day, he became more religiously obsessed. Dylan surrounded himself with ceremonies and religious symbols that held hidden meanings he could not begin to explain to her. Kathryn wasn't remotely interested except she felt she must keep a close eye on this further plummet into a madness she could not understand. She was a regular patron at church in her hometown, but this religion Dylan followed was frighteningly bizarre.

He now woke before her, using the early morning hours to pray and sing chants at an altar assembled in the living room. The morning ritual ended by the time she called him to breakfast. His religion became an overpowering passion that consumed his every thought and action. Preaching to her continually, he wanted her to learn the intricacies of his world. He lectured her as she bathed, ate, worked, and tried to sleep.

By his own admission, things had grown worse for him. Nightmares plagued his sleep while visions haunted his waking hours. No longer allowing Kathryn from his sight, Dylan saw her as his only protection against the forces that tormented him. Screaming in the middle of the night, he would rage against the things crawling around his room. He pleaded with the walls, begging them to stop breathing, to stop their infernal swaying in and out. By hollering futile defiance at visions standing in his doorway, he kept her awake all night long.

Kathryn would unsuccessfully try to bury her head under pillows and blankets during his nocturnal encounters, but nothing would drown out his noise. Thrashing in her own bed until she could stand it no longer, she would finally kick the covers off in a fit of tired anger and stumble to his room down the hall. When she entered his open door, he would scramble away in a mad panic because, in his eyes, she appeared as a different ghoul each night. Making her way to him, Kathryn would sit on the side of the bed, reach out and take his hands. Her grip stayed firm as he fought her touch. Eventually, he would settle down and she would hold him in her arms, cradling his head against her breast. Then, as any good mother, she would hum while rocking him to sleep, continuing her duty until the gentle rumble of his snoring filled the room.

Dylan started to open up to her. His efforts were at first halting and disjointed, but progressed to nonstop repetition. During times of sharing who he was and why, his voice adopted an abrupt, flat tone, as though he were emotionally separated. His stories about himself and family were, at best, outlandish. They consisted of small fragments of events picked from random situations and woven together with curt, shocking words to elicit optimum reaction and sympathy from the listener.

Kathryn had difficulty deciding whether or not they were true. It was very difficult to believe that his family was as coldhearted as he portrayed. There had to be some truth in what he said, but it would take a lot of sifting to find it because she doubted he remembered things as they really happened.

In the last three months, his periods of lucidity were growing increasingly longer. Dylan insisted that he could hear her mind and attacked her for what he believed she was thinking. It didn't matter if he were wrong. He took great lengths to study every action, twitch and body movement she made, translating each one into a continual dialogue of thought and motive. His constant verbal rhetoric defied logic and normal response, making her feel as if she walked on eggshells twenty-four hours a day.

His nights began earlier as he spent more time trying to compensate for lost sleep. Terrified that she would try to escape, and, screaming that he knew of her plans to leave him, he increased measures to prevent the possibility. When his mood of paranoia escalated to such a level that it forced him to take specific action against her, Kathryn found it difficult not to loathe him. Growing unreasonably possessive of Kathryn, he locked her in the cage, allowing his fear of losing her to overshadow his need for her protection. He oppressed her and everything around him for days on end, growing more quiet and distant with each passing hour.

Kathryn complained about his renewed abuse of her. She tried to convince him that she had long ago accepted there was no place for her to go. Showing him the bruises caused by sleeping on the cell floor would cause him to feel instant remorse, but did nothing to improve her circumstance. All her protests meant nothing. Instead, they bounced off the wall Dylan had built around himself.

Unwilling to accept returning to the unbearable conditions of when she first became his *guest*, Kathryn decided upon a working solution to the dual needs of her proper rest and his comfort. She decided they would both sleep in her bed, and, if added assurance was required, he could handcuff their wrists together.

Dylan abhorred the idea. He wanted her close but he couldn't bear the thought of being so intimate. He objected to her suggestion with a raging vehemence.

Confused, Kathryn could not understand his reasoning. This man had watched her bathe and use the toilet, and had kept her naked a good part of the time. He had examined every inch of her body. She had held him and rocked him to sleep countless times. Privacy was an unknown commodity and she had no reason to believe she could ever expect it. Yet he drew the line on deliberately sleeping in the same bed with her.

Dylan fought the idea with unreasonable arguments. Repeating his illogical thinking in an endless refrain, he refused to be persuaded. They argued for hours, but Kathryn was adamant that she should not return to sleeping on a Plexiglas floor under any circumstance. She insisted he concede on this issue, because there was no other alternative available.

Dylan hung his head and stared at his feet as they scuffed at imaginary stones. When he finally agreed, she was shocked that he bowed to her authority. The decision made, she moved out of the cell once again, grateful to see the bookcase close behind her. Dylan shuffled sheepishly to her bed as if he were the one being forced into a compromising position.

The first night together, Dylan clung to his edge of the bed too nervous to breathe or move. The tension bristling within him made the entire night strained and unpleasant. Prepared for any physical advance he might make, she was surprised by his labored distance. It was as if he were afraid of her. A week later, feeling comfortable enough to demand her hand, he insisted it was his lifeline to the real world—a world he didn't understand but was terrified of losing.

Holding her right hand all night, Dylan slept on his stomach while forcing her to remain on her back. He clutched her hand under his body, not moving from that stiff position until it was time for his morning devotions. It was an awkward sleep at best, but both became accustomed to it, and after awhile, it was the only way he could sleep.

Occasionally, Kathryn insisted on being alone as a very rare privilege. He was haunted by horrifying terrors that had him cowering in the corner of his own bed until she was compelled to come in and lay down near him.

His paranoia increased daily. Fearing he might be lost forever inside a psychotic episode, she had to consider where that would leave her. *Can I overcome someone who is completely insane?* She wasn't sure. Already having witnessed exhibits of his superior strength, she was aware that people under mental duress tended to have increased strength. During her short stay on a psychiatric ward in Seattle, Kathryn had witnessed one notable ninety-eight-pound woman who ripped a sink off the wall. It had taken four interns to sedate the poor woman.

Adding to the limitation of his physical superiority, Dylan kept the house weapon-sterile—even the hangers could not be removed from the rods. He had thought of every solution before she could even come up with the possibility.

In one attempt to escape, Kathryn had tried to break a window, smashing it with the brass candlestick she just finished dusting. It was a sudden, desperate gesture, an impotent need to destroy something that belonged to him. An alarm immediately blared throughout the house. Dylan had not only barred the windows with steel, the glass was made of the same bulletproof Plexiglas as her cell. She could no more break out than someone could break into the house. He had run into the living room, upset and devastated by her attempt to leave, and walked her through the electronic precautions he had taken to prevent any such endeavor. That was the day Kathryn learned that the house was more secure than an armory.

Another time, while spring-cleaning the kitchen, she had tried to pick the lock on the kitchen door but discovered she had neither the necessary aptitude nor experience. Without weapons or tools, Kathryn could not afford for him to die or be lost in a mental catacomb.

Her nights passed with a certain amount of empty agony. Sometimes, she would wake up aching for David's touch only to remember it was Dylan who slept in her bed. At times, that didn't matter. She would squeeze his hand in hers, grateful for any human touch in the early hours of morning. Lost in weakening heartache, she would hear the distant waves of the ocean beat against the shore or smell the saltiness in the air...or hear Meaghan's sweet voice all out from her room down the hall—"Mommy! Mommy!"

Kathryn had to work at staying sane on a minute-by-minute basis. It was far too easy to slip into the spiraling madness right along side of Dylan. There were times when she prayed she too could become crazy so the pain of being his prisoner wouldn't touch her. But it was that anguish that kept her focused and spurred on, giving her the necessary will to fight.

Finally pushing herself from the comfort of bed, Kathryn slipped faded jeans over bare legs and headed down the hallway. Dylan still insisted she sleep in only a white T-shirt.

Today would be spent in the greenhouse. Hoping for a crop of fresh salad vegetables all winter long, she decided to plant a wide variety of seeds in prepared hothouse trays. It was her first experience with this type of gardening, and she was excited to see what could be produced. She had her doubts about a hothouse being plausible in the mountains, but Dylan allowed for special heating and glass to keep temperatures in the 50s.

Hungry, she decided to poach eggs for breakfast. Dylan no longer questioned her meal choices, but ate every meal with equal relish, happy to have the decision made. He rarely made a special request and that suited her just fine. As she set the table, she called to Dylan so they could get breakfast finished and she could get out to the greenhouse.

Pouring a cup of coffee, Kathryn sat at the table and watched the birds just beyond the clearing. The morning was cool. It would be an early winter this year. Sipping at the coffee cradled in her hands, she let her thoughts wander absently. She heard the sound of feet shuffling down the hall to the kitchen door.

Good, she thought, anxious to get the morning underway.

"Well, well. Good morning. And who might you be?" the strange voice laughed behind her.

Kathryn turned, dropping the cup from her hands when she saw the unfamiliar shape in the doorway...*the clear blue eyes that smiled; the short brown hair that meticulously stayed in the determined style; the slight, square frame that looked strong and intimidating; the broad nose that accented his almond shaped eyes...*

He was perhaps the most beautiful person she had ever seen in her life.

Chapter Eighteen

"Oh my God! Please, help me. I'm being held prisoner in this house by a madman," she whispered as desperate tears of relieved shock streamed down her face. Kathryn ran to the unfamiliar man in the doorway without really thinking about it. It was a natural reaction she would have acted upon toward anyone who was not Dylan. Kathryn had been cloistered for so long, she began to doubt that there were people still left in the world.

As she stood looking into this man's face, she knew it was a foolish move. This stranger was most likely Dylan's partner—the mysterious "George" Dylan talked about so often. Although she had learned that George had undertaken Dylan's education at a very early age, she had never seen the man. He had never dropped by, and, according to Dylan, there was no reason to expect his appearance in the future. George was *inside* Dylan, and that was the only contact he needed. As this man stood before her now, Kathryn thought Dylan probably meant the word *inside* as a metaphor referring to his close relationship with George.

She knew Dylan had no friends. There were never any visitors to his house. What little family he had lived back east, and they didn't keep in touch with one another. Dylan had not talked to his family since the day he left home over twenty years ago.

This anonymous man could be anybody, but she saw him as her knight in shining armor. He was the man who was going to scoop her up in powerful arms, whisk her through the door to his four-wheeled steed, and carry her off to freedom.

Overwhelming emotions charged through her, racing from paramount relief to riveting anxiety and back again. Her passions switched so quickly, Kathryn couldn't tell what she was feeling. Fear mingled with joy and caused her stomach to bind with nervous excitement.

The man's deep blue eyes flashed—strong, intelligent eyes that could evaluate a problem and straightaway find the most expedient, efficient solution. His thick, arched eyebrows underscored the frown chiseled into a strong, masculine forehead. He was a man who had seen trouble, but as his face lit up into a broad, gentle smile, she knew he was a champion. He would defeat her enemy.

Kathryn, too pleased at seeing another person, didn't consider proper caution. She decided instantly that she liked this man. She loved how smiling creases eased into long, deep dimples on either side of his full lips as he clicked his tongue and shook his head in a slow, amused way.

Perhaps, he didn't understand what I said? she thought, perplexed by his lack of concern for the perilous situation surrounding them. His smile captivated and troubled her at the same time.

"Where is he?" the strange man asked. His voice was strong and authoritative. The soothing, careful way he spoke put her at immediate ease. It told her that her life was about to change, and that change would come because of this man's intervention.

Kathryn envisioned the inevitable confrontation between Dylan and the stranger. This confidant, calm man could have no idea to what lengths Dylan would go to keep her. Dylan was not about to let someone simply take her by the hand and walk out the door. Dylan would put up a terrific fight, one she hoped he alone would not survive. She had to make this man understand the seriousness of the situation here.

"He has a rifle," she whispered, afraid to raise her voice. She didn't want Dylan to surprise them and perhaps overpower the stranger.

The man gazed around the kitchen, nodding his head in obvious approval.

"If we leave before he comes down, the police can come back for him," she gasped, urgent desperation crusting her whispers. "How did you get in? Did Dylan let you in last night?" As her eyes begged him to move toward the door, little beads of perspiration surfaced around them. She was anxious to leave the house.

"The house looks great! He's done a lot of work on the old place. Fixed it up nice. So where is he? Upstairs? Outside?" he laughed, ignoring her panic.

Shocked that this man did not seem to grasp the full weight of her words, Kathryn wondered if she might be speaking a foreign language. She tried to think through the man's hesitation. He seemed more interested in the decor than her plight.

Kathryn looked around, glancing over his shoulder to see if Dylan was coming through the living room. *Why can't this man understand we have to get out of here? He can worry about Dylan later when I'm far away and safe.*

Kathryn started to grab for his shirt collar to emphasize their need to hurry, but his sudden chilling scowl warned her away. His eyes blazoned with an instant hardness that evaporated as quickly as it had come. He laughed a hearty guttural roar, shook his head, and turned as he headed toward the staircase. She watched in stunned silence, suddenly unsure of her hero as he walked through the house with familiar ease.

He's not here to help me. He not only knows Dylan, he doesn't believe me, she realized in dismay.

"He's always been such a kidder. I see his friends have the same overdramatic sense of humor," he chuckled. "Mom always said Dylan and his friends were weird." Swinging his right foot onto the first step, he started to climb the stairs.

Mom. He said Mom. He must be Dylan's brother, her mind scrambled, trying to piece together the added clue to the puzzle. *If he's a brother, then he can't be George, and if he's not George, then he will help me,* she rationalized with an added dose of hope.

"This is not a joke. Your brother is a lunatic. He's kept me locked in this house for over a year. You have to help me get out of here," she screamed in as loud a whisper as she dared, pleading with the man as he climbed. She wanted to grab onto his leg and stop him from climbing, but the memory of the *look* stopped her.

Why doesn't he understand that as Dylan's brother, he has a moral obligation to help me? He can't just let me remain here under these conditions. No longer afraid of retaliation from Dylan, the urgent need to make this man understand her predicament loomed in her mind. She stumbled up the staircase after him.

The handsome stranger continued to head to the bedrooms, oblivious to the hysterical sobs behind him.

Kathryn gave up, turned and charged the front door in the hopes that this stranger had left it open or, at the very least, unlocked. Perhaps, with Dylan's attention distracted by a family reunion, she could escape unnoticed. Through blinding tears, she found more nails in her coffin.

"Dylan!" the man hollered, glancing back to see her pulling and kicking at the locked front door.

Dylan staggered from the bedroom in numbed surprise. Stopping at the head of stairs, he glared down at the uninvited and obviously unwelcome guest. "What the hell are you doing here, James?"

The brother halted midway up the staircase and laughed, a long, villainous chortle from his gut. "Glad to see you too!"

Kathryn cried. Hanging her head low, she shuffled to the foot of the stairs and slumped on the bottom step in total defeat. The deep-seated hatred brewed fresh and bitter within her as she glanced at the two men who were now both her enemies.

"I wanted to see what you were doing with the old homestead. I see you've made some improvements. Nice work," the strange man grunted.

"Planning on staying?" Dylan grimaced, ignoring the compliment. Dylan's eyes squinted as if the thought of James staying was particularly distasteful to him.

"Why, yes, I am. I assume that won't be a problem," he said through a grin. Turning on his heel, James descended back down the stairs.

"It is a problem. There's no room. I've made some changes. Took out a bedroom. You can't stay." Dylan scuttled down the carpeted stairs after his brother.

Kathryn jumped out of the way and stood in a bewildered daze in the middle of the front hallway.

"I want a cup of coffee. Are you coming down, or is it still too early for you?" the brother snarled in response to Dylan's attitude. Bit by bit, James was losing his earlier cool composure to an irritated annoyance.

Dylan followed the man into the kitchen, with Kathryn a resigned distance behind them.

Appalled by the escalated situation, Kathryn cleaned up the spilled coffee from the table. Rinsing the cloth under the kitchen tap, she remained in shock at the turn of events. Her actions were slow as if she were moving against the water's current. Emotionally crushed, she carried two mugs and the pot of coffee to the table. Feeling like an unwilling bondservant, she poured a cup for each of the men. Returning to her position by the sink, waiting for orders, or at least for someone to make some sense of this new situation, she started to tremble as a cold chill washed through her.

In one fluid motion, the two men stretched back and swung their feet up to rest on opposite chairs. Dylan pulled out a cigarette from a half-full pack sitting on the table. He held the thin tube between nervous, twitching fingers, and offered the pack to his brother as a courtesy he obviously didn't feel.

"Got any rum for the coffee, or are you going to drink it flavorless?" the man asked with a certain mixture of sarcasm and command in his voice. He waved the pack away, refusing his brother's dubious generosity. Running well-manicured fingers through his short curly hair, James let out a relaxed sigh and took his own pack of British cigarettes from his pocket.

"What are you here for, James?" Dylan snapped, already tired of the game they were playing. Dylan could not take his eyes off the other man. Shooting malicious contempt at James, it was obvious Dylan wished his look could kill. There was an underlying fear of his brother that cracked in Dylan's voice, but he tried to hide it behind a false bravado.

"I'm here to take my rightful position as head of the house. I'm here to take over the estate," he answered in a cool, confident voice.

James slowly exhaled white smoke into half-a-dozen perfectly shaped circles into the air between himself and his brother.

Dylan bristled from the obvious slap in the face. He had tried to perfect that little smoke ring trick since Kathryn knew him, and for years before that, she suspected. Hate planted itself on his pursed thin lips, and Dylan's dark scowl frightened her. She could see the depths of anger into which he was plummeting, perhaps the deepest and quickest that she had witnessed.

"You gave up that right years ago, James. This is my house and no one is going to take it away from me," Dylan snarled as he clenched his hands into tight little balls.

"Mmm. No, I don't think so. I'm the four star brigadier here, not you. Surely you know that makes me top dog, old son," James said through a deep-throated laugh. He was a man who didn't dwell on the darker side of life and its problems because he just took what he wanted, not caring about the cost to others. His laugh was cold and evil, rising from his stomach with robust enthusiasm.

Kathryn refilled Dylan's cup and again stepped back to the sidelines. Neither man seemed to notice she was even in the same room. She wondered if James thought she was simply a spacey, submissive girlfriend. She loved his voice. His tone had deep resonant sounds and it sent a shiver up her back. Unable to help herself, she liked to hear him speak with his curt British accent.

She studied the two men as they parlayed and lunged at each other. Only their similar style of clothing suggested they were brothers. The two men were as opposite as night and day. Dylan was much more slender and a head shorter than James. Dylan's eyes were darker and didn't have the glint of steel flashing from an arrogant, mischievous stare. James' countenance was fair, almost transparent white with a hint of ruddiness suggesting he must have been a redhead in his youth. James, who had a much sturdier build than Dylan, possessed a lighter attitude. He didn't have to struggle with self-identity like Dylan. James knew who he was without any hesitation, and he expected everyone else to recognize his station as well.

The men argued, laughed, and chatted, reminiscing about things she could not understand. They talked about theologies and abstract inconsistencies as if they were old college buddies sharing a keg of beer and a large steak. To her surprise, Dylan had laughed more in the last half hour than she'd heard him laugh in the entire time she had known him.

"What do you want, James?" Dylan finally shouted. Tiny veins throbbed at his temples. His face was flushed with a deep hue of red. He jumped to his feet in a sudden, threatening gesture, with hopes of intimidating his older brother.

James remained unruffled, smiling in a queer, knowing manner. He had the upper hand and enjoyed shoving it in Dylan's face. The more agitated Dylan became, the more James enjoyed himself.

"Why, brother dear, I wanted to come home and be with my family. I've been away far too long. Haven't you missed me?" James chuckled, already knowing the answer. He turned and signaled for her to fill Dylan's cup with more coffee.

His earlier charm quickly faded. Kathryn was beginning to suspect that James was as crazy as his brother. She again filled the cup and then moved back to her place by the sink, waiting for the outcome of something she didn't understand.

Perhaps James is just biding his time, waiting for the right moment to help me. Surely, he can't condone Dylan's treatment of me? Kathryn thought with growing shock. Shifting from one foot to the other, she became more uncomfortable the longer the two men talked.

"No, I haven't missed you. In fact, I don't want to see you or anyone else for that matter. I've behaved myself. I don't deserve this intrusion into my affairs," Dylan screamed, unable to contain his agitation within socially acceptable limits.

Dylan lit another cigarette from the tip of the last one. Kathryn wondered what kind of values these two men had learned at home. Trying to envision their parents, she speculated about what kind of examples the boys must have seen. *Perhaps I've been a little unjust with Dylan. Maybe he's told me more truth than I cared to believe. How else could one family have created two monsters?*

"It doesn't matter. I have the claim that gives me jurisdiction over everything. I was away in England. You were here. But now that's all over. I've found you. I know you tried to hide, and you were very clever about it, too. But now I'm here and I'm in charge," James sneered, knowing his carefully chosen words were digging right into Dylan's heart. "You and your girlfriend here are mine for the taking. And I plan to do just that as soon as possible."

Dylan's eyes opened wide in horror.

Kathryn's heart skipped a beat as her mouth fell open. James was crazier than his brother.

"I...I...I..." Dylan moaned, his eyes distant and empty.

James looked at her over his shoulder, and then back at Dylan. He shook his head in a slow rhythmic sweep, his tongue clicking out a knowing beat of "Tsk, tsk."

Kathryn wanted to run screaming to the table and beat her circumstances into James' thick skull, so he would understand that she was not Dylan's girlfriend. She was not even his friend. She was his prisoner and his brother was a lunatic. Surely James did not fully appreciate his brother's state of mind. Perhaps Dylan's sickness was a new development in James' mind.

Dylan slammed his fists against the table in angry defiance. He did not want to simply hand over his entire life to James. But without James, he could not stay in the house. Without the house, he had no prison. Without the cell and wilderness, he could not hold her hostage. He would lose her forced love, and in his eyes, that meant he would lose everything.

"Dylan, Dylan, Dylan. She's not your girlfriend, is she? You've done it again, haven't you? When will you ever learn?" James asked with a sniff.

Chapter Nineteen

Kathryn smashed her fists against the wall of mirror. Kicking at the glass in a last-ditch effort to release pent-up anger, she turned, disheartened, and slumped to the floor. The smooth, cool surface of the mirror supported her back that had grown stiff from infuriated indignation.

She hadn't gone into the cell willingly. Fighting them like a wildcat, she inflicted several deep scratches and bites on Dylan's arms and hands. James stayed away from her wrath and supervised her imprisonment from a safe distance. The injuries didn't matter. Nothing she did could stop them. They tossed her into the room like a discarded sack of potatoes, watching and laughing as she sprawled face-first onto the floor in a humiliating heap. She could hear James' boisterous voice fill the room with cruel jokes at her expense before they shut the door, sealing her into isolated silence.

She may have known theoretically how to hurt a man, but in the face of blatant opportunity, the knowledge was useless without practical experience. In retrospect, she wished she had made the time to take defense classes when she had the opportunity at college. David had taken up her spare time, and when she wasn't with him, studying for two majors was her main focus. Unfortunately, self-defense simply wasn't a high priority back then.

Dylan had changed. She was so afraid of him in the beginning and was still frightened when he lapsed into one of his *moods*. During the last year, he had grown softer and gentler, almost likable. He treated her with a certain degree of unexpected kindness and respect. It was a subtle change she could not explain.

However, Dylan, the man who had ripped her from the comfort of her own life and subjugated her to a prisoner profile, had now himself become the unwilling prisoner of James. He was totally subservient to his older brother, making her wonder what hold James had over Dylan. There was no question of the pecking order—James was the unchallenged master of everything.

Apparently, *everything* now included Kathryn. Dylan had relinquished ownership of her with visible reluctance, but, nevertheless, unquestioned submissiveness. He had looked at her through a broken, longing gaze as he agreed with James that, since she could not leave the house, Kathryn was therefore part of the estate. This meant if Dylan left, he had to leave her behind. As if to cement the agreement, she was dragged, kicking and screaming, up the stairs and locked in the cell.

When she first saw James, it seemed as though he simply appeared in the kitchen doorway. There had been no dramatic sound to announce his entrance. There had been no warning of his presence. She had been thrilled to see him, but her excitement about the possibilities he presented overshadowed what she otherwise should have been able to see immediately. She didn't think anyone could be worse than Dylan, yet in the short time she had spent with James, he had proven that theory wrong.

Once together, the two brothers talked about her as if she were not in the same room. That had infuriated her. She served them coffee, cooked them breakfast, and washed their dishes while listening to their pathetic bickering about the ownership of the house or her. James did not even have the decency to eat what she had prepared. Instead, he only laughed as he watched her throw out his coffee and scrape off his plate.

James stated his claim to the estate while Dylan whined and argued about the unfairness of James' position. It was more than she could bear. They talked about her as if she were an object with less value than the stove she cooked their food on.

Dylan lamented her loss to his brother, but James refused to back down. He didn't have to. Dylan seemed used to being controlled by his brother, as if it was a war that had long ago been fought and lost.

If Dylan was not going to fight, Kathryn decided she would. However, finally summoning the courage to express her indignation to the two brothers, she was rewarded with instant lockup without a chance to eat.

Kathryn wondered what was going to change under the regime of her new *master*. She harbored the uneasy feeling that however things changed, it would, without any doubt, be considerably worse for her.

She thought back to the few attempts she had made to escape under one captor. *Whatever will I do under two?* Kathryn pleaded with the silence of the Plexiglas cell. *That is, of course, if Dylan is allowed to stay.*

To her surprise, Kathryn was imprisoned for only a short time. Dylan came for her by early evening.

The eerie "whoosh" of the door opening woke her from a light sleep. Without uttering a single sound, Dylan stood in the shadowed doorway and motioned for her to come. His eyes were black and haunting. Looking very much like a whipped dog with bowed head and rounded shoulders, he attempted to shield himself from the exposing brilliance of her prison.

The tormented shadows that accented his pale pallor made her apprehensive—a feeling she had almost forgotten. She hesitated to leave the frail security of her cell, but with two of them to contend with, she knew better than to disobey or delay.

Dylan reached out and grabbed her by the elbow as she passed him. Drawing her arms behind her back, he slapped the cuffs around her wrists. Pushing her ahead of him with rough insistence, he forced her to keep moving at a quick pace. Ushering her down the stairs and into the living room, Dylan signaled for her to sit on the plush footstool already placed close to the fireplace.

Pivoting on one heel with the bravado of a retired soldier, a grim depression hovered over Dylan as he marched to his own reserved place. He strode to the sofa opposite James and dropped on the cushion with a heavy grunt. His eyes were lowered with shame. Sheepishly afraid to look up from a predetermined spot on the carpet, he chewed his lower lip until spots of blood oozed from the self-inflicted wounds.

Kathryn stared at Dylan, unable to combat the concern she was feeling for him. Confused as to why she should be so worried about him, Kathryn wondered if they were both in the same danger.

James exuded an air of cool command. The musical clink of ice cubes knocking against the wall of a glass filled the silence as James swirled chilled Scotch inside the crystal tumbler held loosely in his hand. His piercing, frosty eyes revealed a deep-seated rage lurking just under the surface.

The very sight of him caused an icy shiver to creep up Kathryn's already quivering spine. The stars shone brightly through the windows set into the cathedral ceiling of the living room. Light from the blazing fire danced off the glass around the large room like a gentle visual echo. Lamps were low and romantic. It was a beautiful evening, one that should have been shared under better circumstances.

The presence of James shattered the ambiance of the room. Kathryn had thought earlier that he was a handsome man, but studying his features now, she decided she hadn't looked very closely. His face was cold and lifeless, like Dylan's, but with an added intensity of cool rage and overpowering disgust for everything.

The two brothers, side by side, had striking differences. Both had intelligent eyes, but Dylan's were softer and less menacing. Dylan looked almost effeminate beside his rugged older brother. James had dark chestnut hair that contrasted his pasty color, and although he looked pale, he still had a healthier appearance than Dylan. His thick, curly hair was kept professionally, unlike Dylan's self-inflicted hairstyle.

Watching the motions and antics of both men, it was plainly visible that Dylan was a "wannabe" of his older brother. She could see the despair in his eyes as he looked at James, viewing his brother as having reached the pinnacle he himself could never attain. Dylan propped one elbow on the sofa arm and moved his fingers in mock calculation as if he were having a lively discussion with someone she could not see. His eyes drilled into the invisible spot on the carpet as he let his thoughts slide into oblivion.

James was the first to break the heavy silence hovering over the room. Kathryn stretched the stiffness from her back and sat taller on the stool, preparing for the inevitable worst. She expected them to disclose her already-decided fate, wishing she could fill her ears with anything to keep the sound of their words from reaching her. Anger collided with anxiety as the fire intensely heated her back, but couldn't stop the ravaging shivers coursing through her.

How dare they decide my life. She felt like a chained dog about to be put down by a disgruntled owner. There was no way she could fight them. Impotent emotion left her weak.

"So, Kathryn. Dylan tells me you were married and had a child. Is that right?" James gave a grin that dug into her flesh like tarnished spurs. The searching gaze of his smugness robbed her of every small dignity she had regained over the past nine months.

"Yes, I am married and I have a daughter," she said, unsure of exactly what was expected. If possible, Kathryn didn't want to say anything to further jeopardize her position. Unwilling to reveal any more about herself than what Dylan might have already shared, yet she didn't want James to steal what little self-respect she had left.

Dylan stole an awkward glance at her from the corner of his eye. Cowering on the sofa, he wrung his hands together in utter defeat. Shadows playing on his drawn features accented the darkness of his inner doubts.

Kathryn wondered what happened during her afternoon incarceration. Whatever it was, Dylan was the obvious loser. It was odd to see him this way. Concern again tugged at her heart, making the doctor in her surface more than the prisoner. Regardless, it still angered her to discover that she had been held hostage by an impotent little man, whose only power and authority had been usurped.

"No, I believe you *had* a family. But that is not the issue here. The issue is that Dylan has told me you and he have not had sex. He swears that there has been no physical activity of any kind between you. Is that true?" he asked point blank. His voice was hard and uncompromising. James sipped at the Scotch in his glass, grimacing with appreciation at the biting liquid. His cold, calculating eyes cut through people as if they were transparently inconsequential.

Kathryn felt soiled under his gaze. Shuddering uncontrollably, her body tried to repel the disgust brewing inside her heart. Eyeing his Scotch with envy, she wished he would offer her one. But he didn't care to consider her with the same kindness or consideration Dylan usually did. James hadn't even offered his brother one, which was probably wise under the circumstances. Dylan looked very much like he'd had too much to drink already.

Her mind raced over the possibilities of what James might want her to say. It was difficult to ascertain what answer was most acceptable. If she agreed with Dylan, which happened to be the truth, perhaps James would see it as grounds for her release. *Maybe,* she hoped, *he's looking for reasons to clean up Dylan's mess in the least scandalous way possible.*

Dylan shifted nervously in his seat as his bloodshot eyes again searched for that precious spot on the carpet. His fingers wrapped around each other. The perspiration on his skin began to glisten in the dancing light of the fire licking hungrily at the well-laid logs. His eyes were sunken and hollow. Their large, black pupils left no color against the whitish background.

"Yes, it's true. I have not willingly had sex with Dylan, and he has been enough of a gentleman not to force himself on me," she sighed, not appreciating the vein of discussion. There was something in James' voice she couldn't quite identify. The worry about Dylan's welfare as he gulped with a loud, choking repercussion, refused to be dismissed from her thoughts. It was obvious that he was not doing well.

Kathryn hoped James might see Dylan's lack of excessive abuse toward her as grounds for release. She could argue that, without any visible proof, the police might disbelieve her story of being abducted and held prisoner for over a year. There would certainly be psychological damage, but she had no idea how deep it was without being able to attempt to fit into normal life. There had been no ransom note which would collaborate her story. Without sufficient evidence or any identities, the police would most likely not pursue them on criminal grounds.

After all, I don't know Dylan's last name, his address, or even what state I'm in, she rationalized, feeling good about the lack of knowledge for the first time. *I guess everything does have a good side. Hell, I don't even know what country I'm in.* She was suddenly aware of the total ignorance of her position.

He might have kept her prisoner, but she did not look physically abused, considering the year-long ordeal. She had scars from the bullets, but the wounds had been treated and were well healed. The police might consider the injury the result of a lovers' disagreement that was taken care of medically, or even by herself. They would simply not believe her for lack of evidence. She was sure of it and she had to make certain James also understood that. They might say she ran away from home and changed her mind after her lover abandoned her.

It was a plausible theory. James would see that.

Dylan again coughed and hung his head in trembling hands. His puffy, reddened skin twitched frantically. It looked clammy and cold. He nervously scratched at himself as though he was suffering from an invisible reaction.

As if she too was catching his fever, she became increasingly agitated. Kathryn found it difficult to stay on the appointed stool.

"Well, I'm glad to hear that," James said, sighing as he crossed one leg over the other. He filled his glass almost to the rim with another healthy quantity of Scotch, stirring the ice cubes with his pointer finger. With emphasized patience, he sucked the liquid from his finger with a loud, annoying smack. James aimed a broad, upper-hand smirk at his younger brother as if he had just revealed a dark, ugly secret from Dylan's closet.

"Does that mean you'll let me go?" Kathryn asked hopefully, trying to look grateful before the fact as an added encouragement to James. *If they let me go, I couldn't care less if Dylan was coming down with the bubonic plague.*

"No, I don't think so. We can't have you running off and putting my poor brother here in prison, can we? No, I have much better things arranged for him. However, the information does mean that you haven't been spoiled," James said in a smug tone. He swallowed a large mouthful of Scotch, swishing it around in his mouth with a loud splashing sound as if he were absurdly checking the body and bouquet of a fine wine.

"Spoiled? What do you mean?" she asked, angry that he was being such a pompous jerk. His answers were more elusive than Dylan's ever were, and it was beginning to irritate her.

All the work she had accomplished with Dylan was slipping away. With James now in the picture, she would have to start at the beginning again, but she doubted she could ever get the upper hand over this man. Dylan was weaker and lacked the confidence of his older brother. Time would have allowed her to use Dylan's own weakness against him, but how would she find a chink in the armor of this hardened master?

Maybe I can pit one brother against the other.

Dylan sat on his legs in an attempt to make himself as small and unnoticeable as possible. The sweat was flowing down his face. His hollow eyes began to look despondent and distant.

. "You mean, you don't know?" James slapped his knee and sat up to make the laugh full bodied from the depths of his diaphragm. He guffawed and hooped, truly pleased with the discovery only he, and perhaps Dylan, understood.

Missing the meaning behind this private joke renewed her indignant anger.

Dylan's eyes shot heavenward, and, for a moment, Kathryn thought she could see his lips moving quickly as if mouthing a prayer, or perhaps a curse. He wanted James to finish his agonizing torture.

"Oh God, this is precious," James laughed in a gut-wrenching, cackling snort that lasted far too long to be natural.

The deviant sound bristled the hairs on the back of Kathryn's neck. Her entire body stiffened against the offense of what James' considered humorous.

Dylan moaned, shaking his head back and forth in outright despair. His dark circled eyes glared at his brother. Hate from his murky soul mirrored on the agonized expression on his face. He balled his hands into damp fists, raising them in mock defiance against the insult of his brother. It was apparent that he wanted nothing less than to wear his knuckles down on James' face. The utter loathing for his older brother flushed his skin with a darker hue of red. It was equally obvious that he could do nothing to vent his feelings as impotence atrophied his responses and locked his jaw into a violent grimace.

Kathryn prepared for an altercation between the two, hoping she alone would emerge as victor.

"How much do you know about my dear brother? Not much, I imagine. He likes to keep his ugly little secrets to himself, that one. Likes to have everyone think he's some big, bad dude just strutting around like a ravaging panther preying on innocent victims," James said. He was the only one enjoying himself. Pouring yet another Scotch, he drew a deep drag on a cigarette and again let the smoke drift from his mouth in perfect circles.

Each circle infuriated Dylan more until Kathryn thought he might erupt like a geyser of unvented fury.

"Dammit, I am an innocent victim!" Kathryn screamed, wishing she were not so helpless. Dylan was far too careful about giving her any chances of escape. She had waited for over a year for an opening to happen, but each opportunity was fraught with too large of a degree of risk, making it unacceptable and distasteful.

"Yeah, yeah. So I've heard. Spare me the details. No one is innocent. Everyone gets exactly what they deserve. Or hasn't Dylan taught you that yet? It was the first lesson he learned, wasn't it Dylan? Remember? You kept whining that no one loved you and George told you that you got what you deserved. Remember that? Or have you forgotten? Remember how they used to scare the hell right out of you, until you'd lose control and scream at the mirror, and the window. Hell, you were always hollering about something when you were a kid," James said, sarcastic disgust edging his voice. He grinned broadly. James was enjoying his moment in the spotlight at Dylan's expense. "Although no one believed you. God, you were a riot. Always coming up with those weird things, like the time you had everyone in the neighborhood burning those ridiculous bulrushes in some mystical ceremony. Didn't you ever feel embarrassed by the things you did?"

Dylan glared at his brother through black eyes of passionate resentment. His jaw clenched into a red line of raging emotion that spent what little strength the fever did not consume. His entire body quivered with the effort to keep himself together and refrain from lunging at James, and Kathryn found herself wishing he would attack his brother. The distraction might prove beneficial.

Kathryn pulled her eyes away from Dylan, afraid she would tip Dylan's possible hand of action. She looked back at James. A gulp lodged in her throat. His eyes were stripping off her clothes, making her feel dirty and used. His look felt corporeal, making her tremble under its power. She could not shake the ugly sensation and intrusive touch left on her skin in the wake of his ogling stare.

"I have to go to the bathroom," she whispered, shuddering from the rape of his eyes and begging for permission to get out of the room.

"You aren't the first one, you know. Dylan keeps hoping for some *savior* because he can't admit his particular brand of perversion. He seems to think that if he can get someone to teach him a different way, he'll change by osmosis and be free from all the dark, ugly feelings living inside him. What a joke! Nothing stops the cancer. The *feelings* control everything you do. They have their origin in the *Grey Land*, and they eat away at your soul until there's nothing left of you. You either go along with the need, feeding its every burning demand, and live a long and eventful life, or you fight the insatiable urges and die young and miserable. Dylan here, well, he just wants to betray what is inside him and die early. I admit all my perversions. I have an abundant appetite for life, and I live it to the fullest. I do whatever I want when I want with no remorse. I tell myself the truth. I don't have to lie to feel good, like Dylan here, who doesn't feel good even with the lie. Do you, Dylan?" James asked, his eyes drilling through the walled barriers Dylan put up to protect himself.

Dylan snorted his servile affirmation and looked out the window on the far wall, avoiding his brother's eyes. Perspiration bathed his forehead, and he swiped at it absently. Fidgeting on the sofa like a naughty child, he wanted to lash out and beat someone, or run away from the confrontation altogether.

She knew the feeling only too well. If James wasn't here, she had no doubt Dylan would beat her. He always did when he felt this cornered. He could resist until a certain point, but then he would have to give into the *voices* that nagged him and the need that consumed him. And all the while he was hitting her, he would apologize for hurting her, explaining to her that the pain he was inflicting on her body was by far less than what *they* were doing to him...and he couldn't stand *their* pain any longer. Luckily, that had happened very few times in the last six months. She had learned how to pacify him before he lost complete control.

The cuffs around her wrists began to ache as the metal dug into her skin. Dylan always tightened them too much. "I really do have to go to the bathroom," she repeated, trying to make her tone more tender.

"Well, what shall I say? Do you want to know all about my dear, little brother here? Or do you just want to believe the lies he's told you?" James asked, oblivious of her request.

By the superior way James was sitting, Kathryn thought that he would look more at home wearing a satin smoking jacket, black slacks and ascot. His movements were easy and sophisticated, but his words were boorish and demeaning. She found her dislike for the man growing, making it more difficult to sit and listen to his verbal diarrhea.

"You're as crazy as your brother," she muttered, wishing she were not witness to this parlor game James insisted on playing. "Listen, I really have to pee! If you don't let me go, I'll just do it right here."

"As much as I would like to see that, Dylan, take her to the bathroom and wait for her," James ordered, waving his hand to dismiss them from his presence as if he were lord of the manor.

Dylan rose unsteadily, his hands holding the sofa to support himself. Easing himself to a steady stance, he motioned for her to follow. His head was bowed and his gait was slow as he led her up the stairs. His left hand clung to the banister with visible desperation, as if he'd fall down if he didn't use the railing as a crutch to pull himself up the stairs.

She followed the obligatory two steps behind until they were well out of earshot of the living room. Catching up to Dylan with one extended pace, she whispered in his ear with hushed tones.

"If you let me take off the cuffs, and promise to let me go, I'll help you overtake James. He can't beat us both. Together we can take him. Then you can let me go. We can both be free. You will have the entire estate to yourself and I can go back to my family. We can both come out of this thing a winner, but only if we work together," she whispered, desperation coating her words with the urgency of their situation. Teaming up together was her only opportunity to come out of this thing. It was the only chance for either of them. She hoped Dylan would realize that and help her.

Dylan stopped at the top of the stairs without warning. He looked deep into her eyes with a vacant, eerie glare and shook his head in a slow, agonized, hopeless gesture. She could not remember ever seeing him look so awful. It was as if he had already decided that he could not stand any more of what was happening to him.

He reached out his hand and yanked her elbow toward him. He moved his face so close to hers she could smell the pungent odor of coffee mixed with stale beer on his breath. Unwashed sweat mingled with faded cologne and heavy smoke, giving his body a sharp, acidic air that she found repugnant and nauseating on an empty stomach. But she stood her ground and refused to take a step back in case it offended him.

As her stomach lurched, Kathryn realized she hadn't eaten all day. They hadn't bothered to feed her when she was in the cell.

Dylan pursed his lips as if he were going to speak, but changed his mind and pushed her into the bathroom. Following her into the room, he closed the door behind them, reached in his pocket and pulled out the key to the handcuffs. He undid one hand and leaned against the sink to steady himself, unable to unlock the other cuff. Kathryn headed to the toilet, concerned with how pale Dylan looked.

"Dylan, say something," she begged. Bells and whistles blared in her head as her doctor's instinct sounded the danger alarms. There was something seriously wrong with Dylan and she had no idea what it was, except that he was quickly losing control. By the look in his eyes and the slowness of his speech, she suspected it was drug related.

"What makes you think that I could turn against my brother? Either way, I lose you. If I help you, you leave me, and if I don't, he takes you. It's a no-win situation for me. I lose no matter what happens. If I go with James, I don't go to jail. Maybe he'll keep me around so I can at least be near you. But the point is a moot one anyway. Nothing matters now," he said in a voice so low it was as if he didn't have enough energy to speak and breathe at the same time.

Kathryn grew alarmed at his appearance. He looked paler than before as the color completely drained from his face. His eyes were glazed and dull just before they rolled back into his head. His hand shot out to grip the counter a little too late. His knees buckled and his body deflated, causing him to slip to the floor in slow motion.

Stunned, Kathryn rushed over to the body of her unconscious guard as her physician instincts took control of her actions. His skin was clammy and cold, almost rubbery to the touch. Kathryn opened his eyelids, but he remained unresponsive. His pulse was slow but strong.

"Overdose. You idiot. You took an overdose of pills. You bloody coward. Is suicide the best way out? If it was, I would have taken that escape myself, but I'm a fighter. I want to live. And you just bloody well blew my chance by taking your own life," she whispered as the anger welled up inside her.

Her knees creaked too loud in the tense quiet as she knelt beside his hips to fish the keys to the handcuffs out of his pocket. Kathryn let a subdued gasp escape. Her heart pounded as trembling fingers clenched around a clump of keys. She pulled out her hand and unwrapped her fingers to expose three individual rings of keys that she assumed belonged to her handcuffs, the house and the van. He must have separated the keys after she had tried to escape in order to keep available only the ones he needed at the time.

Another security method. James! He must have told Dylan to keep the keys in his pocket. Foolish move, she thought, very glad for his mistake.

An apprehensive guilt clouded her thinking for only a moment as she debated whether or not to leave Dylan, dying in a drug-overdosed heap in the bathroom. Every fiber of her being ordered her to help him, while her mind argued for her to forget such theological nonsense and help herself out of here as soon as possible. His collapse provided her with an unexpected opportunity she had no choice but to seize.

Kathryn dragged his body to the back of the bathroom, leaving him on the floor behind the raised tub. She slipped down the carpeted stairs, one careful step at a time, listening with each new descent for any sound of James stirring in the far end of the living room. She could see him in the chair on the other side of the room with his back to the stairs. James was leisurely blowing smoke rings and sipping Scotch, completely unaware of her.

Barefoot, she tiptoed around the corner toward the kitchen, planning to leave through the door which was the most isolated from James' hearing. Once in the kitchen, she dashed to the far door leading to the garden area. Key in hand to speed up her exit, she nervously anticipated what lay ahead.

Unlocking the deadbolt, Kathryn pushed through the open door. Hoping to slow anyone down from following her, she was careful to lock the door behind her before starting for the garage. She made certain that she stayed close to the outside wall. The grass was cold to her bare feet, but she didn't want to take the time to find a pair of shoes from the closet in her room. He always made certain everything was accounted for and there was nothing lying around that she could just grab to quickly flee his control.

It doesn't matter. I don't need shoes to drive, Kathryn reasoned, not planning to leave the van until she could run right into the first sheriff's station she saw.

Reaching the living room window where James was sitting, she crouched to the ground and crawled past on her hands and knees, careful to keep herself well below his line of vision. Once, on the far side of the bay window, Kathryn again leapt to her feet and charged for the garage as fast as she could run.

The open door revealed the van that failed to carry her away so very long ago. But she didn't have time to think about that or to search the garage for whatever else might be of use. She just prayed that it would start the first time.

Climbing into the driver's seat, she pulled the third set of keys from her left hand, throwing the others onto the passenger's seat, and pushed one of the two remaining keys into the ignition. It didn't move. Pulling it out, she shoved the second key into the ignition. The motor turned over and purred into action. She pushed the gear into drive and eased the van from the garage. It felt good to drive, to be in control of her own destination. Creeping down the driveway without lights until she was out of sight, Kathryn hoped to move quietly enough so as not to distract James from his drinking.

Once out of sight and earshot, Kathryn turned on the high beams and floored the gas pedal, causing the van to fishtail in the loose dirt and gravel. The house was secluded at the end of a long grooved path that looked very much like an unused logging road.

She pushed the van down the rutted road as fast as she dared. Barely maintaining control as she headed down the mountain, Kathryn was afraid to go any slower. The ominous black forest was dense and uninviting in the moonless night. She inhaled the crisp mountain air of freedom, drawing it deep into her lungs and exhaling in a slow, satisfied sigh. This time, she was going to make it. The taste of freedom was already in her mouth.

No lights appeared behind her. She was completely alone in the darkness of her new freedom.

The dirt road wove through the trees until it divided into a fork. Stopping close to the edge, Kathryn studied the two routes as quick as possible in the limited light of her headlights. The left trail continued downward; the right leveled off, perhaps heading back up the mountain. In an instant, Kathryn decided to take the left fork that continued down the mountain. Glancing behind her once again, there were no lights piercing the inky blackness of the forested night. Apparently, they were not yet in pursuit. She eased the window down and listened, not hearing any noise except the soft hum of the van's own motor.

The vehicle jerked forward as her anxious foot slammed a little too heavily on the pedal. She had enough of a head start on the two lunatics she had left at the house that they shouldn't be able to catch up to her. Kathryn breathed a sigh of relief as she drove down the mountain to freedom, feeling better than she had in over a year.

Picturing Dylan again in her mind, she wondered whether or not he was dead yet. James would have noticed soon enough that they were not downstairs, and he would have gone up to see what was keeping them. Walking into the bathroom and seeing Dylan on the floor behind the tub and he would either check on Dylan to see what was wrong, or he would search the house for her. Either way, by now he should be in his car searching for her.

And considering how James feels about Dylan, he probably just left him on the floor to die, she guessed. It would make his life so much simpler. Then he wouldn't have to fight Dylan for the estate.

"He might just let me go," she said, the words suddenly making sense to her. After all, she was Dylan's mistake, and James seemed like the kind of man who didn't want complications in his life. This could prove the easiest way to be rid of her. He could just let her and the problem she presented disappear.

As she rounded a bend that clung to the lip of a deep basin, Kathryn felt suddenly liberated as if she could soar through the air like an eagle.

Chapter Twenty

The road became uncomfortably narrow in several places. In others, the abundance of potholes caused the center strip to scrape the bottom of the vehicle. Kathryn slowed to a mere crawl and clung onto the steering wheel in a desperate attempt to maintain control as the van bounced along the hazardous trail. Banking to a sharp left, the road began to climb abruptly at a steep angle. The path wound around the mountain and finally leveled before it smoothed into a heavily graveled roadway. Relieved, Kathryn pressed her foot onto the gas pedal in a race to put the last bit of distance to the highway behind her.

Weaving through the dark tunnel of trees for another five minutes, the road finally led to a clearing of tall grass. In the sweeping light of her halogen high beams, she could see an unkempt cabin at the edge of the tree line just before a black lake. The windows had long since been smashed completely so there were no shards of glass remaining to reflect her lights. The splintered door listed outward, held only by a broken brown-crusted lower hinge. A faded blue rowboat that had seen better days lay off to one side of the house, close to a collapsed dock at the water's edge.

She had chosen the wrong fork and stumbled onto a dead end that had been someone's summer cabin many years earlier. *Probably part of the estate.* She was angry at being lost in this forsaken place instead of speeding along the blacktop to town.

Deserted and left to rot, she suspected she wouldn't find anything of use in the dilapidated shack. There would be no phone or gun, just broken furniture and discarded dishes.

"Dammit!" she swore, incensed at the loss of precious time. She half-expected James to creep up behind her at any minute.

Kathryn rammed the gear into reverse and backed onto the grass to turn around. The tires slid on the thick growth and fishtailed. The van finally stopped, spinning its wheels in a rut of soft dirt. She gunned the engine and the wheels spun wildly, locking the vehicle into a hollow of dirt and grass.

James has certainly found Dylan by now. If he came after me, he probably continued down the mountain, thinking I went that way. And if that's the case, he most assuredly has reached the highway by now. Maybe I can use that to my advantage, she thought, forcing her thoughts and emotions to remain calm so she could think clearly.

The darkness taunted her. She could hear the shadows mocking her foiled attempt to escape after being given such a wide open door of opportunity. The moment of relief and joy she had cherished at the onset of her trip evaporated, disappearing into the shadows of the abandoned cabin. In a sudden outburst of fury, Kathryn beat the steering wheel until her hands were bruised and sore. Wishing she had stopped for shoes, Kathryn opened the door and jumped out to better examine her position in the tall grass. To her dismay, the rear wheels were entrenched in a hollowed-out mud pit.

Kicking the side panel housing the rear wheel well, she swallowed her frustration and headed to the cabin in search of something that might help. Fear ate away at her resolve, making her wonder if this was like the *cancer* James talked about. Dylan had often told her about the insatiable *need* that seethed within him, allowing him neither rest nor peace. She hadn't understood what the two brothers talked about, but perhaps this fear was the closest she had come to experiencing what they'd talked about.

Her love for David was possibly close as well. There were times when her heart ached to have David near, times when the thoughts of David and Meaghan consumed her, times when the memories of special occasions and intimate moments possessed her. Love was different from obsession, which had a firm grip on Dylan, but it still had a similar level of underlying, controlling commitment.

Ironically, she was surprised to discover that she understood Dylan more than she had first believed possible. The irony helped cut the tension and, right now, she needed any release. An owl hooted, causing her to jump at the sudden loudness of noise filling the silence.

As she gingerly walked through the dark, Kathryn tried to keep her mind off the rising fear by thinking about little things she had not had time to analyze before. She realized that although Dylan frightened her, she found James terrifying. Despite her desire to see Dylan dead, and much to her distaste, another thought told her that she was becoming concerned about Dylan. Perhaps it was more a matter that she didn't hate Dylan with the same passion she once had, instead of actually being fond of him.

What shocked her most was the awareness that no matter how excited she was about going home again, Kathryn was actually apprehensive to leave the estate. The contradiction didn't make sense. She loathed being a prisoner at the mercy of first Dylan and now James, but there was a certain familiarity with it that nagged her. The inner voice told her that David would not be as excited to see her come back from the dead as she anticipated. He might not believe that she had been a prisoner for over a year...or that she just now managed to walk away.

He might have a girlfriend. He might have believed I was dead and sought solace in another woman's arms. Meaghan might not even recognize me anymore. She was only two when I was taken. Perhaps David's new girlfriend has taken my place as mother to my baby. She was feeling more miserable with each passing yard. After everything she'd been through, Kathryn didn't know if she could take an unwanted homecoming.

Maybe there's no room for me in their lives anymore. Dad might have died after hearing the news of my disappearance. It's been so long. Perhaps I'm just deluding myself into thinking that I really do have a life to run back to. Maybe James was right when he said I have no husband or daughter. Dylan could have killed them all and didn't tell me. The absurd suggestions drove her crazy. In her heart she knew it wasn't true, but her insecure fear pushed the image of each ugly notion deeper into her heart.

Logic was lost to worry; she forgot that Dylan fed her every day of solitary, at least after the first weeks. He had no time to leave and kill her family, but she couldn't shake the terrifying pictures that loomed in her mind.

Kathryn placed her full weight on the first step. The creak resounded in the solemn darkness. The moon had finally risen above the trees and illuminated the night into varying shades of shadows. Hoping to find some planks to stabilize the wheels, she searched the porch for any loose boards. Yanking the door out of the way, it gave way easily as she pulled it off the one remaining hinge. Stepping over the rickety wood, she tripped into the one-room hovel.

It was too black to see anything. She was tired. The van was stuck. James was most likely looking for her up and down the highway or had given up the hunt altogether. Angry and frustrated, she decided to go back to the van and get some sleep. It would be easier to see what she was doing in daylight.

First light gently prodded her awake. It was cold. The chilly night had left her poorly clad body stiff. Groaning, she stretched the ache from her knees and ankles. It had been difficult to get any sleep while uncovered on the back seat. Her joints offered a disgruntled creak in response to being forced to move. The "clicking" noise irritated her. It hadn't been there a year ago. She would have to remember to thank Dylan for that particular gift when the police rousted him from his private fortress. There were so many things to thank him for...

"Good morning. My God, did you know you snore like a banshee?" a voice asked from the front passenger seat.

Kathryn jumped, gasping in shock. She hadn't heard James enter the van and wondered how long he'd been sitting there, waiting for her to wake up. It would be no good to make a break for it. He'd be on her in a minute, even before she got the sliding door open. Wiping at the sleep in her eyes, she bit her lip to hold back the onslaught of tears wanting to burst through her inner dam of strength. Freedom had been so close...*to just be snatched away like this. Oh, God, what do I do now?*

"Well, it's been a fun excursion, but now, it's time to head back," James said smugly. He sat sideways in the front seat. Around his shoulders, he wore a pale green blanket over a camel hair coat to ward off the early morning crispness. His smile was sinister as he played absently with the small border of hunter-green ribbon rosettes. Whipping the blanket off his shoulders, James draped it in the air and folded it with great panache. Through his exaggerated motions, an emerald colored "MSEB" was exposed, embroidered into a heart shaped area on a fluffy white bunny's chest.

A gasp of recognition seared her still-sleepy mind. She sat bolt upright. The blanket belonged to Meaghan. There was no mistaking it. Kathryn had packed it the morning David delivered their daughter to New Mexico to stay with his parents. Meaghan used to lie in bed and twirl the rosettes between her tiny fingers as she drifted off to a pleasant slumber, playing with one after another like a string of prayer beads. Blankie was Meaghan's constant companion as she watched the many children shows.

The horror of the only viable reality smacked her. *Meaghan would never knowingly...or willingly...*part with Blankie. *Oh, my God! Meaghan!*

James finished folding the blanket into a neat small square and placed it on his lap as if it were his most prized possession.

"Wh...where did you get that blanket?" she whispered through a hand of trembling fingers. Her body shook from unexpected implication.

"This? Oh, I got this from your daughter. It's very nice. Soft. It still has that peculiar little kid smell. Interesting. David's mother made this, didn't she?" he asked as he patted the blanket with tender emphasis. A sinister glint in his eyes made him look just plain evil.

"M...Me...Meaghan? Is she...is she all right?" Kathryn gulped through the flood of blinding tears. A fresh panic claimed her, one she hadn't experienced for a long time. It was an issue that had been put to rest after discovering that Dylan was not interested in her baby at all. It was Kathryn he wanted, and that meant her family was safe now that she was in his possession.

"Yes, she's fine. At least for a while. Her health depends entirely on your attitude and actions." He smiled.

"Have...you...hurt her?" Kathryn asked, more afraid to hear the answer than not. Every fiber of her body wanted to jump up and lunge for James' throat, but the blanket forced her into a fragile state of control.

"Not yet. It depends on what you do. Understand that I'm not going to force you to do anything. From this moment on, everything you do is entirely up to you. No one is going to hold a gun to your head and force you to do anything. You're quite free to go home, if that's what you want. Right now, if you like. Simply drive this van out of here. Or you can return with me to the mansion." James grinned easily.

She was bewildered by what he was saying. His words belied what his features said. The cool expression worn on his face was more than menacing, it was a blatant threat. Wiping a snotty nose on the back of her hand, her eyes again became glued to the pale green blanket. Cuddled under the familiar comfort of Blankie, Meaghan would curl up on Kathryn's lap and be rocked asleep to a favorite melody. The green blanket was made by David's mother when she learned a granddaughter was on the way. The "MSEB" was added after Meaghan was born and given the name of Meaghan Samantha Elayne Breslin. Kathryn wrapped her new little baby girl in the special blanket and carried her home from the hospital, and as the months passed, it became Meaghan's favorite security companion.

"What do you mean I can go home?" she asked with a nervous catch in her voice. "You're letting me go? Just like that?" *Perhaps James isn't as bad as I thought,* she thought, amazed at his magnanimous gesture.

As she again wiped her nose, James' malicious laugh echoed in the tight confines of the van. The hair on the back of her neck bristled from the cruel sound.

"Of course you have a choice. I'm not a monster. If you don't want to come back with me, I don't want you here. You won't be any good to me if I have to force you. No, no, you only have to do what you want," he said in a sweet, almost convincing tone. Leaning back against the door, he adjusted the blanket on his lap and continued to pat it in a subliminal gesture.

"Why would you just let me go?" she asked, unable to take her eyes from his hand.

"It doesn't matter to me either way. Oh, you can go. Of course, that means I'll have to take someone to replace you. Meaghan, perhaps. Yes, she would be good. I would probably kill her after a while. I'll scare the crap out of her for the first couple of years, though. Then it depends whether or not I get bored. If I do, I'll just kill her. If not, well, who knows what game might prove interesting," he said in an off-handed way, fluttering his hand. The broad grin turned up at the corner of his mouth. He knew he was driving her to the brink of insane wrath. "So don't you worry. You're quite free to go."

"You'll take Meaghan?" A new wave of shock swamped her.

"Well, of course. Didn't Dylan explain the rules to you? It's either you or your daughter. And if you don't want to stay, well then, Meaghan will. Of course, if you do stay, then she will remain free in New Mexico. As I said, the choice is yours."

Kathryn's mind exploded under the impact of his vile insinuations and pregnant threats. Dylan had told her what his demons did to him on a continual basis. *They* would offer him a choice: *they* would either torture him or he would torture someone else. *They* didn't care what he decided because *they* got *their* entertainment whatever his choice. *And now James would get his entertainment whatever what I decide.*

The freedom she had dreamed about for over a year was just within her grasp. She could taste the sweetness of its memory; feel the gentle breeze of liberty upon her face. All she had to do was leave. He would simply let her walk out of here. She could turn her back on Dylan and James forever. But that would bring Meaghan to the very hell she desperately longed to be rid of, while leaving Kathryn in a worse mental hell. Kathryn could never let Meaghan be in this place. There was no choice. James knew that. As a mother, she could do nothing that would jeopardize her baby girl.

"Well, what will it be, Kathryn? Are you going to come back with me or do I go after your daughter? We haven't got all day to sit here and mull this thing over," he said. James tossed the blanket on the floor. In his attempt to place one knee over the other, he ground the blanket under one heel for emphasis.

Kathryn choked at the obvious insinuation of his action. Hate engulfed her. The level of impotent fury dissipated, leaving her weak and vulnerable. Her will was being drained until she could no longer control the actions of her own body. As if watching someone else speak for her, she could see her own lips mouth the simple but bitter words of surrender.

She became a passive bystander as her body obeyed James' every order and headed back to the cabin to find the boards she couldn't locate in the blackness of night. A numbness pervaded her senses as she dragged the planks back to the van and shoved them under the rear tires. Climbing into the driver's seat, she eased the van out of the ruts and onto the boards. Still in a fog of shocked disbelief, she turned the van around and drove down the old logging trail back to the mansion...and home...to the waiting cell.

Chapter Twenty-One

Her mind numbed as she drove the van as slowly as possible, retracing last night's flight. The last thing she needed was for James to accuse her of abusing his precious property.

Kathryn now knew, without any doubt, that she would have to kill both Dylan and James, assuming Dylan lived through the overdose ordeal. It was the only way she could ever leave alive. Meaghan would not be safe from these two lunatics even if Kathryn herself died at their hands. They would simply bring her little girl back to the estate after they buried the mother in a shallow grave beside the septic tank.

The van arrived back at the house as snow clouds gathered to darken the midmorning sky. The thudding beat of her heart overshadowed the songs of a dozen birds that darted about in their endless search for autumn food. Her head pounded, the throbbing intensity increasing from the front to the back of her skull with each accented heartbeat. The stress of submitting without question pressed down on her.

James got out and slammed the van door behind him. As he walked to the house, he swung Meaghan's crumpled Blankie in one mocking fist. Sauntering toward the house, he expected Kathryn to be right behind him.

She watched as he headed round the corner of the garage. Taking a deep breath, she sighed and climbed out of the van. Without argument, she followed him back to the waiting prison she had briefly thought was far behind. Her mind ceased to function beyond the concentration of placing one foot ahead of the other. Stopping in the middle of the room, she watched as he continued to stroll through the kitchen to the solarium and sat at the table.

"I'm hungry. Make something to eat. And pour me some Scotch. Two cubes, a splash of water," James demanded as he took a cigarette from the crumpled pack in his breast pocket and lit it with a flurry of exaggerated fanfare. The burning match in his hand disappeared into thin air as he proudly pulled off a slight-of-hand magician's trick in a sarcastic attempt to dazzle her.

She sneered at him, letting James know she wasn't the least bit impressed by his amateurish effort. The scornful look she flung at him drained her of even the energy needed to swear at him. Instead, she lifted two bowls from the shelf, two spoons from the drawer, a box of cereal and cup of sugar from the cupboard, and a gallon of milk from the fridge. Balancing everything in her hands and under one arm, she carried them to the dining area. Dropping the collection of items onto the table without any pretense of grace, she straightened out the breakfast utensils by tossing him a spoon and bowl before scooping up her own and flopping onto a chair opposite James. She didn't care if he objected to her style or to what she served for breakfast. She had ceased to care about anything.

Pouring cereal almost to the rim of her bowl, she filled the remaining space with milk. Devouring one full bowl of cereal and ready for another, she poured a second before James started preparing his first. She hadn't eaten since the day before yesterday.

James rolled the smoke from a second cigarette in his mouth, enjoying the taste with passion and altering his expression with the glazed look of ecstasy. He was a man who reveled in as many vices as he chose, relishing the exquisite pleasure and sensation each one offered. James regarded them not as something that should be given up, but habits that should be honed to a fine art of cherished delight. The more destructive, the better he liked them.

Kathryn was well into her second bowl before sitting back semi-satisfied. She stared at the man across from her, waiting for him to say something. James inhaled deeply and held the smoke for a long time before finally releasing it in different shapes into the air. He returned her scrutinizing gaze while curling his lips into a slimy grimace and throwing her a small kiss. She shuddered from the obvious thoughts that were passing through his mind.

"I'm horny," he stated with sudden abruptness. "Go get ready. I'll be there in a minute."

She fixed her eyes on the disgusting leer hidden behind the hazy smoke clouding his features. He assumed she would obey without question. A wave of revulsion flooded over her. He neither insisted nor added a single word or gesture. To him, the *request* had already been made and it was simply left for her to comply. There was no debate, discussion, or choice. The threat hanging over Meaghan's head as he fingered the soft satin rosettes along the edge of the blanket left Kathryn in the position of total surrender.

Pushing herself up from the table, Kathryn took one last look at the monster sitting before her. She slowly marched to the stairs and up to the bedroom she had been allowed to occupy for the last several months. The time was finally here. *Anything to survive. Anything for Meaghan,* Kathryn reminded herself as she tramped up the stairs, more afraid and depressed than she had ever been.

Stopping at the doorway, she again sighed. The bookcase was open and the Plexiglas cell illuminated the bedroom with its brilliance. Debating whether she was to go into the cell or use the bed, she walked around the corner of the bookcase while still trying to decide.

Dylan hung over the rim of the toilet inside the barrenness of the locked room. Vomiting and groaning, he clung to the porcelain bowl as if his life depended on it.

He's still alive. She groaned, unsure whether she should be relieved or upset by the news. However, since Dylan was in the cell, Kathryn decided they should use the bed...unless, of course, James expressed a different desire.

Suddenly, very much afraid, she had to go to the bathroom. It was a natural response to the anxiety of what lay ahead. Retracing her steps down the hallway, Kathryn entered the small room and closed the door, realizing it might be the last time she could ever again have privacy.

Returning to the bedroom, she saw that James was already standing at the foot of the bed. "Close the curtains and shut the bookcase. I don't want light. Shut the door behind you and take off your clothes. Everything. Then get into bed."

Kathryn bit her lip as she obeyed each instruction. The room was pitch black by the time she felt her way to the bed and pulled down the blankets. She climbed beneath the sheets and waited for James to join her. Laying back into the softness of the bed, she braced herself for the inescapable. She squeezed her eyes shut against the moment, not wanting to see him close to her. Holding her breath, she didn't even want to smell him. Every fiber of her being prayed that he would be quick so she could put the entire sordid incident behind her and get on with her plans for his death.

The intrusion of his touch began with the big toe of her left foot. James fondled her skin much like Dylan had when Dylan examined her, only this was no examination. Her flesh began to tremble as her disgust and fear mounted. The sensation of his fingers continued along her foot and up her leg to the ticklish nerve ends of her tummy. His touch was so light and gentle that it felt as if it carried right past the barrier of her skin into her inner tissues.

His fingers outlined the shape of her mouth and eyes, tenderly following the contour of her throat to the strong sweep of her breasts. He caressed her nipples and tickled her stomach. His hands fondled every part of her body at once...both inside and out. Her mind could not distinguish where his caresses began or ended. There was no obvious weight to either his body or the pressure of his roving fingers. Every part of her body tingled and vibrated with the subtle stroke of his intentions and the speed with which he tenderly brushed her flesh. He instinctively knew where all her most sensitive areas were, and he concentrated on each one at the same time.

Her thighs burned with desire, and although she hated herself for doing it, she parted her legs to allow him easier access. Some desperate need deep within her could forget who she was with in the blackness of this room. The way he touched her drove her to a level of unbridled lust she had never before experienced. He pinned her against the mattress and manipulated her need and emotions as if he were a master and this was his preferred art medium.

Kathryn could no longer identify what he was doing. Every inch of her body was a flame of urgent need. His fingers reached beneath her and traveled along her spine in a sensual massage as he manipulated her thighs wider apart. He filled her, burying himself deeply into her now-hungry passion. Her mind exploded with the uncompromising totality of his touch and the utter confusion of ecstasy erupting within her. It had been so long since she had known the pleasure of orgasmic release. James brought her to the explosive peak half a dozen times before he finished with her.

She hadn't felt him climb on or off the bed—he was simply with her and then gone in an instant. Kathryn had no idea how long they had been together, or even what time of day it was. Closing her eyes and turning onto her right side, she faced away from the edge of the bed where James stood, hidden by the blackness. She could feel his eyes on her, stripping her of what little dignity she had left.

Muffled by the carpet, his steps treaded out of the bedroom, leaving her alone in the darkness. She cradled a pillow in her arms and wept with shame as she tried to rock away the ugliness.

Rape was the inevitable result of her situation. She had expected and prepared for it for over a year. She hadn't prepared herself for the shameful reality of enjoying it. She had enjoyed sex with a monster who, just hours earlier, had threatened the life of her only daughter. The pleasure was beyond her control. It was as if he overrode all her natural emotions and physical responses.

Curling into a fetal position, while still grasping the pillow close to her heart, Kathryn cried herself to a troubled sleep where the nightmares were kinder than truth. She sobbed before blessed unconsciousness claimed her, "Oh, God, David, I'm so sorry."

Kathryn groaned from the memory of last night. She felt dirty, and a chill covered her skin. With her head still buried beneath the pillow, Kathryn knew she was without covers. It was an old sensation from the early days of the Plexiglas cell, although she gratefully recognized that she was still lying on top of the bed instead of the floor. She had half-expected James to slip her a drug and lock her in the cell with Dylan.

Stretching on top of the sheets, Kathryn forced her eyes open to again face the world. A small lamp from the night table bathed the room in a soft glow. She was not surprised to see James ogling her from the far corner of the bedroom. He leisurely rolled a lit cigarette between three fingers as he sneered at her like a street gang member leering at the bloodied body of his latest victim.

"Get up. Let Dylan out of his damned prison and get down to the kitchen and make some breakfast. I want something to eat," James growled, standing in the doorway. His voice was low and commanding. He was neatly dressed in the manner she had grown accustomed to: earth-toned plaid shirt buttoned to the throat; solid gold vest; chocolate brown, thin ribbed cord pants; spotlessly clean gold socks the exact shade of the vest. The colors may have varied over the past year, but the style remained constant. Both James and Dylan dressed in strong, contrasting colors. Dylan's laundry showed that he was meticulously coordinated, right down to his socks and underwear.

At first, she thought that it should mean Dylan was predictable, but she soon discovered that he surrounded himself with constant, unchanging things in order to contrast the instability that raged inside. Dylan's world—his house, clothes, belongings, habits, rituals, and methods—was all by the book. Everything had to be *proper*, and was guided by rules and regulations only James and Dylan could understand or remember. It was how he kept his world from completely falling apart. He could not control the rages, passions or sensations that plagued his every moment, so he enclosed himself in a bubble of ceremonies that could be accomplished automatically without the need for thought.

It was the only way he could survive in the world. By living day to day in multitudinous routine, he could appear almost normal. As long as no one looked too closely. She snorted as she removed the pillow from her forehead and tossed it to one side.

She suspected James was the same as Dylan in that respect. There were definite differences between the two brothers, but they had obvious habitual similarities, and she wondered if she could use those rituals and habits against them somehow.

Kathryn was unwilling to compel herself to move. She desperately wanted to sleep but doubted James was inclined to allow her to do anything other than cater to his selfish demands.

"I said get up!" James shouted. He tossed his burning cigarette under the bed and stomped over to where she was still lying. His black eyes were possessive and almost wild looking in the dim light of the lamp. Forming formidable fists on each hip, he created an illusion of complete authority.

"All right, all right. I'm moving. I'm up, letting Dylan out, and getting breakfast," she whispered through gritted teeth that suppressed the deep-rooted anger.

"That's breakfast for everyone but you. I don't remember inviting you to eat with us," he stated more cruelly than before. He stared into her now-frightened eyes.

Kathryn gulped back her hunger to obey the latest barrage of orders. Things were going to be worse than horrible under James' rule. She got up to dress in the clothes she had worn last night.

"I don't think so. You can either wear the T-shirt or go naked. The choice is yours." He laughed with enough malignancy in his voice to reinforce the weight of his words.

Dressing in only the T-shirt and disappointed that she was back to bare essentials, she headed to the bookcase to let Dylan out. On one hand, she was relieved to be able to check his condition. The fact that he was vomiting last night was a good sign. His system rejected the drugs and he would live. She still had no idea what quantities of what drugs were ingested. Determined to at least minimally examine him, Kathryn opened the bookcase wall.

Dylan already had the door unlocked in anticipation of the wall being opened. The bookcase could not be unlatched from inside the cell, as Dylan had not anticipated being on the wrong side of the door. It was planned instead to be an added precaution against her escaping should he be incapacitated and the card-key fall into her hands.

"God, I feel awful," Dylan moaned as he staggered through the bedroom and into the hallway. His eyes were circled with dark pads and his color was paler than she'd seen him in a long time. Dylan's steps were unsure and he needed the wall to support himself. The smell of pungent bile emanated from his clothes and breath, and wafted into the air as he passed.

Kathryn wanted to wash and alleviate the pressing urgency of her bladder before heading to the kitchen, but Dylan had struggled to the bathroom and locked the door behind him. She stomped downstairs to the half-bathroom off the utility room that was beside the locked storage room. By the time Dylan managed to stumble into the kitchen, James was already on his second Scotch and had inhaled at least six cigarettes.

Kathryn made a large pan of Dylan's favorite egg concoction and left it heating in the oven until Dylan arrived. As Dylan made his way to the table, she brought him a cup of coffee before filling two plates with egg and toast and carrying them to the brothers. Returning to her place by the sink, she decided to clean up the dishes while they ate and talked.

Dylan looked better after a shower and dressed in clean clothes— a faded blue denim outfit that he wore when he and Kathryn had gone camping or took long walks in the surrounding forest. It was a complete statement of defiance against his older brother, and, if the point was not wasted on her, James was certain to notice. Dylan picked at his eggs. He kept his eyes firmly focused on his brother. Disgust and loathing were plainly carved into his features.

James laughed in a loud, unnatural voice that echoed off the solarium walls. "My, my, Dylan. I do believe your feelings are showing." He snickered at his brother's expense. "By the way, Kathryn is very good in bed. It's a shame you didn't get around to tasting her. I think with time, we can start a real relationship."

"I don't want you touching her. I found her. I brought her here. She's mine. You have no claim on her," Dylan answered through clenched teeth. He began to shovel food into his mouth to conceal his hatred and anger.

"Well, I think it's more a case of the better man winning," James said through a haze of smoke aimed right at Dylan's face.

Dylan flushed with deep scarlet. He dropped his fork to the table and jumped up, kicking the chair to the floor behind him. "You bastard!"

"Precisely. I am the king of bastards." James laughed heinously, slapping his knee with his hand. There was no question about how much he was enjoying himself.

Flying into an unparalleled rage, Dylan flew across the room. He threw open the cupboard, grabbed a glass and threw it into the empty sink. The glass shattered into a dozen shards of potential weapons. Dylan snatched a large jagged piece from the debris and glared at James with unequaled vehemence. Instead of lunging at the object of his hate, Dylan raised the broken glass and jammed the knifelike point into the back of his left hand.

Chapter Twenty-Two

The darkness surrounded them, making the room small and claustrophobic. Kathryn tensed, expecting Dylan to answer James' challenge and attack her at any moment through the black veil. It was a nonverbal threat that had long ago been laid to rest, but the added James element could change everything. Dylan might now feel he had something to prove.

She backed into the corner, keeping guard where the wall and mirror came together. Protecting herself on two sides from his intrusive touch, she crouched, ready to spring into action. Her mind ran over the measurements of the room that were once committed to automatic memory, but rarely used in recent months. Dylan's labored breaths revealed his position, and she concentrated on his every movement in order to give herself enough time to run should he try to make a wrong move.

Dylan stirred in the far side of the room. His hands made a hushed slapping noise in the dark as they grabbed against the stainless steel sink. A low groan escaped as he stood on his feet and smacked his hand against the wall to steady himself.

"You should let me examine your hand," Kathryn offered, feeling suddenly sorry for him. She kept her voice low, whispering just loud enough so he could hear. "You shouldn't be banging it around like that."

Answering with a rough grunt, his socks made a soft padded noise as he walked around the toilet. With a clumsy flop onto the seat, he urinated into the bowl with a resounding echo that shattered the silence. Kathryn appreciated his care in not standing, missing the bowl, and peeing all over the seat and floor in the dark.

Crossing the floor with a noisy panic underlying each step, he acted like someone who had recently been blinded and was unused to the sudden blackness. Stumbling into the stainless steel table, he offered a curse at his own ineptness and the detested darkness.

Kathryn was baffled by their new living conditions. She couldn't understand why James had locked her and Dylan into the cell together. It seemed that James hated them both with equal passion.

All hopes of James the Conqueror vanished as she realized that James considered her merely a bonus that had just been dropped into his lap with neither strings nor cost. James acted as if the best thing that ever happened to him was returning to the estate and finding her there, and yet he wasn't the least bit appreciative to his brother. James treated Dylan as if he too was put on earth for the sole purpose of James' explicit entertainment.

There was so much she wanted to ask Dylan, but *Rule Number Four* prevented her from speaking. Dylan was sent into the cell for a failed suicide and she was incarcerated for a blundered escape. They were both being punished for losing their individual battles with James, who would not set any predetermined confinement period. They were at James' mercy, and she suspected he did not even know how to spell the word.

All the information she gathered in the past year involved only Dylan. He hadn't mentioned his older brother specifically when he talked about his family, and the two brothers were different enough to make James an unknown element.

"You should conserve the food. We don't know when we'll be fed next," she whispered, daring to break the rule only long enough to save her life. She'd been through this before and knew the uncertainties. She knew how difficult it was to depend on a keeper who was mentally disturbed.

Kathryn and Dylan had walked into the cell at James' command. There was no physical coercion on his part; James had simply ordered them into the cell. Kathryn was allowed to prepare some food, Dylan was allowed to wrap his hand, and they were ushered into the dark and told to close the door behind them. James' orders were obeyed without the need to raise a finger against them. Now, in the solitude of thought, she wondered what magic power James had that forced them to comply so easily with his demented desires.

However, that was not her immediate concern. Dylan needed proper medical attention and they had to restrict their food consumption.

What would happen when the hunger overcame them, and death loomed at the door? Would they end up fighting each other like vicious animals, scrapping over a single dry bread crust? Would they be willing to kill each other for a cold bowl of broth? Oh, God. She moaned, knowing that it could quite possibly come to that if they were locked up long enough. She wondered when the animal instinct would come out in her own nature, and how long it would take Dylan to revert to considering his own needs before hers.

"Don't worry, he won't kill us. It'd spoil the game," Dylan said, as if he had read her mind. "And the game is everything. It keeps *them* amused, and that is the only reason *they* allow us to live."

She could hear him try to swallow small bites of sandwich by washing them down with cold coffee. His throat was obviously raw and sore from vomiting all night. Dylan shuffled to the mirrored wall and grunted as he fell to the floor just a few feet away from her.

"Here. Though I don't know what good you can do in this blackness," Dylan snarled as he thrust his hand at her.

Kathryn recoiled at the unwanted surprise of a hand pushing into her right breast. It was an accident. Dylan immediately pulled it away and held it in front of her so she could put it where she wanted. She found his injured hand and pulled it closer for a physical examination.

He leaned toward her. The gurgling noise of his upset stomach grew louder as it competed against the rapid popping of escaping flatulence.

"Must you do that?" she hissed at him. She had little patience for Dylan and was disgusted by his baseness, although aware he was still suffering from the effects of the ingested pills. If he were a patient in the hospital, she would note his bodily functions and ignore them except for the medical information they offered. But here, in this confined space, she more than cared what he did.

As she gently probed the wound on his hand, she fought the urge to talk to him. There was a multitude of new questions needing answers. Dylan flinched and choked on a dry, wrenching cough as she gently poked his skin. If she could not sew the hand's flesh together within six hours of the injury, he would have to wait until after he took a series of antibiotics for probable infection. She felt sorry for Dylan, but there was nothing to be done. They were in the same helpless predicament, and for the first time since she had been a prisoner, she felt equal to her captor.

"He'll never let us die. At least, not until he's damn good and ready. No, he'll humiliate us until we wish we were dead. Even then he'll keep us alive until we no longer amuse him. He's like a vulture picking at any bit of meat left on our bones," Dylan whispered with a voice that was rough and sore.

Kathryn squirmed under the weight of his words, nervous that James would punish her as well for Dylan's crime of speaking. The blackness surrounded them like a shroud, smothering her in its stillness, and making Dylan's words thunder and boom with a fresh horror.

"It wasn't always like this, you know. James was so cool in the beginning; I looked up to him, you know. He was my hero. I always thought he was sort of awesome. The way he talked and dressed. I could listen to him for hours. We were really close. We went everywhere together; did everything together. He took me under his wing and taught me the most wonderful things about the *Grey Land.*

Eventually, all I wanted was to be with him, and to be in *there*. We went *there* together sometimes, and I visited with some of his *friends* and *associates*. He promised me the world back then. I don't exactly know when things changed, but they did. He began to hate me and make me suffer in unspeakable ways," Dylan said, speaking more to the blackness than to his roommate.

Kathryn was confused. She closed her eyes and leaned her head back against the wall, concentrating on finding any spot on her body that didn't hurt, especially against the hard floor.

"I was four when I first met George. I used to hide in the closet because I was afraid of my father. He was an ugly drunk. Confrontation scared me. It still does. When he drank, he was unbearable. I hated to be around him, so I crawled into the closet and buried myself under the pile of dirty clothes. It was comforting in the darkness somehow. Sort of safe. No one could find me. They'd search every room and then I'd hear them go outside, but no one ever found me. I could hide in there the whole day if I didn't have to go to the bathroom. When *those green bastards* came and started to watch me from the mirrors and windows, I'd run to the closet because even *they* couldn't find me there. But then, one day I met George in there. After awhile, he told me he was a ghost from Britain. He told me he had been watching me for a long time. It was three years after that when I finally invited him to come into me, so we could always be together. I was so tired of being alone," Dylan continued, repeating the stories in a monotone.

There was no reprisal from James. He seemed to let Dylan have his say without interference. *Maybe James isn't as bad as I thought,* she hoped.

"I thought you said James was your older brother," she asked, still unable to make sense of what Dylan was mumbling about. She wanted him to fill in the answers to all the questions burning inside her, but doubted he could be that coherent. What confused her the most was how Dylan, after going to such lengths to kidnap her in the first place, could hand her over to someone else. It just didn't make sense.

"I have no brother, at least no blood brother. I have an older sister I can't stand. We fought all the time, even when we were kids. I remember waking up one night, and *they* were looking at me from the mirror beside the bed. It was the first time I ever saw *them*. I was only four then. My sister and I slept in the same bed back then. I was so scared I couldn't move or make a sound. I looked over at her to wake her up in the desperate hope she would protect me. What a laugh! I sure was stupid back then. When I saw her face, it was glowing with a bright, translucent green mask, just like the one in the mirror. *It* had a horrible, toothless grin, and the eyes were black and vacant. It was just like those theater masks, you know, the one that smiles and the other one that frowns.

The ugly *thing* with *its* smooth, glowing features mocked me, begging me to reach over and touch it. But I didn't. I was too terrified, so I ran to my hiding place and that was when I met George. I didn't know who he was back then. He told me that my family hated me; that my sister was one of *them.* He said that was why my family avoided me. George said they couldn't stand to have me around, but were forced to put up with me because I was their kid. But he said that he was my only friend. He wanted to spend as much time with me as he could. He wanted to teach me things I never imagined; things that felt good; things I didn't know about my body." He sighed, as if the memory was too much. His voice was weary and crushed.

Kathryn wanted to reach out to him. In the darkness, listening to his exhausted words, her empathy for the broken man grew. She could close her eyes and see him as a patient who had become completely dysfunctional and irrational. He was someone who desperately needed to discuss his distresses and lost battles. She wanted to rock him and comfort his agony. Instead, she stretched out her legs as the coolness of the room began to dig into her bones. The scanty clothing left her feeling chilled and vulnerable. Rubbing her legs, she attempted to massage some warmth and relief into them.

It was a long night. Dylan rambled endlessly as if he were compelled by an unspoken urgency to explain himself before he died. Perhaps it was the only way he could guarantee his immortality.

Or was he using the cell as his confessional? Maybe he just wants me to know so I won't hate him, she thought, trying to make sense of his aimless rambling. *Or he could be trying to make sense of his own life.*

Kathryn had a difficult time unraveling the Dylan puzzle. He spoke in riddles, half-spoken sentences and images she couldn't comprehend. The words he used were dramatic and chosen for their shock value rather than their accuracy. Taking that into account, she added in the Dylan-factor when translating his dialogue into an understandable series of events. Experience as both mother and doctor played helpful roles in the interpretation of his madness.

Her first clue was found in the story about pulling his teeth—he was missing no adult teeth. That meant that they had to be loose baby teeth, which would explain why his mother wasn't overly concerned about the incident. What had been magnified in his mind as a traumatic, life-shattering event was, in reality, a misunderstood cry for attention. His mother probably considered it a lucky occurrence for her young son since, with further investigation into his memories, Kathryn discovered that his mother had placed a silver dollar under his pillow from the tooth fairy.

Dylan had one sister five years his senior. She was bitter about the loss of her own elevated position of only child when Dylan pushed her from the limelight of everyone's affections. Dylan was a particularly sickly child who demanded constant attention. Because of a miscalculation by the doctor, he was delivered two months prematurely by Cesarean Section. Jaundiced and underdeveloped, he weighed only two pounds and suffered from a number of poorly functioning organs. His liver, eyes, and digestive problems were a constant concern.

Dylan endured a two-year battle with respiratory problems. After being released from a hospital incubator, he was placed on a pillow on the kitchen table. His family fashioned a sheet into a makeshift vapor tent and placed a pot of steaming water under the draped sheet in a twenty-four-hour attempt to keep his lungs clear.

In the fifties, doctors were equipped with medical knowledge that had since been found to be a danger to patients. Kathryn suspected that the homemade hot mist vaporizer was the primary cause of his persistent bronchial condition. Today, she would recommend cold mist humidifier to ease potential breathing problems, since cold mist didn't fill the lungs with inhaled fluid. He had also been fed a daily dose of good, old-fashioned hot toddies, and was bathed in alcohol to combat the effects of a pneumonia that refused to disappear. Today that would no longer be prescribed for a newborn infant. The alcoholic prescription had only aggravated the problems of his underdeveloped liver and added to his jaundiced condition.

Other symptoms he suffered were a direct result from food allergies that were not recognized forty years ago. He had a milk intolerance which spiraled him into twenty-minute cycles of crying, vomiting, and sleeping. His mother would pinch his toes to force him awake long enough to feed him formula, which only caused him physical pain and stomach cramps. This caused exhaustion due to excessive vomiting, which led to sleep. The cycle carried on twenty-four-hours a day for over two years.

For the first few months, he was a frail child who, when fully stretched, fit into the palm of his father's hands. Due to Dylan's slight size, his mother laid him on a red velvet cushion. She was afraid he might break if his tiny body was handled too much. However, Dylan translated his family's overprotective care as a lack of love since they rarely touched him. The only human touch he knew was when they fed him or changed his diaper. Today, this lack of physical bonding would be considered as the cause of his emotional disturbance and lack of conscience. It was a problem that was a current phenomenon in a small segment of North American children, and it was one psychologists were failing to remedy.

The more Dylan talked, the more she realized that he obviously grossly misinterpreted their actions. His mother doted on him while his father began drinking only after Dylan was born—probably a stressed reaction to mounting medical bills. He was well cared for by all his relatives, who took a personal interest in his health.

Though his words eventually revealed the truth, he uncovered it in a disoriented manner that showed he did not have a realistic grasp of the people in his life. Dylan filtered everything through the delusional vision enforced upon him by his imaginary friend George, causing him to react defensively in every situation. Every thought, action, and motive of the people around him was translated through George as the opposite of caring intentions. He painted not only everyone around him in the darkest possible picture, but himself as well.

Dylan's view of the world had always been through myopic eyes. *Perhaps the intense attention he received so early in life developed his concept that the universe revolved around him,* she decided.

His aunts took turns keeping a twenty-four-hour vigilance on him, giving him alcohol baths, diaper changes, plenty of water to flush the jaundice, and small amounts of food every half-hour.

Dylan's life expectancy was nil because, in the fifties, the country doctor's method of care in his hometown was inadequate. It was only through the patient dedication of his parents that Dylan had survived.

By the age of three, Dylan received radiation treatment for skin cancer. Two years later he became diabetic; by seven he had severe iron deficiency and anemia, probably a result of malnutrition. He had developed an early distaste for food, which Kathryn suspected was a direct result of the intestinal cramps experienced as a baby.

At age four, he began an association with a *ghost* in the closet named George who soon did become his only friend, because George forced Dylan to push everyone else out of his life. His parents thought it was cute that Dylan had an *invisible friend*, not realizing that, to their son, George was indeed very real.

Spending most of his first seven years sleeping, Dylan countered the physical isolation and emotional separation imposed on him by plunging into a make-believe world of dreams and fantasy.

Kathryn had difficulty establishing the reality of George. There was no physical proof to support Dylan's claim, and it was not something she was inclined to believe. Horror movies and books capitalized on people's natural fear of the supernatural, but Dylan totally believed he had embraced the very *entity* others only envisioned. He refused to watch certain movies because they closely revealed the *reality* he had witnessed and endured, and that terrified him.

Dylan had an insatiable need to be loved due to his early years of isolation. The crazed, obsessive need colored all his interaction with family and friends. He identified the inability of his family to physically hold him as neglect and apathy. George filled Dylan's fragile emotional state with images of angry distrust, so that by age seven, Dylan willingly opened his soul to be possessed by George.

His innocent demeanor changed almost instantly and he became uncontrollable. He developed a crisp, proper British accent and seemed older than his years. Dylan's natural instincts mutated into ugly cravings for retribution. He plunged into a pit of vices, presumably enjoyed by the *demon*, George, who controlled him. Shoplifting became second nature; smoking soon developed into a habit; an unusual sexual curiosity blossomed into an abhorrent appetite that invaded his dreams and controlled his physical world. Dylan explored various pleasures usually unavailable to a seven year old, involving himself with kids in their early teens who appreciated a chance to experiment on a willing partner more naive than themselves.

Visions of translucent *green faces* haunted his nightmares and waking hours; *hands* crawled across the floor and up the furniture to attack him; *arms* hung from the walls, reaching extended *fingers* to grab him as he cowered under the covers; *voices* tormented his mind with slanders, suggestions, demands, and constant babbling noise. *They* invaded his only escape, turning his dreams into terrifying nightmares until the horrors that plagued him became the accepted norm.

Dylan was expelled from school every year throughout elementary and junior high, developing a reputation as an incorrigible student. His high IQ caused him additional problems. Growing distant, he plunged himself into the world called *Grey Land*, the spirit world he craved to be part of forever. Separating himself from his family and the world, Dylan eventually lost all rational perception of events and circumstances around him.

Classmates avoided him as too weird to associate with, forcing him deeper into the invisible world of demons. His parents lost all control of Dylan as he became more recluse with each passing year. He developed a ballooned concept of his own evil, acting as if he had to prove how really evil he could be and feeling the worse he was the better he was.

In the repetitive monologue of his history, Dylan still avoided answering her questions about James. It was a topic he was afraid to discuss to any great extent, and she made a mental note to pursue the matter.

Kathryn stretched. Lying on the floor, she cradled her aching head in her arms. Trying to unscramble the maze of Dylan's emotions and memories had given her a headache. Dylan was already breathing the slow, labored breaths that bordered on the verge of a low snore. Closing her eyes, she tried to silence her mind so she too could get some sleep.

An eerie feeling crept up her spine, making the hair stand up on the back of her neck. Someone was staring at her, and she suspected that James was sitting in the easy chair on the other side of the mirror studying her. Opening her eyes to glare at the blackened mirror, she screamed in horrified shock.

A black eyed *translucent green mask* wearing a ghoulish Shakespearean grin glowed at her from the Plexiglas wall. Its empty eyes studying her and Dylan as if the room was awash in light.

Part Five

*The Second Anniversary *

Chapter Twenty-Three

Life had settled into a dubious routine. Dylan became reticent and removed from the daily events involving the household. James spent his hours drinking, smoking, and engaging in his favorite hobby, which was ridiculing Dylan. Kathryn took care of the house, sent Dylan for supplies, and lived in the cell when she finished her daily assignments. If her chores took two hours, she got one meal; anything over six hours earned her two meals. She tried to extend her duties in order to earn the extra meal, but especially so she could extend her time in the light outside of her room. The cell's constant darkness was depressing.

Privileges were nonexistent. To escape James' continual verbal abuse, Dylan was forced to take refuge in the cell with Kathryn. Dylan would curl up beside her on the floor and lay his head in her lap. Insisting she sleep sitting up, he would beg her to stroke his forehead until he would slip into a questionable sleep. Requiring her to keep one hand in his the entire night forced her into a position that denied her the night of rest he selfishly sought and obtained.

Every morning, Dylan used his card-key to free them from the dark room. Kathryn would shower and change, and as she headed to the kitchen to make breakfast, Dylan would look after his own needs. After breakfast Kathryn would clean the house, do laundry, and return to the cell unless James had a more personal and distasteful use for her.

Sex had become, at best, a daily misery that lasted anywhere from a few minutes to two hours. James' gentle, mystical touch was now laced with expanding bouts of deliberately caused pain. James cultivated the level of her agony and fear to satisfy his ever-burgeoning need for brutality and excitement.

Dylan obeyed James' every order, while the older brother went out of his way to humiliate and belittle Dylan at every opportunity. James pushed Dylan to the breaking point repeatedly, forcing Kathryn to worry about another possible suicide attempt. She could only imagine what life would be like without Dylan around to

shoulder the brunt of James' animosity, and didn't want the chance
to experience it firsthand.

Stretching her limbs, she tried to get the feeling back into her
arm. "Time to get up," she said, shoving Dylan's head off her lap. Her
bladder had become an accurate alarm clock, although James rarely
cared about time. He didn't seem to care about anything other than
satisfying his own peculiar needs.

"No, Katie. Not yet. It's too early. I don't want to get up," Dylan
moaned.

"I have to pee, and I need a shower. I want to get to work early
this morning," she argued. Pushing herself from the floor, Kathryn
shuffled to the toilet and relieved her bladder's urgent call. At one
time, her motivation to work was driven by a deep-rooted pride; now,
however, the incentive was simply a need to see daylight.

Dylan hollered as he stumbled into the table on his way to the
door. It, too, was part of the morning routine he adopted because he
just couldn't get his bearings in the dark. Without offering any
explanation, he had quieted Kathryn's continual complaints about
the lights-out situation by confessing that it was at his insistence, not
James'.

The door hissed open and Dylan headed out to the bedroom.
Flushing the toilet, Kathryn limped behind him into the hallway. The
increased hours of immobility spent on the hard çold floor with
Dylan, making certain he was comfortable, had a horrid stiffening
result on her body. Her joints, unbending and sore, wanted nothing
more than a good soak in the hot Jacuzzi to ease their aches and
pains, but James had taken away that privilege several months ago.
She felt lucky to still have the shower. Having been without for so
long, she no longer took anything for granted.

Kathryn stepped into the steamy water. The heat felt wonderful
as it cascaded over her taut muscles. The shower puff lathered suds
over her skin as it invigorated her. She was dismayed that her
coloring had returned to internment gray. Anxious to get outside and
do something, she planned to get all her chores done as quickly as
possible. James hadn't agreed to the idea, but she hoped to convince
him by midmorning.

As she entered the kitchen, Kathryn crossed another day off the
calendar. Today was the mark of her second anniversary as Dylan's
prisoner. It wasn't a day she particularly wanted to celebrate, but she
did hope that they would soften and give her a few well-earned
concessions, at least for a while.

The first order of business was to make a spectacular breakfast. In
the eight months James had been at the helm, Kathryn had not been
able to make one single meal or cup of coffee good enough to please
him. She tried tea, cereal, hot chocolate, toast, anything, but James

only drank Scotch if it was poured by his own hand and, she assumed, ate his own cooking. There was never any kitchen mess to support the idea that he cooked for himself, but he had to live on something.

Every dish of food she prepared for James was scraped into the garbage. It was frustrating because Kathryn knew she was a good cook. Friends had enjoyed coming for dinner parties when she was with David. Dylan always devoured her meals, and she hoped it was more than his desire to simply avoid conversation. And she liked what she made. Grunting with annoyance at James' attitude, she dismissed his opinion while deciding what to make this morning.

Everyone enjoys crepes, she decided. *And there are frozen strawberries and peaches in the freezer.*

She settled on Ukrainian fruit compote for the topping. It was a favorite recipe of David's grandmother and it was far tastier than simple jam. The grand old lady had taught Kathryn a number of recipes from the Old Country before being fatally wounded in an untimely auto accident in Seattle. David's grandmother died only a year after their marriage, missing the joy of seeing her first great-granddaughter.

The two men sauntered into the kitchen. James carried a half-empty glass of Scotch with him, while Dylan asked for a cup of coffee by the time he sat at the table. Kathryn poured the coffee and handed it to Dylan, who sipped it gratefully. She smiled broadly and used a not-so-subtle attempt to win favor with the men from the start. Dishing out two plates of food, she carried them to the table while humming softly—Dylan always liked to hear her hum.

Returning to the counter, she nibbled quick bites between cleaning up the kitchen. James had long ago banned her from the privilege of joining them at the table, enforcing the stigma of slave into her self-image.

Dylan finished his crepes and asked for more while James lit up a third cigarette. It seemed that breakfast was once again not to James' liking.

Damn, that doesn't help. Kathryn grimaced. She couldn't figure out what kind of food James liked. She tried everything, but nothing passed his careful scrutiny. *Maybe he eats something disgusting like raw liver.* She chuckled, wondering what he could possibly eat that she couldn't prepare. James would not discuss with her what he liked. He just continued to label everything unacceptable.

Not allowed to interrupt them, Kathryn waited three hours to bring up the subject of the garden. By then it was almost noon. Determined not to let the request die unspoken, she continued to clean the house and feed Dylan coffee until the two men were available to listen. As Dylan rose from the table, Kathryn stepped beside him and asked to work outside.

James laughed, truly enjoying her words as if she intended them as a joke.

Kathryn pouted and shifted her feet, not exactly sure what to do next. The sun was shining and warm. It was a beautiful day. Having been locked up in the dark for months now, she couldn't just go back to the cell. *I'll go mad. I'll kill myself. No, James will have to let me go outside and do this. I have to get outside.*

"Give it a rest, James. Let her go work in the garden. She really likes that sort of thing," Dylan whispered with enough annoyance crusting his voice to cause James to laugh again.

"If I don't start the garden soon, it'll be too late. There won't be a crop to harvest if I wait much longer. And I have to start from scratch since everything in the greenhouse is dead," she said, trying to maintain a gentle respect in her voice. It was a kindness she did not feel. Kathryn found it difficult to manufacture the constant façade of forgiveness James expected.

The last time Kathryn was allowed outside was during the short walk from the garage to the kitchen the day James escorted her back from the cabin. James stripped her of everything after that. Much to her distress, the greenhouse was abandoned, outings were canceled, and human decency was suspended indefinitely.

"Get a life, Dylan. In fact, that's not a bad idea. It's your second anniversary here with my brother, isn't it Katie? Well, I think it's high time you and Dylan have a bonk in the old sheets, what? That'd be a real knee-slapper. Wouldn't that be better than planting a stupid garden you'll never get the benefit from?" James asked through another chorus of sadistic laughter.

Kathryn and Dylan exchanged nervous glances. Neither wanted to indulge that particular command, but both knew there would be no options if James insisted. He would simply pull out Blankie to convince Kathryn and torture Dylan with internal pain.

"Give her a break, James. Let her go outside for awhile," Dylan suggested. As he chewed his bottom lip, a drop of sweat slid from his temple down his cheek. A hunted look crept into his eyes.

He had let his hair grow into a curly, thick, unkempt mop. Leaving his beard uncared for, scraggly bits of hair stuck out on his lower chin, shabby sideburns, and the corners of his upper lip. It was the worst crop of facial hair Kathryn had ever seen on a man, and she understood his previous passion of keeping himself completely clean-shaven. He had even shaved his head several times a day. Of course, Dylan's excuse was that he didn't want to leave any stray hairs at a crime scene, but she suspected it was because he looked awful otherwise.

"What do you mean I won't get the benefit from the garden? Are you finally going to kill me and give me some damned peace?" she asked, knowing she should be stunned by the threat. But there was nothing left anymore. She was already empty inside, and had been for a long time. Now used to being a prisoner, the fear of death no longer hung over her head. Things had drifted into a numbing routine. There was a certain mindless comfort that possessed her life. Everything outside the estate had ceased to be a concern. It was enough to get through today and tomorrow, one day at a time.

"Your life doesn't concern me. Whether you live or die is inconsequential to the game. You will die sooner or later. Does it really matter when or how?" James laughed, enjoying his own metaphorical morbidity at her expense. He was a master of mental and physical torture, prolonging his precious, demented games to the utmost limits for his own pleasure.

Kathryn again knew, at that precise moment, that her days as their prisoner was limited. James was planning her demise before autumn. There was no other way to interpret his words. *And, if that's the case, I better make my move.* She sighed, reminding herself that neither James nor Dylan could be allowed to walk out alive, even if she should die with them. It was the only way to assure Meaghan's safety, and that was all that mattered.

"All right. Let's say I willingly have sex with Dylan and that provides you with a new form of perverse entertainment. What's in it for me?" she asked. "What will you give me in return?"

Dylan looked up at her, horrified by the thought. He cowered at the implications of having to finally perform.

"Nothing. Absolutely nothing. What, do I look like a game show host to you?" James asked with cruel smugness in his cold, inhuman eyes.

"Then screw you! No more. As of today, it stops. Kill me if you want. I don't care, anymore. Understand? I'm through," she snapped. *Being nice hasn't helped. Maybe if I push back. He's so sick he just might respect that.*

Dylan screamed, grabbed his head, and collapsed to the floor. Writhing for no explainable reason, he continued to scream as an internal pain attacked him without mercy. His feet lashed out in a flurry of kicks. Pounding bent elbows on the kitchen floor tile, he wrapped his forearms around his head. A red rash rose from his neck up his face.

"I think you'll find Dylan doesn't share your misguided sentiment. You see, I can cause unbelievable agony to assault his senses until he goes absolutely mad. He'll do anything to stop the pain. And that's precisely how I want him. You see, it doesn't matter whether or not you are agreeable. He'll force you to do whatever I want to stop his own pain. And if it comes down to the choice between you and him, make no mistake, he'll choose himself every time. Won't you, Dylan?" James asked with a deep-throated laugh. "Just like when the time comes, you will pick yourself over Meaghan and David."

Dylan looked up from the floor through the pleading eyes of a wounded child. The internal agony bared itself in his shattered features, and Kathryn knew he would soon capitulate to James' demands. Dylan, unfortunately, had a very low threshold for pain. His face and clothes were bathed in sweat. A band of dryness wrapped around his chest in a ring, and would have made him look comical if he wasn't already so pathetic.

"Stop it! I can't stand anymore. It hurts. Oh, God, it hurts so bad. Wh...What...do you...want?" Dylan stuttered, barely able to make himself heard. He doubled over as the anguish settled in his guts. Regardless of what happened to Dylan, this was always the typical ending.

Kathryn had witnessed these rashes, burns, cramps, vomiting, and bruises as part of the many mysterious illnesses Dylan frequently exhibited. However, she had yet to find any physical cause for the complaints that plagued him almost daily. The illnesses, aches, and disorders disappeared as quickly as they came, and without proper equipment or books, she had no idea what disease he might have...if any.

She was beginning to understand that the things plaguing him were not at all real. Instead, they had a psychosomatic origin that seemed to be triggered by some signal or word from James or George. The symptoms he suffered were too real to be invented, although he would never allow her to examine him properly. Not only did Dylan describe the illnesses accurately, his body provided temporary proof of their existence. If he had been a patient, Kathryn would have wondered if he were had a borderline Somatization Disorder.

Today's show was no stranger than others. But she knew that no matter how strong his resolve, he would crumple under the imagined pain eventually doing whatever it took to stop the *burning* sensation in his head. It was always just a matter of time.

"All right. Anything. Just make it stop," Dylan whined, groveling on the floor as if he were trying to escape under the tiles.

Dylan stopped writhing and stretched his muscles to relax their tightness. His breathing became slow and even. Wiping a wet forehead on his shirtsleeve, Dylan pushed himself to a sitting position. A look of utter disgust and loathing crawled across his distorted features, giving him the hopeless, haunted look of cornered prey.

"I will not participate. I'm through with both of you. Kill me if you have to. I DON'T CARE. Got it? I refuse to play your sick little games any more!" she screamed at the two men. James revealed that he had already planned to bring David and Meaghan here to add a new dimension to the games. It didn't matter what she did. There was no possible way she could kill one of them let alone both. There were no poisons or weapons available. She couldn't get out of the house even if she did kill them. *Oh, God. What am I going to do?* She was drowning in the utter despair that swamped her.

Turning abruptly, she stormed from the kitchen. There was no place to run. It was a futile exercise at best. It would only prolong the inevitable. But she was so very frustrated with everything. Emotionally bankrupt, she screamed as she rampaged through the house. There was nothing else for her to do. It was the last small step into the abyss of insanity.

James had finally won.

Her auburn hair, now long and uneven from two years of unkempt growth, was dull and dry. There were pronounced crows-feet at the edges of her eyes. Her skin had aged and grown sallow from lack of healthy living conditions and of course, the emotional tension burdening her biological systems. The loss of hope and joy had depleted her self-worth of any remnant of who once would have been recognized as Kathryn, until there was no more life left within the shell of her body. Kathryn, the woman now shrieking throughout the house in a helter-skelter spectacle, was no longer able to hang onto the prized yet fragile seed of sanity she had stored in her heart so very long ago at the beginning of this ordeal.

Rounding the staircase, she ran through the living room toward the utility hallway that would bring her back around into the kitchen again. Dylan grabbed her by the arm, but she yanked herself free from his loose grasp. Launching into a more enthusiastic sprint, Kathryn burst into the hallway. Dylan turned and headed back to the kitchen to catch her as she ran through the opposite hallway door. Kathryn sidestepped him as he rushed toward her. She lunged past him, missing his left hand, and dashed back through the kitchen doorway. She was prepared to race the same circle until her body gave out somewhere along the pointless, endless trail.

Dylan turned and buried his fingers into her thick hair, jerking her to a quick stop. Yanking Kathryn off her feet, she fell backward onto the cold hard tile with a bruising thump. He wound his fingers through her hair to strengthen his hold and hauled her through the kitchen and up the stairs. Kathryn scrambled behind him, desperately holding onto his wrists to alleviate the agonizing pull on her own head. She climbed and fell up the stairs behind him. Dylan dragged her along the carpeted hallway floor into the bedroom, stopping just at the foot of the bed. Picking her up, he tossed her onto the bed before slamming the bedroom door shut behind them.

Kathryn stopped screaming and scrambled to a sitting position at the head of the bed. She pulled her T-shirt down over her knees almost to her ankles. Dylan closed the curtains and turned out the lights. They were plunged into total darkness.

Dylan was not all that distasteful to her. For the last two years, she had held him, comforted him, and cared for his needs. More than anything else, she had become used to him. And that familiarity lent a certain comfort to their relationship. She had seen herself making love to Dylan. The thought had crossed her mind from time to time, in the dark, in the cell, while stroking his brow, holding his hand...

Unlike James, who had forced himself on her, Dylan had always remained a gentleman. *Pathetic, perhaps. Maybe even contemptible at times. But he's always showed me some degree of decency in an indecent situation. I can appreciate that...should appreciate it. Maybe even reward it.*

Kathryn didn't think she would have minded so much if it had just happened, or if Dylan had simply asked her. But for both to be forced to perform solely for James' entertainment...*That's just appalling!* She hugged her knees close to her breast.

Sex with James was precisely that—cold, meaningless, calculated, animalistic, physical lust. She needed someone to make love to; she wanted someone to make love to. It had been so very long since she knew the warmth of that rare and priceless passion. It was like she was wrapped in a plastic body bag that was smothering everything human about her. It felt as if she had been holding her breath for two long years, unable to breathe any life, or love, or desire.

In the darkness, listening to his soft, snoring thrum, she found herself wanting to place her arms around Dylan, to hold him tight. She needed to hang onto someone like a drowning person needs to hang onto a life preserver. *Oh, God.* She didn't want to admit it. It was a disgusting, shameful thing to say—*I want to make love to you.*

Dylan stumbled to the bed. He lost all sense of direction and footing in the dark. His flailing arm struck the corner post and caused the bed to tremble under the blow of his panic. He crawled onto the bed in slow, cautious motion, not wanting to accidentally touch her. The bed bounced as he stopped and flopped crossed-legged just in front of her. Making no further move toward her, his nervous trembling sliced through the darkness and touched her.

She could smell the acidic, salty odor of his sweat. *Fear. He's more scared than I am.*

In the two years she had been at his estate, Dylan was always properly and fully dressed. His shirts were buttoned to the neck and were always long sleeved. He always wore socks and long pants. She saw very little of his body. On the very rare occasion, he might roll up a sleeve or a pant leg to the knee, but that was the extent of his self-exposure. Now she wondered if there was more to his shyness. *Was it really an embarrassing shame over some physical deformity? James must certainly be aware of the problem, and that's why he's pushing Dylan into this. The bastard!*

She felt sorry for Dylan. She felt sorry for herself.

Dylan held his breath and stayed motionless. He bunched himself into a tight ball of nervous energy.

"Have you ever been with a woman before?" she asked in a gentle hush. She could feel him bristle in response across the bed.

"N...no. Well, yes. I mean, no, not like that. I've thought about it. I've always wanted to. But never could," he mumbled. His voice was smothered by the oppressive fear that assaulted him.

"Why?" she probed, still hugging her knees close to her breast.

"It wasn't right. I mean, I just couldn't," he continued, his solemn words heavy and pained.

Kathryn reached her hand across the chasm of darkness between them. She touched his arm. His arms were intertwined into a tight knot across his chest. He resisted her touch. His muscles stiffened. He fought against lashing out and physically thrusting her away. Undaunted, she locked her palm around his arm, reassuring him with her gentle but secure touch. She wanted him to know she didn't altogether object. She wanted him to realize that she understood and was going to help him.

"Come. Lie down and relax," she whispered. One hand patted the mattress beside her as an added encouragement. Her voice was soft and low. Her fingers pulled him forward, firm in their insistence.

Dylan shook his head. He pulled himself back from her hand, wrapping his arms tighter around his chest. His breathing became rapid and nervous. His skin trembled beneath the damp material of his shirt. Gulping, he hunched into a protective cocoon.

Kathryn again laid her hand upon his shoulder, this time just comforting rather than rushing him.

Dylan shook his head violently. His tongue clicked against his teeth. He sucked his cheeks. Fidgeting, he resettled himself in an even tighter cross-legged position.

"No, no. Relax. Come. Lie here beside me. We don't have to do anything. It's okay. Don't worry," she encouraged.

"I can't. You don't understand. You're just trying to make fun of me. I will not become the butt of your jokes, too. It's bad enough I have to put up with James," Dylan snarled. The increased level of his discomfort emitted an elevated body temperature through his shirt.

"This is no joke, Dylan. I am not making fun of you and James isn't here. I want to do this. I want to be with you. I want to put my arms around you and hold you close. To make everything all right. I need this as much as you do. I'm doing this as much for me as for you. I'm so alone. I hurt so much inside. I miss David so much. Sometimes, at night, I can smell him beside me. I think I feel his touch on my leg...but then I wake up, and it's your hand on my thigh. You hold me like he did, sometimes. Oh, you don't know it, but you do," Kathryn said. His soft voice cut through the fear, releasing the inner tension that was winding him to the snapping point.

"You don't want to do this! You just think you have to because I want you to. Well, I don't. I don't need your charity. I don't matter to you. Or anyone. You don't want to be with me any more than anyone else does. God, why can't someone just love me for who I am?" His shoulders beat up and down like exhausted wings as he sobbed in turmoil.

Kathryn felt empathy for the wretched specimen sitting across from her. The depth of his lonely sorrow weighed on her, pulling her into the vortex of his emptiness. She could sense the overpowering emotions swelling within his confused mind as they seared his heart with the brutality of their nakedness. Dylan did not handle emotions well. He avoided facing or admitting them, going to ridiculous lengths to ignore the more normal aspects of his humanity. The fight within him to deny what he was feeling raged and filled the room with an oppressive heaviness.

"I do want to do this," she whispered. He fingers brushed the hair from his forehead, and followed the thin trail left by the ascending tears trickling down his burning cheeks, knowing they would be blushed from the heat in his skin.

She followed the line of his cheekbone down to his lips. Her fingertip caressed the full bottom lip of his mouth, separating his lips gently.

Dylan stiffened his neck, holding his head at a taut angle of resistance. Tears ran down his cheeks. His bottom lip shivered under the gracefulness of her free touch. He loosened his arms. Stretching his back, he relaxed his vigilance of defiance.

Kathryn followed the line of his features down his neck and along his shoulder to his elbow. Taking his arm in her hand, she ushered his upper body the short distance to the pillows with tender persuasion. Slowly, he submitted to her lead.

"I can't do this," he muttered, trying to rise from this more vulnerable position.

"Shhh," Kathryn placed one finger across his lips. Bending over him, Kathryn found his mouth with hers and kissed him a long time. His nervous reluctance yielded to a sensual release, and soon Dylan responded with the urgent need that he had denied for longer than she could imagine. Her own reluctance relented to the demands within her heart as passion overcame her logic, and she let herself be lost to the moment at hand.

Dylan reached his hand to her face and caressed her skin. Flipping her on her back, he leaned on one elbow beside her head. He outlined her eyes and cheeks, found her lips and kissed her again. His lips brushed her neck, and in an awkward moment, he reached down and removed her T-shirt.

Kathryn responded to his gentleness, passion controlling her own movements and longings.

Dylan ran the smooth edge of his nails down her arms and back again, changing his attentions to her collarbone and breasts. He kissed her breasts and stomach, his lips trembling with excitement. He savored her taste with the eager patience of someone who truly knew the pain of love and giving. Dylan was not in a rush. He wanted to explore every millimeter of her body, knowing her body as his.

. Kathryn reached out and unbuttoned the top of his shirt, but he stopped her fingers, kissing the palms of her hands before returning to her hungry lips. He played with her nipple, keeping his weight away from her body. She held his head in her hands as their lips embraced with a passion she had long since buried.

James never let her participate in the act. He performed everything, refusing her even the release of submitting with proper physical responses. She could never touch him and was only allowed to experience the results of James' interest.

But now, she could reach out and touch someone warm. There was gentleness about Dylan that she had long believed was there. The sweep of his fingers trembled with a sensitive understanding of how she felt. They were one in anticipation and appreciation as he was orchestrating a sonnet of experience. He knew how to tease her with an increasing excitement as his hands roamed over her body. He learned to delight in her yielding reactions to his physical urging. He moaned with joy as she responded to his inquiring fingers and asked for more.

Kathryn reached up and undid another button of his shirt. This time he did not resist. She continued down his shirt until she reached the top of his cords. Slipping her fingers into his pants, she eased the button open, ready to search more intimately and reciprocate her growing passion.

Dylan stopped abruptly. His hand clamped onto her fingers and yanked them away from his body. His harshness hurt her. He kneeled beside her and threw her hands away from him.

"What's the matter?" Kathryn asked desperately. "What did I do?" She began to cry from the shock of his sudden refusal. His rejection pierced her heart, deflating her tenuous balloon of worth.

"I...can't...do...this," he hissed, angry with himself. His self-hate filled the room.

Raging at the top of his lungs, Dylan leapt from the bed. He screamed for James, bellowing the name over and over.

Kathryn pulled herself into a ball under the sheets and trembled at the head of the bed. She no longer recognized her emotions. They were a soup of confusion.

Dylan switched on the night table lamp, washing the room in an unobtrusive light. The T-shirt under his plaid flannel shirt was stained with sweat. His hands shook as his fists flailed the air in futile frustration. He roared at the ceiling. Rage possessed him. Stumbling to the end of the bookcase, he flipped the lock and threw the bookcase open, dragging it to its widest limit. Turning on the room's lights, he slipped his card through the lock and swung the cell door open.

Kathryn buried her head into the pillow she clutched close to her breast, shielding her nakedness from the vulgarity of the room. She wept. Bewilderment staked a claim in her mind while his rebuff overwhelmed her heart.

Dylan hollered for James and challenged him. His words made no sense to Kathryn, who could no longer hear his ranting above her own sobs. She didn't know whether to pity or hate Dylan. She couldn't decide whether she should pity or hate herself.

Stomping to the hallway door, Dylan yanked the door open and continued to bellow his challenge out the door. "Get up here, you bastard! It's you and me. I want out! I want to be free!"

Kathryn buried her head into the folded pillow to protect her ears from the sounds of a madman. Rocking back and forth, she sobbed and wailed, howling long, low roars of unstoppable inner torment.

The noise of angry words grew louder in her ears. Looking up, she saw James and Dylan in the cell in hand-to-hand combat. They struggled and wrestled, neither one giving way to the other.

Chapter Twenty-Four

The two men struggled in the brilliant light of the sterile Plexiglas cell. Dylan had broken into a heavy sweat under the intense labor of their physical battle. James took the wrestling in his stride, as if it was an amiable joust with an adoring lover.

Dylan backed into the stainless steel table and screamed from the sudden jab of pain in his kidneys. The sound of James' laughter flooded through the mirrored doorway, mocking not only Dylan, but Kathryn as well.

"Shut up. Shut the bloody hell up!" she screamed, unable to bear one more sound. The noise of their arguing grew in its intensity until it was all she could hear.

Kathryn jumped from the bed. Standing in front of the see-through mirror, she screamed at the dueling pair hysterically, to no avail. They ignored her, forcing her to witness their foolish, angry explosion. Emptied of stamina, she grabbed the end of the bookcase and slammed the wall shut. The sharp thud of its closure reverberated in the sudden silence of the bedroom. Several books toppled from the rows of shelves onto the floor at her feet.

Lost in the momentum of her desperation, she stood in front of the wall and screamed, "Shut up!" until her voice was hoarse.

The need for the bathroom broke the trance that had catatonically seized Kathryn. She had no idea how long she had been sitting on the bed staring at the bookcase. Stumbling through the hallway to the bathroom, she was shocked to see it was night outside.

Running down to the kitchen, she turned the light on and stood ogling the clock above the sink. It was 9:00 P.M. She had been almost nine hours on the bed watching and waiting for the victor to emerge from the cell. Afraid it would be James, she tried to prepare herself for the unthinkable possibility.

Creeping up one step at a time, she returned to the bedroom, expecting to be met at the door by one of them. The room was empty. She tiptoed to the bed, and sat on the edge. Nibbling her lower lip until it bled, Kathryn tried to decide what to do. Another hour passed before she noticed she was naked.

No one came through the bookcase. Without thinking, Kathryn rose like an automaton and began to push the bed, chairs, dressers, tables and anything moveable she could find against the bookcase to block it off. It took her an hour to pile everything from the bedroom and hallway in front of the shelves. Edging away backward, she left the room until she backed into the hall banister. In a swift, unexpected move, one which surprised even her, she yanked the door shut and once again cowered by the banister. Staring at the recessed door panels, she found it difficult to pull her eyes away, still watching for any telltale signs of the door opening. She was afraid they would sneak up on her.

It was six in the morning before Kathryn could pull herself away from the vigil of guarding the bedroom. She had no idea what she planned to do if one of the brothers rushed through the door. She couldn't think that far ahead. Switching on the coffeepot, she pulled three cups from the cupboard. Too anxious to sit, she paced while the coffee brewed. She poured herself a cup and she sipped it at the sink while watching the sunrise.

A pale glimmer of light bathed the clearing. It was a warm day. The temperature was already rising quickly.

She half-finished the ten-cup pot and started a second in case they came down later. After nibbling two pieces of toast by the sink, she headed back upstairs to see what was happening. The door was still closed. Opening it, she cautiously crept into the bedroom. Nothing had moved. If Dylan and James had tried to escape through the bookcase wall, they failed.

She couldn't believe they would not know another way out of the room. Just because she hadn't found it didn't mean there wasn't one. *God knows what sort of surprises Dylan created before I got here. Probably just another of their damn games*, she reasoned. She expected a hand to reach out and grab her at any moment.

Not wanting to make a single sound, she carefully pulled clothes from the dressers and hurriedly dressed. Being in the bedroom gave her an unpleasant eerie feeling. She had to get out of there.

Kathryn roamed the house without any clear direction. The windows were barred. The doors had deadbolts. Dylan had gone all out to ensure her captivity without him. She wandered from window to door in every room on the main floor. Although the alarms no longer posed a threat, without tools of any kind, she was as much a prisoner now as before.

Tears rolled down her cheeks with burning defeat. Pouring another cup of coffee, she looked at the view beyond the solarium. Toasting the ironic hopelessness of the situation, she took a large swallow of coffee and burned her tongue. Her anger erupted. Without thinking, her hand lifted the cup from her lips and flung it across the room at the door.

Kathryn instinctively retrieved a broom and garbage can. Armed with a roll of paper towels, she skulked to the door to clean up her mess before James and Dylan came down. Tears blinded her as she worked to pick up the broken bits of pottery and wipe up the coffee from the tile. Blubbering uncontrollably, she rinsed a cloth in the bucket of hot soapy water and wiped the door and tiles until there was no sign of spill or broken cup anywhere.

Her hand stopped moving. Not sure what she was seeing, she pivoted her head in hopes that a new angle might clear her thoughts and focus her view. The pin on the bottom hinge was protruding above the metal bracket about an eighth of an inch.

Dropping the cloth, she jumped up and ran to the counter. Ripping open the drawer, the contents of silverware spilled onto the floor. Searching through the pile, she picked up a dinner knife and sped back to the door. Dropping to her knees, she placed the knife tip under the pin and pounded the handle with the palm of her hand. The effort caused her more pain than assistance. Leaping up in frustration, she ran to the pantry and grabbed a can of beans to use as a hammer. Returning to the hinge, she tried her new idea until the handle punctured the can and bean juice oozed over her hand.

She slumped on the floor and slammed her head into the door repeatedly. "So close. So close. So close," she chanted. "Probably wouldn't work anyway." She felt beaten with failure. Leaning against the door, she tried to regain control. She concentrated on slowing her breathing. Sighing, she opened her eyes and stared at the island light. She liked this kitchen. Dylan had done a beautiful job decorating. The island was conveniently placed and the diffused light was bright without being annoying. The expensive pots were a pleasure to cook in, and...*The pots. The stainless steel pots.*

Kathryn jumped up and pulled down a quart pan. Placing the knife blade under the pin and smashing the pot bottom against the handle, it was an easy matter to hammer both bottom and top pins out of their hinges. Sticking the knife into the slit of the door jam, she worked the door open until it could be slid out of the locks with little effort.

By noon, Kathryn stood outside the house on a beautiful, sunny May day. It was the most beautiful air she could ever remember breathing, and she filled her lungs. Little patches of crocuses shot through the earth all over the clearing. Birds called to each other in the forest. She was alone with the beauty of the outside world.

Deciding not to leave without shoes this time, Kathryn tiptoed upstairs to the bedroom closet. Finding her walking boots, she pulled them out and shoved her feet into them. Stopping and listening one more time for any movement on the other side of the wall, she turned and skipped down the stairs. Kathryn pranced through the door and along the front of the house, twirling and waving her arms. Freedom felt so wonderful!

The open garage door offered her a mixed opportunity. The van was parked in the closest stall, but unless Dylan or James left a key in the ignition, she would still have to walk to town. The doors to the van were locked. Searching further into the back shadows, Kathryn found the snowmobile Dylan had used buried under a tarp. Again, there were no keys, and she doubted she would get far on the runners anyway. Her hands slapped on the sides of her thighs. *Bicycle. Maybe he has a bike.* It would be easier than walking, so she decided to search the garage for a mountain bike.

Dylan kept his garage well organized. Everything had its special niche on the wall, floor, or post. He was a very meticulous man. Once something was given a place to live, it could not be removed from the spot unless it was guaranteed to be returned. She wasn't sure if it was a rule or an exercise in laziness because he didn't want to search for anything.

A half-dozen tires leaned against a small, built-in wooden box. Lifting the unlocked latch, the side fell to the floor to reveal an older-model and very dusty dirt bike. Grabbing the handles, she hauled it from the crate. It could have been enameled in gold gloss, but without keys, it might as well have been a piece of art. She didn't hold much hope for finding keys.

As she examined the dirt bike, a familiar smile crept across her lips. During her early teen years, she had spent several summers on her uncle's farm with three cousins. They spent the time chasing cows, playing with wiener pigs, and fishing down by the creek. She learned to ride their dirt bike along the back trail through a number of adjoining farms. The bike had been an older model that required a flip of a switch here, a turn of a lever there, and a good old American kick-start.

Just like this one. Except this bike was painted midnight metallic blue.

Kathryn rolled the bike to the edge of the garage, swung a leg over the rear wheel, and plunked down on the dirty seat. Turning the switch on and opening the gas valve, she readied herself to kick the bar into action. Jumping up while holding the handlebars, she put her weight on the metal bar, jerking it downward. Nothing happened. Again and again she tried. It took four jump-starts before the bike rumbled into action. The gas gauge pointed to empty.

Kathryn searched through the cupboards and corners and cupboards of the garage until she found a couple cans of gas. She filled the tank and eased the dirt bike out of the garage.

With only a passing glance backward to make sure nobody was running after her, Kathryn revved the bike down the driveway, remembering to take the right fork this time.

The sun was warm. Birds darted in and around the trees. Small, lazy clouds drifted by high in the sky blue atmosphere. The noise of the dirt bike filled her ears. The wind was cool as it whipped past her. A cloud of dust tailed the speeding machine as she shot around the many potholes. Traveling the route to the highway was faster this time than it was several months earlier.

She expected to find an electrified gate looming in the distance at the end of the trail. Considering the precautions Dylan built into the house, Kathryn expected it to be close to impossible to leave the estate. As she drove to the highway intersection, there was no fence or gate. Dylan was using anonymity to hide his estate rather than announcing to the world that he was here.

She skidded onto the blacktop, leaving a shower of loose stones and dirt flying through the air behind her. Deciding to go east, Kathryn opened the throttle, shifted the gears, and settled into the top speed of forty miles an hour heading toward a vague hope of where the town might be located.

"Thank you," she said, smiling in appreciation. The pleasant-looking young man with no sideburns handed her the first diet cola bottle she had held in two years. Her fingers trembled as she brought the bottle to her lips and sipped the sweet, cold liquid. It tasted good. She licked the drops from her lips, not wanting to lose any of the carbonated freshness. It was an old flavor. The corner of her mouth raised in sly correction. *No, it is a new flavor.* It was her first taste of freedom.

The police department of the small town was generous in their friendliness and understanding. The sheriff didn't even flutter an eyelash as she told her story. He was very polite and attentive. As she listened to the words tumbling from her mouth, Kathryn found it difficult to believe her own story. And yet, this fatherly man in the gray uniform looked at her solemnly as if he'd heard the same tale a hundred times and was quite familiar with it. His gentle eyes put her at immediate ease and she appreciated that.

Now, sipping her drink, she was awed to be among real people again. The half-dozen deputies milling around the office was overwhelming. She felt almost invisible because no one intimidated her. The sheer number of people in the station unsettled her, and Kathryn found her level of anxiety rising every time someone walked passed them. She found herself looking away when someone came into the room. The noise level of even the small town hustle and bustle grated on her nerves, making her wish she were not actually here. The estate was so quiet and peaceful. Kathryn began to wonder if she'd made the right decision in coming out into the world again.

After giving her statement, the sheriff decided it would be most prudent if they got out to the estate as soon as possible. They had no idea who Dylan or James were. There were no records of anyone by those names in this area. Kathryn was unfamiliar with the area and couldn't successfully describe the location. Her mind was focused on getting away than remembering a map back to prison.

The sheriff organized four cars to leave for the estate and find the two men in question. But first they'd have to find the house, and that meant she had to show them the way.

Kathryn agreed to take them back to the estate.

The trip back to the estate was a quiet one. Kathryn felt increasingly uncomfortable with each added mile back to the house. The fact that she couldn't open the windows or doors in the back of the patrol car crowded her, making her feel claustrophobic. The confinement pressed down on her, making her feel frightened and vulnerable. She tried to convince herself that it was ridiculous. *Don't be silly, Katie. You're safe now. This is a police car, not a prison. They're here to protect you. They won't just turn you over to Dylan.*

But she couldn't shake the terror that was burgeoning inside. Panic corrupted her ability to think rationally. Her throat closed. Sweat beaded her face. A deep-rooted trembling seized her. She began to shake more violently the closer to the estate they drove.

The lead car turned right onto an unmarked logging road. The stabilizer bars beneath the car steadied over the potholes. It continued its relentless journey.

Kathryn felt as if she would hyperventilate with the tension. She couldn't breathe.

The car wound through the trees and broke through a clearing. In the middle of the expansive grounds stood a large brick mansion. A van occupied one open stall. There was no sign of activity on the grounds. The sheriff instructed Kathryn to stay in the car and wait until they come out.

The eight police dispersed around the house, coordinating their efforts according to a preplanned design of attack determined before they left town.

Kathryn watched them peer into the windows until they eventually disappeared around the various corners of the house. She tried to get out of the car, just to be outside, but couldn't. She would have to wait until they returned.

It seemed to take forever before the sheriff returned to the car. They had searched the house and things were not exactly as she had described. He asked her to follow him into the estate and explain a few things.

Unsure of what to expect, she fought against stepping one foot back into that house. She could feel someone staring at her from an upstairs window, but when she looked up, there was no one at the windows. Kathryn obediently though reluctantly followed the sheriff around to the kitchen door, the same door she had used just hours earlier to escape. They walked into the front foyer and up the stairs, a path she knew only too well. Turning left at the top of the stairs, she followed the uniformed man into the bedroom. When she hesitated at the door, he assured her that it would all right. She swallowed hard and walked the unbearable last few steps to the opened bookcase and around to face her captors.

Chapter Twenty-Five

The familiar smell of the hospital was more than reassuring; it was comforting. The nurses treated her as if she were a visiting celebrity. The sheriff, who was dubious in the beginning, became a little less cordial after the discovery of Dylan's body at the estate. He insisted Kathryn be a guest of the town until the end of the week, by which time the police expected to have all the loose ends of her story tied up.

Still unable to believe she was in a hospital, she refused to let them shut the door and close her into the room. Her room was across from the nursing station. Kathryn could hear the continual whispers from the desk all night long. Her ordeal was the main topic of discussion on this, and, she suspected, every floor. Being a small town, strange and exciting things were a rare occurrence. The phone, bells, and buzzers echoed throughout the eerie silence of the night shift, and for a moment, she was back on duty in ER on a slow night. The soft glow of the hall lights bounced off the pastel two-toned walls and the black reflecting windows. She watched the hallway activity from their reflections until it reminded her of the people Dylan talked about. She shivered. It was a most distressing feeling, like a sudden ominous omen of something awful promising to happen.

How much has he affected my life? Will I ever be rid of him? she asked, moaning at the awareness of his haunting presence even after proof of his death. The idea of his being part of her reactions, emotions, and thoughts was an unpleasant possibility she was not prepared to accept. She wanted to be rid of him forever, but was afraid that the aftertaste of this experience would flavor everything she would ever do.

Kathryn shifted under the crisp sheets stretched tightly over the firm hospital mattress. It was narrow, warm, but best of all, empty. No one crowded into her space. She wasn't required to run down the hallway to anybody's rescue if they should scream out in the middle of the night. On the contrary, the bell fastened to the pillow assured her of instant attention to her own needs.

But she was afraid to sleep. Kathryn didn't want to awake only to find that being safely secured in this hospital bed was the dream. She didn't want to discover that the people just beyond the door who were concerned about her welfare in a wonderfully *normal* way existed only in her mind. They made Kathryn feel part of the real world, and she didn't want to lose that.

Every hour a nurse armed with a flashlight and quiet step would slip past the door and check on Kathryn. She was still awake. Excitement, disbelief, fear—they all churned together to rob her of a good night's sleep. Kathryn refused a sedative to help her sleep. She was afraid to submit to a drug, regardless of who administered it. Her mind wandered over every detail of the last two years, trying to make sense of everything in the light of yesterday.

There was only one body in the cell—Dylan's. Kathryn had identified the body as that of the man who kidnapped her and held her hostage for two years. He was dead. Probable cause was loss of blood from severed arteries in both his wrists. Found on the floor a short distance from his hand was a small pocketknife—the presumed weapon. The precise cause, circumstance, and time of death could not be determined without a full forensic analysis.

The police were unsure whether Kathryn killed the victim after a lover's spat and fled, hoping they would believe the outlandish tale she concocted. They weren't sure what they did believe. The immediate physical evidence did not support her story, and yet the tale was bizarre enough to be real. The sheriff would reserve judgment until after a full investigation.

Kathryn was examined by the doctor on duty, who followed the procedures and tests set out by the standard rape kit. They gathered smears, nail scrapings, tissue samples, and other pertinent information in a collection of labeled tubes with her identification. Pictures were taken of the multiple scars from injuries, weapons and scratches, and each cause was noted in the report. Then she was admitted to a private room on Three-West for observation.

Morning came early in a hospital, even one in a small Midwest town. The reserved minimum lighting used for nighttime changed to full-blown hall and room lights as the next shift began to rouse patients for morning routines. Not expecting a visit from the doctor, Kathryn was hoping for one from the sheriff.

She was more confused than the police about the discovery of Dylan's body alone in the cell. All night long she had pondered where James had disappeared to. *How did he get out of the damned cell? The sheriff said they found all the furniture still piled up against the bookcase. I've been in that room for two years, and not once could I find any way out of that damned place. Where could it have been hidden?* She had examined every inch of that room more times than she cared to count and had found nothing. Her mind struggled to determine where the exit could have been.

Dressed in the clothes worn from the estate, she thumbed through a magazine and waited for breakfast to be come. It was a busy morning. Several nurses, one ward aide, one porter, the doctor on call from last night, a staff psychiatrist, and the sheriff visited. The sheriff had more questions about her two-year-internment after finishing a background check on her. He discovered that Sheriff John Tyler had never closed the books on her disappearance. There had been evidence to suggest that she had been dragged out of the house to a waiting vehicle, which confirmed part of her story.

The sheriff notified her family as to her current situation, and he expected them to fly in later that day. However, he had more bad news than good. There had been three bodies found at the Breslin property that night two years ago. Deputy Mike Shaw, the officer on duty; her husband, David; and a houseguest, Wendy Smithers, were all found dead by the officer who reported in for the four-o'clock shift.

Kathryn's face flushed a deep scarlet. Her mouth fell open and her hand flew up to conceal the escaping gasp of shock. The pain of loss seared her mind. Tears welled over the rim of her eyes. A sudden ache rent her heart, and she wailed inconsolably. Hysteria captured her and she became uncontrollable. She tried to leave. The doctor ordered a sedative, and Kathryn soon drifted off into a troubled sleep until early evening.

Still groggy, Kathryn awoke to the unfamiliar surroundings. The sheets rasped as she moved between them, adjusting from her side to her back. Yawning, she opened her eyes, taking in the pale green ceiling, the small square light above her head, and the conventional medical valves and tubes on the wall behind the headboard. She found it hard to remember where she was and why. The disorientation slowly passed as the drowsiness of the sedative wore off. Her throat was thick and dry and she smacked her lips together in mild annoyance.

"Do you want something to drink, Baby?" a broken voice asked.

Kathryn opened her eyes and turned her head toward the chair by the window. It was a voice she recognized from a different lifetime. Her heart skipped a beat. She was no longer Kathryn Breslin, the married woman and mother who was kidnapped. She was daddy's little girl, and all her resolve disappeared as tears streamed down her face.

Her father was sitting beside the bed, watching her with strained concern. Anxiety was cut into his weary, seasoned face. His voice cracked under the weight of his long-endured fears and final relief. His cheeks were wet from crying. His eyes were haunted from nights without sleep. The lost glint of life in his eyes was renewed with the freshness of hope.

Tears of mixed emotions stormed within her at the sight of her father. The once distinguished-looking man was drawn and fragmented. It was obvious the feeble old man had aged many years in the last twenty-four months.

"Oh, Daddy," she sobbed. Her arms stretched toward her father. A symphony of disjointed emotions exploded in her. After giving up hope of ever escaping, she had thought she would never see anyone she knew again. In the last two years, she became increasingly confused about what reality truly was. But now, seeing her father beside her...it was as if she had just woken up from a very long and emotionally draining coma.

Reaching his arms around his daughter, the old man hugged her with unashamed desperation. Together they wept with mutual joy and relief that they had found each other alive.

Kathryn was terrified to let go of her father. She could still wake up and find this is just another cruel joke played on her by Dylan and James. She was certain that would cause an irreversible shattering of her fragile mind.

"Katie, I thought I'd never see you again. I'd almost given up hope," the old man sobbed. His cheeks were red and tear-soaked. His chin quivered from the effort of holding himself together. They cried in each other's arms, just as they had done when they lost Kathryn's mother.

In the hours that passed, Kathryn's father brought her up to date with the events after her disappearance. After the dual funeral of Wendy and David, Meaghan remained with her grandparents in New Mexico for a while. However, the family decided it would be more suitable for Meaghan to be with a younger family where there were children around her own age. It was arranged for Meaghan to stay with Kathryn's older sister, Shannon, and her husband Brian. Two months ago, Shannon had a new baby daughter to add to her two sons. Becky, Kathryn's younger sister, had married a young accountant last year. They had moved to North Dakota as a result of his promotion three months ago.

Aunt Lottie had died last year after a bout with breast cancer diagnosed too late for treatment. David's sister, Candice, had given birth to twins early this year. Life in Nantok Falls was tainted. Everyone still talked about what had happened that night, although they graciously stopped talking when Kathryn's father came around. But he could still hear the whispers, and he knew that people didn't leave their doors unlocked anymore. Life in Nantok Falls had been changed. The town had lost some of its innocence that night.

Bill continued running the shop at the request of David's parents, although business had certainly suffered since the incident. David was the main business genius behind the press. Bill hired a woman to replace David, someone by the name of Annie Holt. She was doing a fine job of rebuilding the business to a successful state. Annie and Bill had started going out a couple of months ago, and everyone was pleased to see Bill finally starting to put his life back together after his loss of Wendy. They made a fine couple. Everyone in town liked Bill, and they were pleased to see him smile again.

The clinic suffered immediately after Kathryn's loss as well. Her father became sick right after the shock of Kathryn's disappearance and was forced to hire two people to take their place. When he was back on his feet, he decided to work only half-days. The clinic eventually expanded to accommodate the new physician, naturopath, and her father's part-time hours.

There was some concern and family discussion about what to do with the Breslin businesses and estate. The death insurance paid for the house mortgage. Insurance even covered David's outstanding line of credit, mortgage, and equipment lease of the printing business. However, under the circumstances, everything now belonged to Meaghan, although the estate was held in limbo pending the discovery of Kathryn's body and the official death certificate. Before anything could be disposed of and transferred to the daughter, they would have to wait seven years for Kathryn to be declared legally dead. So the family had made arrangements for everything to be taken care of until that time. David's parents were managing the printing business, Kathryn's father looked after the clinic, and David's sister looked after the house and property.

The Nantok community itself had been severely wounded by the incident and loss. People were a little more afraid of strangers. They even began to look at each other with a certain amount of suspicion. Since no clues were ever found to suggest a reason behind the multiple murder/kidnapping, an air of hushed fear settled on the small seaside town. The common bond had gone out of the community. Their lives had been changed forever. As each year passed and there was still no word about Kathryn, many had given up all hope. She had been much loved and respected by the townspeople, and the tragedy left a definite emotional scar.

Kathryn wept long after her father left for a local hotel that night. Refusing a sedative, she sobbed through the night, barely aware when a nurse came into the room. She mourned David and Wendy with a woeful intensity. Although wishing they were alive, she realized that she had known for a while that they were dead. It was a feeling she'd had in her gut for a very long time.

Early the next morning, the sheriff returned with the forensic reports. His fatherly features were drawn and concerned. Although her story held up on the Washington State end of things, it was far from being clear on this end.

The body at the estate belonged not to a man by the name of Dylan Johnson, but to a woman named Heather Hunter from Sherrill, New York. She had become the sole heir to the Hunter fortune after her parents and sister died in a plane crash twenty years earlier. The estate where Kathryn had been held was owned by a shell company out of Nevada, which could be traced back to one of the several companies owned by the Hunter estate.

There were only two sets of prints found anywhere in the house. One set belonged to Kathryn and the other set to Ms. Hunter. There was no evidence of a third party ever having been in the house or even in contact with the deceased.

The rape examination and initial investigation revealed that all of Kathryn's physical wounds were old and well tended, but there was no sign of recent intercourse, forced or otherwise. The psychological report said she was suffering from long-term mental and emotional stress. There was no doubt that Kathryn believed she had been held prisoner for the last two years. However, generally speaking, she was in good physical condition.

The coroner's final report stated that Heather Hunter died within half an hour prior to the police arrival on the scene, which ruled out Kathryn's participation. She had been in the police car en route to the estate at the time. The cause of death was ruled as suicide resulting from loss of blood caused by the opening of arteries in her wrists. The most probable reason was the victim's fear of facing the legal consequences following Kathryn's escape from the estate.

A series of diaries kept by the deceased were found in one of the locked rooms. They bore witness to the outlandish report Kathryn gave the police, so she was free to leave whenever she wanted. The sheriff expressed his apologies, but hoped she understood that they had no other recourse than to act the way they had.

Kathryn accepted the sheriff's explanation. She was more than glad to have it finally behind her.

Part Six

❧The Autumn ❧

Chapter Twenty-Six

Kathryn hugged her knees into her chest and stared out the window. Rocking gently back and forth, she felt a familiar nervous stir. It would soon be time for her to leave. Fear lurked in the pit of her stomach, nagging at her fragile security. She sighed, not exactly convinced she was ready or even wanting to leave. Shannon and her husband, Brian, had been wonderful. They had taken Kathryn into their home without a second thought and cared for her with an overprotective concern that was very much appreciated.

Shannon treated her sister with kid gloves. She pampered Kathryn with much needed love and understanding, helping her younger sister to heal and forget.

Kathryn held Meaghan for hours, afraid to let her go. It was a painful reacquaintance. Meaghan had forgotten her mother, having mourned for both parents two years earlier. She still harbored a deep-seated anger against her parents for leaving her, not knowing what awful thing she could have done to make them send her away like that. As time passed she became part of Shannon's family. Contentment again filled the little girl's life, although it was obvious that there was still an unfilled emptiness within her. Over the next twenty months she talked about her mother and father, but they became a more distant memory with each story.

When Meaghan again saw her mother, she hid behind Auntie Shannon. It was like a sharp double-edged sword stabbing Kathryn in her breast to watch Meaghan shy away as if Kathryn were a stranger. A sudden outrage exploded within Kathryn's heart for the theft of her daughter, and she cursed Dylan under her breath while outwardly trying to show nothing but love and patience toward her baby.

Smiling, Kathryn would watch from the window of her room as Meaghan played in the back yard with her cousins. While Kathryn cleaned the kitchen, living room, and family room, Meaghan helped Auntie Shannon look after the new baby. The family had been very good to Meaghan, and Kathryn was more grateful than she could ever hope to explain.

Kathryn was still very confused and disoriented. She was not the same person, and she no longer felt a part of the family she had been taken from two years earlier. Kathryn was uncertain whether she could bridge the chasm between the two worlds she now hid in her heart—the one she could never share and the one she was terrified she might forget. With David gone, the memories she had secreted away were all she would ever have of him, and she could no longer remember the sound of his voice.

She mourned not only for the loss of her husband and best friend but also for the savage theft of the memories of them touching her life. The dream of being reunited with her husband and friends was shattered, and Kathryn wept fresh tears from the new heartbreak assaulting her.

Every night, Kathryn still barricaded herself and Meaghan into the bedroom suite over the garage. Shannon had given her that room because it was a large bedroom/sitting room—and it allowed her two exits, in case James entered through one of them. Kathryn was terrified that James was still looking for her and waiting to make his move. He wouldn't just let her go. He enjoyed tormenting her too much, and perhaps more importantly, she could recognize him. The thought of his lurking in the bushes made her jump at every shadow and peripheral movement.

She couldn't stop thinking about the puzzle of the two brothers. James was perhaps the greater enigma of the two. There were so many missing pieces she could not put together. Earlier Kathryn had been too submerged to see through the sludge of confusion. But now, after everything was said and done, her mind couldn't help going over all the odd inconsistencies.

One thing that circled her mind was the cigarette. Kathryn thought James must have cleaned up behind himself, although it certainly didn't seem to fit his characteristics or profile. She had never found a single burn mark or discarded butt from the cigarettes he threw under the bed each time before he abused her. She never washed one ashtray that wasn't filled with Dylan's brand of cigarettes. James smoked an imported British brand, while Dylan smoked homegrown. James never accepted a cigarette from Dylan or offered one to him. She had thought he was just selfish. Perhaps that wasn't the case.

There was also the question of eating. She had never seen James eat or prepare food for himself. It was as if he subsisted on air. *What could he have possibly eaten that I couldn't prepare?* she asked again. The question had nagged her for months without offering any answers.

It had been so long since she had been with David—touched him, smelled him, felt him. Her mind remembered what it was like, but her body had forgotten, and when she was with James, she forgot what it should feel like. It wasn't until Dylan had lain beside her that she realized the one thing missing with James was the body weight. Even Dylan's hand had a warm weight to it, whereas James' touch had neither warmth nor substance. She could never tell precisely what James was doing because he seemed to be everywhere at once. Kathryn was constantly reeling from the exciting result of his touch. She would resist what his touch did to her, but it wouldn't matter. Nothing she did could stop the intensity and excitement of what she felt, and she was too soon lost in the sensations to care about the physics of his maneuvers.

And why did he insist on total darkness? It was so I couldn't see him. But why? The things he did to her and the things he whispered in her ear proved it wasn't shyness that forced him into the dark. Both brothers had the same fetish about being unseen. Dylan's, however, was now understandable.

God, how could I not have known he was a woman? Again, there were so many telltale signs. He squatted on the toilet because he had to, not because he was trying to be considerate. She was never allowed to see him naked, and his clothes were always baggy. The fact that he did not sweat around his chest meant that he bound his breasts so as not to give himself away. Now that she aware of it, she realized she had felt the odd stiffness through his clothes around his chest once or twice but had thought nothing about it at the time.

But he did so many man-things, she argued in defense of her ignorance. *The way he brushed his hair back, cut his toe nails, sat...*Even his attitudes were distinctly male, as was his logical thinking process. He had constantly felt his face for hair growth. There were so many things about Kathryn's way of thinking and emotional outbursts he could not fathom. Looking back, she decided he had concealed his femininity too completely for her to ever have guessed his true identity. *That was why he stopped making love to me that night.* If they had continued, he would have been exposed for what he was—a woman.

So Dylan was a Heather. She shook her head in disbelief. It explained so many things, and yet left so many more unanswered. There was no question that Heather utterly believed she was a man. The continual turmoil caused her a great deal of internal agony because she could not do the one thing she wanted. Heather simply did not have the right equipment, and there was no getting around that one basic fact.

Was it a simple case of penis envy? Kathryn doubted it. There was something much more deeply rooted in Dylan's psyche than that. She wondered if she'd ever understand.

The questions plagued her whether she was awake or asleep. Kathryn would have to find the answers if she were ever going to gain peace of mind again.

Going home was the hardest thing Kathryn ever did. She packed Meaghan's and her belongings into several boxes and two small duffel bags. They said their good-byes, climbed into the sedan Brian retrieved from her Nantok Falls home, and headed north.

Years earlier, Shannon, Brian, David's sister Brenda, and her husband, Frank, had cleaned the house after the police were finished with the crime scene. They didn't want Kathryn to return home to find bloodstains to remind her of David and Wendy's brutal murder. But Kathryn didn't return. As the months turned into years, there was a family debate on what should be done with the family estate.

Last week, Brian had gone north to the Island to make sure that Kathryn's homecoming would be less traumatic and stressful than was necessary. He had straightened up the grounds, hired a housekeeper, and repaired anything that was broken. He arranged for added security and had the locks changed to assure Kathryn would have the only keys in existence. When everything was as ready as Brian could make it, he had driven Kathryn's sedan from Nantok Falls to Santa Anna in Southern California so she would have a vehicle for the return trip.

Following the California coast, Kathryn was thrilled to once again spend time with the ocean. Making the trip home an extended vacation, they stayed at several motels along the way. She was in no hurry to rush back to an empty house. Garibaldi was their favorite place in Oregon, and they stayed at the luxury condominium hotel on the beach for almost a week.

Kathryn shared her joy of the beach and ocean with Meaghan. She taught Meaghan about all the life that lived in the tidal pools. No longer angry with her mother, Meaghan had a good time experiencing all the things the coast had to offer. They rode dune buggies and horseback, flew kites, and experienced a myriad of other things they found along the way.

When they finally reached home, Meaghan was far too excited to wait for Kathryn to open the door to their home. She jumped out of the car and dashed around the side of the house to where she remembered the swingset being. Kathryn stared at the black windows of the empty house. Her hands were still gripped around the steering wheel. In the carport was David's vehicle. The yard badly needed attention. She'd become very aware of landscaping in the last year, and now, seeing her yard, ideas naturally popped into her head.

Taking a deep breath, Kathryn climbed out of the car and reluctantly headed to the front door. The key turned easily in the lock and the door opened. A sense of relief coursed through her. It had been over two years since Kathryn had a key to a front door, or any door for that matter. It offered a sense of security and command over her own life again.

The house was too still. It was devoid of the life that had once filled its walls. The silence slapped her, making her numb as she stood at the foot of the stairs in the front hallway. She wanted to yell that she was home, but no one was there who cared.

She would have to build a new life on the foundation of the last one. *I'll be damned if I forget the happiness we had. Dylan can never steal that away from me. That will be my revenge. I will live and enjoy life. I will not let Dylan destroy me,* she vowed, determined to keep this promise...for herself, and for Meaghan. David and Wendy would want her to overcome.

Kathryn bit her lip as she walked upstairs to the living room and kitchen. There were so many happy memories in all these rooms. David had made their dream house, and together they filled it with life and love. Dylan could never take that away. Now that she was home, there was no question. David would always be part of her.

After moving back into the house, Kathryn attacked the voluminous mound of mail placed in a box on the kitchen table. Bills were separated and taken care of by Brenda as soon as they came. The monies from the printing business and all other funds were placed in the bank. That still left a great heap of social mail from people who did not know what happened to the family, and junk mail from people that wouldn't have cared even if they did know.

There was little else for Kathryn to do, so she set about to tackle the mail as her primary chore before deciding what to do next. It was too early to return to the clinic. *Maybe by the end of the year.* She wondered when she would feel like going out into the world again...or if she ever would.

Kathryn made a cup of tea and sat down at the table. Armed with a garbage can by her side, she tore open the first envelope, tossed it into the garbage, and proceeded with the next one. By the second hour, Kathryn had worked through most of the pile, placing the majority of mail into the garbage as undesirable or out of date.

A pale beige envelope with blue insignia was the next bit of business to be taken care of. It was from a lawyer in Billings, Montana. Kathryn opened the letter hesitantly, not knowing anyone from that part of the country. Shocked by what she read, she dropped the letter from her hand and watched it flutter to the table in slow motion.

The late Heather Hunter had left the entire Hunter estate and businesses to Mrs. Kathryn Breslin. The letter had been sitting in the box on the kitchen table for over two months, waiting for Kathryn to return and find it. Now all she had to do was to go to Montana to sign the papers and claim her inheritance, which was valued in excess of twenty-three million dollars.

Kathryn was stunned. Part of her wanted nothing more to do with either Dylan or his belongings, while another part was glad to have been victorious over his life and possessions. It proved she was the winner of the war waged against her. But there were far too many casualties to allow her to feel good about being the victor.

Chapter Twenty-Seven

It was another week of soul searching before Kathryn notified the lawyer of her intent to claim the inheritance. The money was little consolation for the devastation Dylan had done to Kathryn and her family. There was certain fairness in his placing his affairs into her hands. Kathryn needed to dismantle his life piece by piece, just as he had exterminated hers. She needed to destroy every piece of evidence that Dylan ever existed. Pictures, clothes, personal belongings, house, land, and businesses were all to be put on the auction block for complete elimination. The power she had gained over Dylan after his death made her feel very much like the victorious army razing the enemy king's castle to the ground.

Without risking setting one foot back onto the estate, she eradicated the possession and memory of his belongings and property. As each piece of his life disappeared into the sea of the general populous, Kathryn felt a little piece of herself return from the abyss of despair.

Kathryn had made a vacation of driving to Billings. It was difficult to understand Dylan's reasoning behind leaving everything to her. *Did he expect me to outlive him? Had he planned to let me go all along? Had he decided to commit suicide from the beginning? And what about James? Doesn't he have a claim on the estate? Is he going to contest the will?* There were so many questions that would never be answered. *James would be a fool to show his face.*

Kathryn wished she had never met Dylan, but that was beyond her control. A new level of cynicism entered her thinking as she appreciated the justice meted out. He would be forgotten forever. She would personally see to that.

The lawyer handed Kathryn a large white cardboard file box of private papers, deeds, titles, and bonds. Her fingers trembled as she carried the box to the trunk of her sedan. She had talked herself into believing that the last two years were far too ludicrous to be real. But as she drove back to Nantok Falls, the nagging proof of that painful period of hell was undeniable.

Kathryn would have to sort through Dylan's life and tie up all the loose ends. It was unfair of him to further burden her with the affairs of his death. *Maybe Dylan had no friends or family in his life. Hard to believe that I'm all he had,* she reflected. She was amazed at his complete lack of life. However, she was in no rush to enter his world once again and decided the unpleasant task was best accomplished on familiar ground.

When Kathryn returned home, it was another month before she could open the box that shadowed her peace of mind. It haunted her, but she was still too afraid to look at its contents. The very presence of the papers drove her into the reclusive arms of her home and the pounding solace of the ocean at the base of the cliff.

Finally facing the task, she found several sealed letters amongst the contents. Dylan had addressed them to her personally, and each one was dated and numbered so she could read them in developing sequence. It was an eerie realization to learn that he had prearranged to reach out to her from beyond the grave.

Kathryn fingered the pile of letters after organizing and reorganizing them into numbered order, feeling she had to suffer the letters to earn the inheritance. Unsure she wanted to go back and be part of Dylan's insanity, she hesitated to read them. But curiosity got the better of her and she found herself tearing open the envelopes. Each envelope was stuffed with a thick quantity of folded papers. One by one, she read the volumes of words, morbidly captivated by the lunacy penned on the pages.

Dylan had written things he felt he could never explain to her or anyone. He exposed what was going on inside his heart—his needs, motives, and dreams. The rambling in his writing, more than he ever did in speaking, provided her with a difficult challenge to decipher the truth from the maze of biased memories.

Number 37.

Dear Katie:

I know you think badly of me. I can see it in your eyes every time you look at me. You will never understand what drives me. It is too difficult to explain. It hurts inside, like a knife has cut my heart into a thousand agonizing, still-beating slivers. I ache all the time. I don't know how to stop the constant throbbing pain. I've tried everything, but it's still there. It's always there—when I'm awake...asleep...with you...alone.

I always felt separated from the people around me, like I was completely different. We had nothing in common. I could never understand what they felt or thought, because the words always had a different meaning for me than it did for them. We never talked the same language. It was like we didn't even live in the same world.

My family and I—we were simply strangers existing in the same house. I didn't understand what they were about, and they didn't have the foggiest notion that I was. Hell, I didn't even know who I was. It always seemed like

I reeled from one experience to another like a drunk on skid row, and I was never quite sure how I got there. I never knew what was happening. It was like I just woke up and found myself in an uncomfortable, awkward situation—confused, afraid, and having to react instantly to something I knew nothing about. Poof! There I was. And I was always alone.

The agony of aloneness is awful. It corkscrews your soul into a series of aching spasms until you can't think straight anymore. Everything gets all warped and bent in your thinking. It's like looking at everything through the belly of a tornado. You can only see that tiny area at the bottom of the funnel. Everything else is distorted with debris, garbage, and broken bits of things that make no sense. It swirls around you, and as you dizzily try to look out and see where you are, the whirling wind perverts and muddies everything around. You end up not being able to see anything beyond the wall of your whirlpool prison.

You have no idea what it's like to live in the inescapable eye of the tornado. You have no idea what it's like to have to exist with that kind of depravity shredding you apart every minute of every day of your whole entire life. The images, thoughts, feelings…the burden of their horrors is more than one should have to bear. I couldn't stand seeing people tortured. It wore me down. Every time I closed my eyes, women were being physically and psychologically tortured until I learned to enjoy the image and idea. It became pleasurable. It became desirous. It became the only thing I wanted to think and dream about. It felt good inside.

I was four when it started. I was addicted to the adrenaline rush by the time I was seven.

It sexually stimulated me, although it was a long time before I learned exactly what that was. All I knew for a very long time was that it felt nice physically. Soon I spent most of my time fantasizing about the excitement so I could gain the feeling. Then I learned how to get the same thing from somebody else. I didn't understand much else except I liked it. And that made me feel dirty and ashamed. It drove a greater wedge between me and everyone else, because I knew no one else thought about the same things I did. Regret dogged my steps. Constant guilt churned inside me because I knew I wanted to do something bad, something that wasn't acceptable by anyone else in the whole world.

But then I found that there were others like me. Maybe not quite the same, but they liked odd, unacceptable things as well. I researched materials, books, and articles about things they discovered were interesting. I looked into the history books and found entire centuries and nations that thought the way I did. But that only made me feel worse, because it sounded so sick when they did it. I began feeling like I was an abhorrent, evil creature. I felt worse than I ever did before.

You don't know the first thing about me, and yet you set yourself up to be my judge, jury, and executioner. You tell me what is normal and how I should feel. You think you know what is real and what is not. But that's bullshit! You have no idea what I have seen or what I've been.

You have no idea what it is like to live with the things I think about. There are so many dark things that live in my heart. Secret, ugly things I was forced to witness not only in my mind, but in life as well. I have such a hate for everybody…even you. Maybe it's not hate but anger, because no one understands me and not one person ever helped to stop the insanity that devoured my childhood and life.

All of you live in a world I can never hope to grasp, and you won't explain it to me so I can join in with everyone else. God, I'd give anything to be normal! Just for one single minute. Just to know what it feels like.

You portray everything that I can never have. You are so innocent. You wear it like it's a natural right that belongs to everybody; like it's the badge of honor of a secret club that wouldn't even consider letting me be a member. Well, I don't have it. I never had that innocence. I was evil at a very young age. It lives in my gut like a tight, coiled snake ready to strike at any moment. Its venom is fatal, and it squeezes the spirit right out of me until I have no life left. You keep your badge of honor. I have my snake. It is my badge of dishonor. I belong to a club that would not accept you or your kind. At least I belong somewhere.

The noise of my friends beats me back, crushing me beneath the rubble of insanity. I know I'm crazy. I feel it growing inside me like a cancer eating away at my soul. It hurts. It hurts so much. And it is so very dark where I live, like I'm wandering around an endless, lightless cave inside my heart.

It's like there's a hundred people crowding inside of me, filling me until there's not one square inch of room left for ME. I cannot move or grow, so I remain stunted and small. They scream, yell, and babble at me all the time. Sometimes I can't understand what they say. Sometimes I wish I couldn't understand. They say such foul things, things I never wanted to hear or know. But I have heard and I do know, and it is so hard to scour the filthy black thoughts from my mind and soul. They stay there, building up until I think I will explode with the pain and shame of bearing them.

Oh, God, I wish I was young. I think I could have been a nice person. I dream of that sometimes. I dream that I look after somebody, and I take care of them. They need me and want to have me around. But then my mind puts that person in danger so I have to rescue them, and they feel obligated to like me. They have to like me regardless of finding out that I am not really nice. They forgive my badness because I rescued them, and that is so very important to me. I've never been a child. Never had that sweet innocence. Never saw the beauty and excitement life holds for only the young at heart. I was old before my time. I was possessed by a demon that taught me what it was to be a man, in every way but the one important way. But that was my torture. To need and want to be a man to the most minute detail, but never being able to get close to the reality. George and James filled me with the brutal, sadistic desires of an evil man, but gave me no release or satisfaction.

How can I ever hope you would understand the pain of being me?

You're so pathetically innocent, you never will have the slightest clue what goes on inside me—the war I have to wage every minute of every day just to stay sane. It is so hard to pretend to be normal so other people will never find out who or what I really am. I try so hard to be like everyone else, but then I get tired. The enormous effort drains me of any reserve strength I have until, driven beyond exhaustion, I wish I would die.

I have tried to kill myself. Many times. But they won't let me die. They will never let me sleep and rest. God, I pray for rest and peace and death.

You see, I know George for what he is. Oh, he told me he was the ghost of a British lord who died several hundred years ago. I bought that for a while. But then I met James. He told me he was George's brother. That made us relatives. Go figure.

It took a long time to learn that there are no such things as ghosts of dead people. They're demons that possessed the person in question. And because they possessed that person for so many years, they know everything there is to know about that person. They talk, walk, and act like the person that is no longer alive. They take over the life of the person until death separates them. They search all over to find a body, and then they lie, steal, cajole, and do whatever is necessary to gain control of the new host. They tell whatever story will be accepted by the new host, and their imagination is vast.

There is no such thing as regressive memories of past lives. I know. I've hypnotized people. The demon goes from one body to another, taking with it all the memories, feelings, and emotions of all the people it inhabited before the new host. It's a trick. They always trick us. They want a body and they are prepared to do anything to get one...and keep it.

Then those bastards feed their perverted desires, pushing their new host to the limits. I had sex by the time I was seven. I was smoking by the time I was nine. I was alienated from everyone and everything I knew. I was George's prisoner, and was tricked into overthrowing him by James. Then I became James' prisoner. And you have to know that James was worse than George ever was. I became more deplorable under James, and to top everything, I never did get rid of George. James made me believe that I had exorcised George, but what really happened was that I just invited James into me over top of George. Then all hell broke loose and I was riddled with demons.

I saw them. I felt them. I heard them. They were all around me. They were inside of me. Oh, God, why didn't someone hear my cries and deliver me from the worms crawling beneath my skin? It felt so awful. They slithered under my skin, in my organs, through my brain. They drove me insane and no one would stop the pain. No one heard the screaming agony I bellowed in so many ways.

He taught me about Grey Land. It's a place like a massive, endless hotel where the demons live until they can find a body to possess. And they possess more people than you'd think. People think they're all right. But inside so many of them is this little cancer waiting to take over their whole life. They take an innocent child and turn him into a mass murderer, serial killer, gang member, drug addict, child molester, or drunk, or any kind of monster they can—anything that makes the demon feel successful. And the only thing that makes them feel good about anything is to witness the destruction they can rain down on as many people as possible.

I heard the voices. I saw the faces and hands. I was ordered to maim and kill people. Random people that hadn't hurt me, that made no sense. But I fought against the urges and needs. I could only hurt them. I think if I didn't find you, I would have killed someone eventually. I would be one of those sick serial killers running all over the country killing just for the sake of killing to quiet the voices inside their own heads. I wanted to, but there was something inside me that must have been still decent. And when I met you, I couldn't hurt you. I wanted to protect you.

That's why I took you, you know. I needed you to be my friend. I needed you to understand the war raging inside of me—the part that wanted to hurt you and the part that couldn't stand to even think of that sort of thing. I needed you to understand so you could stop what they were doing to me. I needed you to stop my pain.

I would stay awake nights arguing with them, the horde of demons and voices that badgered me until I would draw blood—yours or mine. So I gave them mine. I would have given them my life in exchange for yours, and if you're reading this letter, then I have given my life for you.

I read papers or watch T.V. and I see the horrendous number of things happening to so many people. It's because there are so many demons that have found homes. And then the person just acts out the things that particular demon wants.

I don't want to hurt people. I don't even want to think about it anymore. I don't want to see the images in my mind anymore. I want it to stop. God, how I beg it to stop. But it excites me sexually. Always sexually. It's gotten that I like pain. It excites me in a sick sort of way.

I don't want to hurt people, but I have to. George, James, and all their bastard friends hurt me until I lash out and hurt someone else. It's like offering up a sacrifice to get someone else to take my place.

James turns my mind against me. I can't fight that. It's like hypnosis or something. My head begins to burn like my brain is on fire, and then something happens somewhere else in my body. It's always a different place so I can't get used to it.

You can get used to pain. It becomes part of you after a while so you hardly even notice it anymore. They don't want that to happen, so they have to keep changing how they attack me. I just can't stand it anymore. It has got to stop. And if you can't help me, then I will do it myself. One way or another.

Know that I am so sorry for hurting you. I never meant to. I hope someday you will forgive me. You are the only person I ever cared about. And I can't pay enough to make up for the crimes I have committed against you, even for the thoughts I have had against you.

I'm sorry. I will always be yours.

Love,

Dylan

Kathryn read the last letter of the pile. It was the clearest he had ever been in all the time she knew Dylan. She almost felt sorry for him. What was worse was the fact that she almost forgave him. Dylan was as much a victim as she was, and perhaps a greater victim in the light that he lost his life and family. She only lost her family.

But something inside her fought against feeling sorry for him. People struggle with all manner of difficult problems without resorting to the things he did. *No. Victim or not, you still have no right to infect me with your diseased fantasies,* she decided as she lay the letter upon the coffee table.

Kathryn stood, her thoughts and emotions numbed by his words. She picked up the pile of letters, stepped around the coffee table, and tossed them into the fireplace. Pulling a match from the container, she knelt down, struck the match, and started the pile into blazing inferno.

Kathryn returned to the sofa. Piece by piece, she began the process of dismantling Dylan's life, disentangling its cancerous hold on hers.

Part Seven

The Third Anniversary

Chapter Twenty-Eight

It was with mixed emotions that Kathryn prepared to celebrate May 12th—the first anniversary after her release. It was the day she was kidnapped, the day David and Wendy were killed, and the day she escaped.

The past nine months had been busy and she was grateful for that. Although it didn't take her mind off things, it did help her get through them.

Reluctantly, Kathryn sold the printing business to Bill. It had been David's dream, and for that reason alone she had entertained the thought of keeping it. To give away the business was to give away one more piece of David. But it wasn't her dream and she knew next to nothing about the business. Bill had done a good job taking care of things after David's death, and Kathryn decided he deserved the business, which had become his passion since Wendy's death.

In the summer, she had tried to return to the clinic. People treated her more like an oddity than a long-lost friend. They either said nothing, which plunged a wedge of uncomfortable silence between them, or over-expressed their condolences, which was equally unsettling. Everyone had an opinion on what had happened whether or not they verbalized their thoughts. It was unnecessary and painful, and Kathryn decided she didn't need the added emotional burden in her life at this time. On top of everything, she discovered that her heart was no longer in her work, and after only one week of part-time hours, Kathryn gave up the endeavor altogether. She legally gave her partnership of the clinic to her father, who sold it to the two new doctors before he too retired. His health was failing. He chose to stay close to home, look after his garden, and visit with Kathryn and Meaghan when time permitted.

Kathryn compensated Shannon and Brian for the two years they had looked after Meaghan and the three months they had cared for her. Then, although unnecessary, she paid Brenda and her husband for managing her property and bills.

While straightening out her own affairs, she sorted out Dylan's. She wanted Dylan's matters out of her life as soon as possible. Without being concerned what price she got, Kathryn sold Dylan's house and various businesses at six different auctions. The house was auctioned complete with furnishings, videos, books, foodstuffs, clothes—she took nothing from the premises. Dismantling his life piece by piece had become a passion that consumed every minute of her days for two months.

Every loose end was taken care of in her own life and Dylan's before she contemplated what to do with the rest of her life. By the time the dust settled, Kathryn had just over nineteen million dollars in the bank and a new life ahead of her.

She still woke up in the middle of the night from the same nightmare of being relentlessly hunted. Whoever the heavily shadowed stranger was, he always caught her. The moment she felt his cold, clawlike, bony fingers clamp on her shoulder, she would wake up screaming in a cold sweat. Suddenly awake, Kathryn could still feel the deep gashes of his inch-long nails indenting her flesh. She would massage her shoulder until it stopped aching. But the memory of the sting lingered until the next night, when the pain would be renewed after a fresh hunt through the darkness of her fears.

Kathryn stayed home to take care of Meaghan. She was afraid to let her daughter out of her sight. They did everything together, although they rarely left the house. Together they became reclusive prisoners of Kathryn's own experience and fears. Protecting herself and Meaghan was her only concern. It soon became her obsession.

The year that passed did not take away the fear and pain of what happened. They both hurt, but Meaghan had healed much quicker than her mother. Meaghan still harbored a deep-seated anger with her father for leaving, but Kathryn knew that would pass as she got older. By then, Kathryn hoped she could explain what happened to them. By then, Kathryn hoped she might understand it herself and overcome her own anger.

It had been a hard year. Kathryn decreed that they needed a good day out. It had been years since they had a day just for themselves in a light, carefree atmosphere. After everything they had been through, Kathryn knew they deserved at least that much.

Deciding to make a day of it, Kathryn put together a picnic basket of all their favorite foods and drinks. Packing a blanket and some toys for Meaghan, she planned to go to Deception Pass and sit on the beach. Meaghan loved the beach, and although it wasn't very warm, it was a nice enough day that they could enjoy themselves. Meaghan was fond of making sand castles, and Kathryn thought they could create an elaborate one if they both spent a good part of the afternoon on it.

The drive was a pleasant one. Kathryn enjoyed her new car. She had sold their two vehicles after cleaning David's clothes from the house. It was too painful to have his personal effects around. She kept some things that were too precious to give up: his Spanish Doubloon necklace, wedding ring, the sweater that still had his smell, his books...

Although it was the most painful thing Kathryn ever did, she gave his clothes and belongings to the Salvation Army. After a great deal of personal debate she relinquished her furniture and refurnished the house with things she and Meaghan picked out. Kathryn wanted to remove all the things that reopened the still-festering wound of David's death.

When they arrived at Deception Pass, Kathryn parked in the picnic area. There were other children playing on the beach. Meaghan, who was so delighted to again see another child, ran over to play with them, armed with a shovel and pail. Kathryn watched carefully, unable to fully drop her guard. But she wanted to relax her vigilance enough to let Meaghan have a good time. It was a constant struggle to remain balanced in her need to protect her daughter, and Kathryn was the first to admit she didn't always succeed in being rational.

They ate, played, and walked along the beach. They talked and laughed, and it felt good. For the first time since everything had happened, Kathryn felt alive and thought just maybe life wasn't going to always be bad. Watching Meaghan play with the other children gave Kathryn hope for both their futures. Meaghan looked so free and happy. As she watched her daughter laugh, she remembered how Meaghan had been around Shannon's family.

The decision was made before she realized. Kathryn would keep the house because it was their home. Her father had been talking about moving to California to be closer to Shannon's family, and although it had hurt her at the time, Kathryn now decided to make the same move. She needed and wanted family around. The relationships between herself and her friends had become strained to nonexistent.

Perhaps with family around, I can remember how to truly live again. Tomorrow I'll call Shannon and Dad and let them know. Meaghan can start next year in California. Maybe she can go to school with her cousins. She'd like that, Kathryn mused, pleased with her new plans. It had been a long time since she was capable of making plans with any hope and enthusiasm.

The rest of the afternoon was more than pleasant. Kathryn felt a true sense of release, as if a great load had just been lifted from her shoulders. Today would also be the day she began her new life. Excitement built within her as her mind ran through all her plans almost quicker than she could grasp. She was going to give her father the option of moving in with her and Meaghan. He would like that. They could leave in the next couple of days and go house hunting. It would lift everyone's spirits because her father had become distant and depressed after retirement. It was as if he had not gotten over his broken heart after Kathryn had disappeared.

Yes, perhaps California will be the best thing for all of us. The more she thought about the possibilities, the freer she felt. It was the most positive move she'd made in three years. It was a wonderful feeling to be able to make a decision about the course of her own life...and Meaghan's life...and know instinctively it was a good one.

As she drove home, Kathryn couldn't help but smile with glad exhilaration the entire way. Meaghan couldn't remember ever having seen her mother so happy, and she kept asking what was so funny.

Kathryn explained her plans, and Meaghan was thrilled to be moving back to Santa Anna to be with Auntie Shannon and the family. She especially missed their dog and asked if they could get a puppy when they moved. Kathryn thought it would be a great idea. She didn't want to remind Meaghan that it was David who was allergic to animal fur. Meaghan had asked for a puppy ever since she discovered what they were, but David's reactions were so severe and unpleasant that they couldn't have one near the house. Now there was no reason, and a dog would be good protection.

They sang songs with the radio as they drove, and Meaghan talked about staying over with her cousins and helping look after the baby once in a while. She had grown up so quickly in her short little life. It was time for her to be a little girl again and let Kathryn bear all the weight of life.

Arriving home early, they made a light supper and watched one of Meaghan's favorite videos. Kathryn had learned to enjoy movies after years of being prisoner before its boxed screen. After the video, Kathryn told Meaghan to get ready for bed and wait to be tucked in. If she pulled out her bedtime favorite story, Mommy would read it to her.

Meaghan ran squealing down the stairs and hallway to her room. She couldn't get the move out of her mind, and she ran chanting the name of her new puppy with each step.

After straightening the kitchen, Kathryn changed into pajamas before going to Meaghan's room. The light from Meaghan's bedroom reflected off the pastel hallway walls. Kathryn almost skipped with a light joy into her daughter's room. She expected to see Meaghan under the covers with the chosen book in her lap and Blankie in her arms. As Kathryn opened the door wider, Meaghan was nowhere to be seen. Stepping backward into the hallway once again, Kathryn checked the bathroom, but the light was out and the room was empty.

"Meaghan, honey? Where are you? Are you playing hide and seek with Mommy?" Kathryn asked in a gentle singsong voice.

"I'm in here Mommy," Meaghan answered from behind the closet doors.

Confused, Kathryn sauntered over to the closet doors and eased them open. The bedroom light lit up the cluttered space enough for Kathryn to be able to see Meaghan sitting cross-legged on the floor in the corner. Blankie was in her arms and a book was in her lap, waiting for her mother to read it.

"What are you doing in here, honey?" Kathryn asked gently as she knelt on the floor beside her daughter. A sudden fear stabbed her through the heart and panic seized her mind.

"I want you to read the story to my new friend, Mommy. He says you know him. He says he likes your stories. He's a nice man, Mommy. He says he likes me a lot and that we'll be great friends. He says he'll come to California with us," Meaghan babbled.

A tear slid down Kathryn's cheek. Her fingers began to tremble. She was almost too afraid to ask, but finally she forced the words passed quaking lips. "What man, Meaghan? Who are you talking about?"

Meaghan looked over at a section of empty space beneath her dresses and blouses. Grinning, she looked back at her mother. Meaghan cupped her little hand in front of her mouth and giggled. "Oh, Mommy. You're being silly. It's George."